The English Modernist Novel as Political Theology

NEW DIRECTIONS IN RELIGION AND LITERATURE

This series aims to showcase new work at the forefront of religion and literature through short studies written by leading and rising scholars in the field. Books will pursue a variety of theoretical approaches as they engage with writing from different religious and literary traditions. Collectively, the series will offer a timely critical intervention to the interdisciplinary crossover between religion and literature, speaking to wider contemporary interests and mapping out new directions for the field in the early twenty-first century.

Series editors: Emma Mason and Mark Knight

ALSO AVAILABLE IN THE SERIES:

The New Atheist Novel, Arthur Bradley and Andrew Tate
Blake. Wordsworth. Religion, Jonathan Roberts
Do the Gods Wear Capes?, Ben Saunders
England's Secular Scripture, Jo Carruthers
Victorian Parables, Susan E. Colón
The Late Walter Benjamin, John Schad
Dante and the Sense of Transgression, William Franke
The Glyph and the Gramophone, Luke Ferretter
John Cage and Buddhist Ecopoetics, Peter Jaeger
Rewriting the Old Testament in Anglo-Saxon Verse, Samantha Zacher
Forgiveness in Victorian Literature, Richard Hughes Gibson
The Gospel According to the Novelist, Magdalena Mączyńska
Jewish Feeling, Richa Dwor
Beyond the Willing Suspension of Disbelief, Michael Tomko
The Gospel According to David Foster Wallace, Adam S. Miller
Pentecostal Modernism, Stephen Shapiro and Philip Barnard
The Bible in the American Short Story, Lesleigh Cushing Stahlberg and Peter S. Hawkins
Faith in Poetry, Michael D. Hurley
Jeanette Winterson and Religion, Emily McAvan
Religion and American Literature since the 1950s, Mark Eaton
Esoteric Islam in Modern French Thought, Ziad Elmarsafy

The Rhetoric of Conversion in English Puritan Writing, David Parry
Djuna Barnes and Theology, Zhao Ng
Food and Fasting in Victorian Religion and Literature, Lesa Scholl
The Economy of Religion in American Literature, Andrew Ball
Christian Heresy, James Joyce, and the Modernist Literary Imagination, Gregory Erikson
Marilynne Robinson's Worldly Gospel, Ryan S. Kemp and Jordon Rodgers

FORTHCOMING:

Chaucer and the Invention of Biblical Narrative, Chad Schrock
Activism and the Literary Self in 20th and 21st Century Literature, Jeff Keuss
Weird Faith in 19th Century Literature, Mark Knight and Emma Mason

The English Modernist Novel as Political Theology

Challenging the Nation

Charles Andrews

BLOOMSBURY ACADEMIC
LONDON • NEW YORK • OXFORD • NEW DELHI • SYDNEY

BLOOMSBURY ACADEMIC
Bloomsbury Publishing Plc, 50 Bedford Square, London, WC1B 3DP, UK
Bloomsbury Publishing Inc, 1385 Broadway, New York, NY 10018, USA
Bloomsbury Publishing Ireland, 29 Earlsfort Terrace, Dublin 2, D02 AY28, Ireland

BLOOMSBURY, BLOOMSBURY ACADEMIC and the Diana logo
are trademarks of Bloomsbury Publishing Plc

First published in Great Britain 2024

Copyright © Charles Andrews, 2024

Charles Andrews has asserted his right under the Copyright,
Designs and Patents Act, 1988, to be identified as Author of this work.

For legal purposes the Acknowledgments on pp. x–xi constitute an
extension of this copyright page.

Cover design: Rebecca Heselton
Cover image: The Cenotaph in Whitehall, pictured swamped in floral tributes
in the days following its unveiling at the Armistice Day ceremony
on 11 November 1920 © Chronicle/ Alamy Stock Photo

All rights reserved. No part of this publication may be: i) reproduced or transmitted in
any form, electronic or mechanical, including photocopying, recording or by means of
any information storage or retrieval system without prior permission in writing from the
publishers; or ii) used or reproduced in any way for the training, development or operation
of artificial intelligence (AI) technologies, including generative AI technologies. The rights
holders expressly reserve this publication from the text and data mining exception as per
Article 4(3) of the Digital Single Market Directive (EU) 2019/790.

Bloomsbury Publishing Plc does not have any control over, or responsibility for,
any third-party websites referred to or in this book. All internet addresses given
in this book were correct at the time of going to press. The author and publisher
regret any inconvenience caused if addresses have changed or sites have ceased
to exist, but can accept no responsibility for any such changes.

A catalogue record for this book is available from the British Library.

Library of Congress Cataloging-in-Publication Data
Names: Andrew, Charles (College teacher) author.
Title: The English modernist novel as political theology : challenging the nation / Charles
Andrew, Whitworth University, USA
Description: London ; New York : Bloomsbury Academic, 2024. |
Includes bibliographical references and index.
Identifiers: LCCN 2023030513 (print) | LCCN 2023030514 (ebook) |
ISBN 9781350362031 (hardback) | ISBN 9781350362079 (paperback) |
ISBN 9781350362048 (pdf) | ISBN 9781350362055 (ebook)
Subjects: LCSH: Politics in literature. | Nationalism in literature. | Civil religion–Great Britain.
| English literature–Political aspects. |
English fiction–20th century–History and criticism. | Modernism (Literature)–Great Britain.
Classification: LCC PR478.P64 A53 2024 (print) | LCC PR478.P64 (ebook) |
DDC 820.9/358–dc23/eng/20230731
LC record available at https://lccn.loc.gov/2023030513
LC ebook record available at https://lccn.loc.gov/2023030514

ISBN: HB: 978-1-3503-6203-1
ePDF: 978-1-3503-6204-8
eBook: 978-1-3503-6205-5

Series: New Directions in Religion and Literature

Typeset by Integra Software Services Pvt. Ltd.

For product safety related questions contact productsafety@bloomsbury.com.

To find out more about our authors and books visit www.bloomsbury.com
and sign up for our newsletters.

For Liv, Arlo, and Robin

Contents

Acknowledgments   x

Introduction: Challenging the "Christian Nation"   1

1   Virginia Woolf and Political Liturgies for the Unredeemed: *Jacob's Room*   29
2   D. H. Lawrence's Political Eschatology: *Apocalypse* and *Lady Chatterley's Lover*   65
3   Evelyn Waugh's Cynical Political Theology: *Decline and Fall* and *Vile Bodies*   99
4   Sylvia Townsend Warner's Queer Anarchist Theology: *Lolly Willowes*   141

Coda: Living the Theopolitical Imagination   177

Bibliography   188
Index   198

Acknowledgments

Our labors of all kinds are best when done in a rich network of friendship, and this has been especially true in my experience of academic work. We teach better among students who trust the relationships among their peers and instructor. And, we write better when communicating with people who are committed to a shared intellectual project and are faithful enough to judge our work sympathetically but honestly. I have been privileged to have such friends through the course of writing this book, and I am deeply grateful to the many readers, listeners, and interlocutors who have sharpened my thinking and shared these years with me.

This book is not a revised dissertation, but some of its earliest seeds were planted while finishing graduate school, and for their nurture I greatly value Pamela L. Caughie, Paul Jay, and Joyce Wexler whose model of care and professionalism continue to shape my work. I am indebted to the many friends and colleagues as well as current and former students who read draft portions of this manuscript and engaged with me in vibrant conversation, including Jake Andrews, Laura Bloxham, Christopher Borth, Thom Caraway, Anthony E. Clark, D. Berton Emerson, Naphtali Forbes-Fields, David P. Henreckson, Jake Jacobs, Fred Johnson, Kjerstin Kauffman, Shannon Kelly, Laurie Lamon, Grace Lillard, Samantha L. Miller, Kari Nixon, Tim Peebles, Patrick R. Query, Nathan Quick, Ana Quiring, Nicole Sheets, and the students in my British fiction seminar who shared their writing lives with me in workshop and, with good humor, discussed Satan, sex, witches, and anarchism. Ann Penfield's industry and cheer make her the ideal assistant, and I have been fortunate to have her aid. My university's librarians have been a constant support, and I could not have completed this book without the grace and alacrity of Amanda C. R. Clark and Cara Elston. K. Elise Leal has been a particularly important thought partner, reading and commenting on much of the manuscript and offering the insight and encouragement that gives energy for the often-daunting task of writing. Having colleagues who are also friends is an immense blessing, and community of this kind is essential for living an integrated life. Above all, I am humbled and honored by the depth of commitment from my writing group of Ria Banerjee, J. Ashley Foster, and Sejal Sutaria, co-conspirators in scholarship and social justice who charitably and critically waded through drafts of the entire manuscript. Sharing in their collective wisdom about writing, field expertise, and care for improving the world has been a highlight of my career, and their capacity to blend scholarly acumen with rich personal friendship is a joy and gift.

This book is dedicated to the people who have given most so that I could complete these labors. Liv Larson Andrews, in her writing, speaking, and life, enacts a theopolitical imagination to which I aspire; her partnership makes this work possible. Our children Arlo and Robin embrace the world both joyfully and critically. May they continue to hunger for justice and imagine new possibilities.

Introduction: Challenging the "Christian Nation"

Armistice Day, November 11, 1920, became a national holy day in England. It was two years after the official end of the Great War, and reckoning with the devastation was still active and raw. The enormity of the war, its unprecedented destruction and global scale, required public ritual that was both grand and capacious, striving to unite the nation by transforming inexplicable chaos into meaningful order. A crowd of thousands gathered in central London to participate in the newly crafted ritual commemoration devised to pay homage to the dead and reassert the sacredness of their sacrifices.[1] The spare and austere Cenotaph in Whitehall was unveiled and wreaths were laid at its base as a carriage bearing the Unknown Warrior processed to Westminster Abbey, site of the warrior's final resting place in the entryway of the national church. This public rite, shared by national leaders, military personnel, clergy, and the general public testified to the need for common work after the devastations of the war, and the structure of this rite exposed a strong desire for something sacred and transcendent. Though the day's rituals clearly had a relationship with Christianity, their "holiness" came from mixing traditional religious faith with nationalism to produce a civil religion that was related to but distinct from any particular historical confession. This commemorative ritual, crafted to give

---

[1] On the actual armistice, November 11, 1918, and its anniversary commemoration in 1919 there were also public rituals including a two-minute silence and the erection of temporary monuments, but the second anniversary established the lasting rituals upheld to this day. See Adrian Gregory, *The Silence of Memory: Armistice Day, 1919–1946* (London: Bloomsbury, 1994). David W. Lloyd puts the number of visitors to Westminster Abbey at 40,000 and another 200,000 the following day. Lloyd, *Battlefield Tourism: Pilgrimage and the Commemoration of the Great War in Britain, Australia and Canada, 1919–1939* (London: Bloomsbury, 1998), 49.

collective, public expression to enormous, incomprehensible grief, became an annual tradition in Britain and a national rite of mourning and unification.[2]

Such rituals, common in many nations and apparent during times of crisis, transition, or tragedy, certainly have a beneficial quality in managing grief and building community, but there is also a sinister side to these displays. Instead of outrage over the wastefulness of the war, protest of governmental and commercial leaders, and mobilization for lasting peace, the Armistice Day rite converted all public energies toward reverence, devotion, and acquiescence. Giorgio Agamben has written of this "double structure of the governmental machine" that moves "between Kingdom and Government and, ultimately, interrogates the very relation […] between *oikonomia* and Glory, between power as government and effective management, and power as ceremonial and liturgical regality."[3] Agamben asks that if political power were merely a matter of force, then why do nation-states thrive on rituals to discipline their citizenry? While the Armistice Day provides an acute moment of "ceremonial and liturgical regality," it is symptomatic of the pervasive enchantments of the state that result in subjugation and willingness to die for the nation or to kill and enslave for its ends. The problem with postwar commemorations is not that they give public space for mourning and remembrance but that they sustain a narrative of national sacrifice as righteous and fuel the ongoing militaristic and imperialist energies.[4] "Politics is a practice of the imagination," writes William T. Cavanaugh, with a nod to the field-defining work of Benedict Anderson, whose account of the nation as an "imagined community" persists in all conversations about nationalism.[5] Commemorative rituals highlight the practices of a national imagination and the construction of national identity, but they also bring into relief the power of aesthetics for this imaginary work.

---

[2] Lloyd reports that the Cenotaph and the Tomb of the Unknown Warrior "were the objectives of the largest pilgrimages in the inter war years" and continue to be crucial to "the ritual of Armistice Day" (*Battlefield Tourism*, 36).

[3] Giorgio Agamben, *The Kingdom and the Glory: For a Theological Genealogy of Economy and Government (Homo Sacer II, 2)*, trans. Lorenzo Chiesa with Matteo Mandarini (Stanford: Stanford University Press, 2007 trans. 2011), xi–xii.

[4] In a response to Agamben, David Newheiser has written that "sacrality is a source of power, and power is dangerous—but power is also the precondition for political action," and thus "the sacred remains an indispensable resource for a politics in pursuit of justice." Newheiser, *Hope in a Secular Age: Deconstruction, Negative Theology, and the Future of Faith* (Cambridge: Cambridge University Press, 2019), 151. Newheiser offers a helpful reminder that good collective action can also arise from sacred auras around politics, though he does not deny there are dangerous forms of such enchantments.

[5] William T. Cavanaugh, *Theopolitical Imagination: Discovering the Liturgy as a Political Act in an Age of Global Consumerism* (London: T&T Clark, 2002), 1. Benedict Anderson, *Imagined Communities: Reflections on the Origin and Spread of Nationalism*, Revised Edition (London: Verso, 2016), 6.

Literature and literary analysis provide resources for further interrogating how such imagination operates at the intersection of national and religious mythologies.[6] The four writers I discuss in this book—Virginia Woolf, D. H. Lawrence, Evelyn Waugh, and Sylvia Townsend Warner—were not people of faith during the period of study, though each were raised in Christian contexts with which they struggled and resisted. They were all shaped to some degree by the Church of England and its mixture of nationalism and religion, and they each reacted in distinctive ways to the militarism and violence perpetuated by English civil religion. Their experiments with literary form through elliptical narrative structures, subjective and shifting points of view, allusiveness, and other breaks with realist conventions invite readers into a heightened sensitivity about the stories that form us while challenging readers to envision new political imaginaries. And, these works act in opposition to aesthetic forms that corroborated and reinforced the sacralized state.

Though there were debates among the creators of the Armistice Day rituals about how distinctly Christian the day should be, there was an undeniable religious aura even in its supposedly neutral or universal elements. Edwin Lutyens courted controversy by designing the Cenotaph to be deliberately free from symbols of religious or national particularity.[7] The monument was eyed suspiciously by some leaders who desired something more explicitly

---

[6] Among the crucial sites of interest in modernist studies for the past two decades has been the relationship between modernism and national identity as well as rival collective imaginings through cosmopolitanism, trans-nationalism, and globalism. Though my arguments in this book are informed by the context of these discussions, I am not primarily concerned with how authors navigated through liberal forms of the nation or for showing their advocacy of collective entities beyond national boundaries. Rather, I focus primarily on how these writers developed alternative political theologies to the ones propagated by the sacralized state. See Pericles Lewis, *Modernism, Nationalism, and the Novel* (Cambridge: Cambridge University Press, 2000); Paul Peppis, *Literature, Politics, and the English Avant-Garde* (Cambridge: Cambridge University Press, 2000); Jed Esty, *A Shrinking Island: Modernism and National Culture in England* (Princeton: Princeton University Press, 2004); Rebecca L. Walkowitz, *Cosmopolitan Style: Modernism beyond the Nation* (New York: Columbia University Press, 2007); Paul Jay, *Global Matters: The Transnational Turn in Literary Studies* (Ithaca, NY: Cornell University Press, 2010); Jessica Berman, *Modernist Commitments: Ethics, Politics, and Transnational Modernism* (New York: Columbia University Press, 2011); Patrick R. Query, *Ritual and the Idea of Europe in Interwar Writing* (Burlington, VT: Ashgate, 2012); Susan Stanford Friedman, *Planetary Modernisms: Provocations on Modernity across Time* (New York: Columbia University Press, 2015); Eric Hayot and Rebecca L. Walkowitz, eds., *A New Vocabulary for Global Modernism* (New York: Columbia University Press, 2016).

[7] Jay Winter notes that the Cenotaph "brought the dead of the 1914–1918 war into history" and "did so without the slightest mark of Christian or contemporary patriotic or romantic symbolism, a feat which did not endear Lutyens or his work to traditional Christians" (104). Winter does not remark, however, on the ways that despite this absence of traditional religious elements, the monument and its veneration still retain a religious character. See Jay Winter, *Sites of Memory, Sites of Mourning: The Great War in European Cultural History* (Cambridge: Cambridge University Press, 1995). On the use of Christian symbols in producing a "cult of the fallen," see George L. Mosse, *Fallen Soldiers: Reshaping the Memory of the World Wars* (New York: Oxford University Press, 1990), 74.

Christian, and Lutyens later remarked, "There was some horror in Church circles. *What!* a pagan monument in the midst of Whitehall!," but he added "that is why we have a rival shrine in the Abbey."[8] Despite these concerns from religious gatekeepers, such a monument and the practices surrounding it— crowds laying wreaths, pausing in silence, and singing hymns—were modeled on familiar religious forms. The aesthetics of the Armistice Day ceremony gave it a religious aura palpable enough to be the focus of the lead article in a special supplement in *The Times* of London. "We have a piece of music," wrote the anonymous *Times* correspondent, "which says in the language, not of any one time or people, but of Eternity, that which is to be said about the funeral of the Unknown representative of all our dead."[9] Music bonds the crowd together, and the correspondent reports that reverential acts for the Unknown Warrior united English people with something "eternal": "Whatever we were thinking before we heard the first sound of it in the distance, that sound uplifted us to the height of the occasion and we were made one people, participants in one act of remembrance."[10] The correspondent is struck by "the sense of unity and of Eternity" that "came through the eye as well as the ear, when all heads were bared and there were thousands of faces lit by the quiet sunlight."[11] More than just a reflection on loss or celebration of victory, the Armistice Day commemorations built national community through imagining "eternity"— that is, generalized language for divinity refashioned for a universal meaning rather than any particular expression of religious faith. National pride necessarily animates the proceedings, and the correspondent describes the day as the expression of a new religion based not in funerals for famous national figures but for an Unknown who may stand in for all soldiers: "For the honour paid to the Unknown was an act of faith; in it we said that, at our highest, we are one; when men die for each other there is to be no distinction between them."[12] This faith made possible by the sacrificial death of combatants sustains national unity and gestures toward eternity and immortality, a religious mythology that creates community and imagines an afterlife. Though the correspondent,

---

[8] Qtd. in Lloyd, *Battlefield Tourism*, 59. For more on the controversy, see Christopher Hussey, *The Life of Sir Edwin Lutyens*. 1950 (Woodbridge, Suffolk: Antique Collectors' Club, 1989), 374–6. Lutyens resisted using crosses for memorials such as the Stone of Remembrance used in the Imperial War Graves cemeteries, claiming that "the Cross is the great anti-Christ of prophecy" and resenting "the inherent cruelty of the *forced* Cross" (*Lutyens*, 375).

[9] Anonymous, "Armistice Day, 1920. The Burial of the Unknown Warrior," *The Times*, November 12, 1920, Supplement, i.

[10] Ibid.

[11] Ibid.

[12] Ibid.

matching Lutyens's intentions for the Cenotaph, resists making the Armistice Day events sound particularly indebted to Christianity, vestiges still remain of traditional religious forms and language: "There was one forgetfulness of self in that quiet ritual, one desire that its prophecy may be fulfilled—that we may come to be one in life as our dead are one in death; that we may, indeed, all become members of one body politic and of one immortal soul."[13] This claim about unity and immortality is theological, a remarkably clear instance where the state holds authority not through raw power and coercion but through enchantment.

What the correspondent theorizes—and, indeed, the entire ritual process of Armistice Day, 1920, entails—is the production of an English civil religion that borrows from Christianity but constructs its own rituals, symbols, language, and mythology. Literature was a vital part of these rites and their sacred aura, evident in *The Times* correspondent's concluding quotation from Edmund Spenser's "Mutability" cantos: "The steadfast rest of all things firmly stayed / Upon the pillars of eternity."[14] Eternal life ought to be in our minds, the writer suggests, when responding to death for the nation, and the quotation vaguely alludes to Christian mythology but stops short of Spenser's more explicitly Christian declaration that all may rest "With Him that is the God of Sabbaoth hight."[15] The literary reference performs a sleight of hand where the writer borrows from the reverential power of Christian mythology without directly appealing to Christianity. A similar move occurred when crafting the much-debated inscription on the Unknown Warrior's tomb, where the end result included references to dying "FOR GOD / FOR KING AND COUNTRY" as well as an allusion to the biblical book of Second Chronicles: "THEY BURIED HIM / AMONG THE KINGS BECAUSE HE / HAD DONE GOOD TOWARD GOD AND TOWARD / HIS HOUSE."[16] Around this inscription appear biblical verses about dying, redemption in Christ, and sacrifice. What this memorial reflects is not merely an attempt to add significance to political community through layers of Christian sentiment. Rather, this use of religious language at a national event in a supposedly secular age means that both the concepts of religion and nationalism are altered by their commingling. The final lines of the plaque remove the original references to David and Israel, turning a

---

[13] Ibid.
[14] Qtd. in Ibid.
[15] Edmund Spenser, *Books I and II of The Faerie Queene, The Mutability Cantos and Selections from the Minor Poetry*, eds. Robert Kellogg and Oliver Steele (New York: Macmillan, 1965), 436.
[16] https://www.westminster-abbey.org/abbey-commemorations/commemorations/unknown-warrior

Judeo-Christian story into a national story. Though the Warrior is unknown, we are told that he is certainly British, and his burial among kings is a final resting place among the ancient royal lineage of Britain. Thus, the religious peoplehood of the Israelites is refashioned as a national peoplehood of Britain, creating a magisterial syncretism of religion and nationalism through a blending of these stories.

Hymn-singing during the Armistice Day rites was the most prominent way that literature contributed to national holiness. The interment for the Unknown Warrior began with "O Valiant Hearts," a setting of a poem by John Stanhope Arkwright, and ended with "Recessional" by Rudyard Kipling, musical bookends that conveyed the interweaving of Christian sacrifice and national service. In Arkwright's text, taken from his collection *The Supreme Sacrifice, and Other Poems in Time of War* (1919), the "valiant hearts" of the title are those fallen dead who have "the great surrender made" and await "the last clear trumpet call of God."[17] These soldiers killed in battle are reassured by the speaker/singer that "Christ, our Redeemer, passed the self same way" and that the deaths of the "valiant" are hallowed as "the Victor's pitying eyes / Look down to bless our lesser Calvaries."[18] The emotive tone and strained reassurance of these lines work to give meaning to war death, joining the sacrifice of soldiers with the sacrifice of Christ in saving the world. This sacrificial rhetoric and analogy between Christ and soldier is far less pronounced in Kipling's more famous text, which instead emphasizes in each stanza a list of admonishments for the nation—"Lest we forget!"[19] But in spite of Kipling's usual reticence about Christianity, the poem consistently pleads to the "Lord God of Hosts" and "Judge of the Nations" under "whose awful Hand" the power of military might appears impotent as "our navies melt away" and earthly power succumbs to divine retribution just as in "Nineveh and Tyre!"[20] Kipling's message is less celebratory than Arkwright's, but his language remains ceremonial and religious, and possibly more distinctly British rather than Arkwright's arguably more global vision of Christian soldiers. John Wolffe claims that the hymns chosen for the gathering around the Cenotaph, "Lead Kindly Light" and "Abide with Me," are "more Christian than patriotic" but "the opening and closing hymns in the Abbey

---

[17] John S. Arkwright, *The Supreme Sacrifice and Other Poems in Time of War* (London: Skeffington, 1919), 17.
[18] Ibid., 18.
[19] Rudyard Kipling, *Kipling: A Selection of His Stories and Poems, Volume II*, ed. John Beecroft (New York: Doubleday, 1956), 450.
[20] Ibid.

[by Arkwright and Kipling] evoked reflections of a more national kind, but in an appropriately reflective vein."[21] This suggestion that Arkwright and Kipling are more nationalistic than Christian is perhaps true by comparison with "Abide with Me," but the melding of Christianity and nationalism is fully displayed in all of the hymns at the Abbey.

While poets such as Arkwright and Kipling lent their talents to national rituals, the novelists I discuss imagined through their fiction various forms of resistance to the seductive power of nationalism and the devastations wrought by militaristic and imperialist violence. These political seductions conscript citizens into aggressive and sacrificial narratives where killing and dying for the nation is elevated to holiness. As Simon Critchley argues, "modern forms of politics—whether liberal democracy, fascism, soviet communism, national socialism and the rest" should be understood as "metamorphoses of sacralization."[22] The transferal of sacred power into all of our political formations is a deep concern for current philosophers, theorists, and theologians, and my argument in this book is that modernist fiction offers an important but under-used dialogue partner for this theorization. Modernist studies is uniquely positioned by its focus on a turbulent political age when various ideologies—socialist, communist, fascist, and liberal—competed for supremacy, and artists imagined counternarratives to these prevailing forces.

My focus is on modernist writers who were not Christians, arguing that their critical and imaginative encounters with English civil religion afford a reading of their fiction as political theology, and I put these novels into dialogue with more recent theopolitical philosophy to suggest the vibrant interplay between these fields of discourse as a contribution to our political imaginations today. As Carl A. Raschke describes it, "political theology is *not* a theology of the political. Instead it aims to inquire into the grounds—or perhaps we should say the *ontological grounding*—of the political as we know it."[23] Instead of a totalizing

---

[21] John Wolffe, *Great Deaths: Grieving, Religion, and Nationhood in Victorian and Edwardian Britain* (New York: Oxford University Press, 2000), 263.

[22] Simon Critchley, *The Faith of the Faithless: Experiments in Political Theology* (London: Verso, 2012), 25. Critchley's nontheistic account of political theology has important similarities with William T. Cavanaugh and Peter Manley Scott's account, despite the difference of their basis in confessional Christianity: "What the term 'political theology' names, then, is the recognition that politics never was drained of the sacred; the primary locus of the sacred merely shifted from church to nation-state and market." William T. Cavanaugh and Peter Manley Scott, "Introduction to the Second Edition," in *The Wiley Blackwell Companion to Political Theology: Second Edition*, ed. William T. Cavanaugh and Peter Manley Scott (Chichester: Wiley, 2019), 2–3.

[23] Carl A. Raschke, *Force of God: Political Theology and the Crisis of Liberal Democracy* (New York: Columbia University Press, 2015), xii.

and absolute secularity, modern political life shows a persistent enchantment. By considering how modernist literary experimentation broadens and refines our capacity to reckon with unimagined possibilities, we may also broaden and refine our capacities to envision political worlds beyond the models we have inherited. Instead of the death-driven narratives of the state, theopolitical fiction envisions dynamic, sensitive, empathetic, and resilient ways to live.

Civil Religion versus the Theopolitical Imagination

England in the early twentieth century is sometimes regarded as a place and time of growing secularity—what Charles Taylor refers to as the "nova effect" of unbelief in modern European societies when traditional expressions of faith are no longer a given but there remains a yearning for transcendence and meaning to face the "malaises of modernity."[24] But whatever amount of religious fracturing was underway, the years of the Great War and its immediate aftermath showed widespread public faith and ritual practice. The war itself was bathed in religious language, and, as the historian Philip Jenkins has shown, "not just incidentally but repeatedly and centrally, official statements and propaganda declare[d] that the war [was] being fought for God's cause, or for his glory" creating "a powerful and consistent strain of holy war ideology during the Great War years."[25] This holy war ideology persisted during the postwar commemorations, and though the term "Christian Nation" may not fit as easily with England in the 1920s than it does in other, more theocratic national contexts, the powerful fusion of Christianity and patriotism remained culturally dominant through the first half of the twentieth century.[26]

Civil religion has been much less discussed as a phenomenon in Britain than in the United States, partly due to the term's history of development and partly because of the broader persistence of Christian language and mythology

---

[24] Charles Taylor, *A Secular Age* (Cambridge, MA: Harvard University Press, 2007), 299. Taylor describes the "ever-widening variety of moral/spiritual options, across the span of the thinkable and perhaps even beyond" that have led to our present time of "a spiritual super-nova, a kind of galloping pluralism on the spiritual plane" (299–300).

[25] Philip Jenkins, *The Great and Holy War: How World War I Became a Religious Crusade* (New York: HarperCollins, 2014), 6–7.

[26] For analysis of the turn toward secularism in the 1960s, see Callum G. Brown, *The Death of Christian Britain: Understanding Secularisation 1800–2000*, Second Edition (New York: Routledge, 2009). See also S. J. D. Green, *The Passing of Protestant England: Secularisation and Social Change c.1920–1960* (Cambridge: Cambridge University Press, 2011).

in US political discourse.²⁷ But even a nation such as England requires public ritual where symbols such as monuments and flags, rites such as coronations, inaugurations, and state funerals, and vows in the form of pledges and anthems are all elements of national worship that produce and sustain political imagination.²⁸ As Jason A. Springs describes the term, "civil religion" "refers to the practices, symbols, myths, rituals, and consecrated spaces and times that serve to unify and integrate the disparate parts and individuals of a society into a cohesive whole," and its Latin roots suggest its function of creating coherence and unity: "*religiare* means 'to bind together'; *civitas* refers to the shared, public life of a community."²⁹ Even in supposedly secular ages, our various acts of commemoration for wars, transfers of power, and historical milestones function religiously. Christianity can become fused with this civil religion, granting the nation an aura of enchantment and transcendence, but Christian faith is not perfectly synonymous with civil religion, even in so-called Christian Nations. Jean-Jacques Rousseau's *The Social Contract* (1762) laid the template for such discussion, arguing that religions such as Christianity might be detrimental to the state, and that the sovereign ought to establish "a purely civil profession of faith [...] without which it is impossible to be either a good Citizen or a loyal subject."³⁰ The dogmas of this civil religion are "the existence of the powerful, intelligent, beneficent, prescient, and provident Divinity, the life to come, the happiness of the just, the punishment of the wicked, the sanctity of the social Contract and the Laws" and the one prohibition is "intolerance: it is a feature of

---

[27] See, for instance, Carolyn Marvin and David W. Ingle, *Blood Sacrifice and the Nation: Totem Rituals and the American Flag* (Cambridge: Cambridge University Press, 1999); Jean Bethke Elshtain, *Just War against Terror: The Burden of American Power in a Violent World* (New York: Basic Books, 2003); Jeffrey Stout, *Blessed Are the Organized: Grassroots Democracy in America* (Princeton: Princeton University Press, 2010).

[28] Norman Bonney argues, for example, that the persistence of religion is always detectable in the United Kingdom during high-profile national events such as coronations and royal weddings, and one might go further to see "the established religious denominations, the Churches of England and Scotland, as forms of civil religion—religion in service to the state [...] officially recognised expressions of the relation between the state and the 'divine' and 'spiritual' spheres and as the authorised media of official state religious expression" (2). Though I am reluctant to see the "established denominations" as synonymous with British civil religion, the overlap between these official churches and the public religion of the nation is undeniable. See Norman Bonney, *Monarchy, Religion and the State: Civil Religion in the United Kingdom, Canada, Australia and the Commonwealth* (Manchester: Manchester University Press, 2013).

[29] Jason A. Springs, "Civil Religion," in *Religion and Culture: Contemporary Practices and Perspectives*, ed. Richard D. Hecht and Vincent F. Biondo III (Minneapolis: Fortress Press, 2012), 29.

[30] Jean-Jacques Rousseau, *The Social Contract and Other Later Political Writings*, trans. and ed. Victor Gourevitch (Cambridge: Cambridge University Press, 1997), 150.

the cult we have rejected."[31] Social cohesion produced by a shared set of values and practices along with vigilance about beliefs and convictions that might disrupt civic unity—these are the promises of civil religion advocated by Rousseau. The most important extension of Rousseau's thought in modern political discourse is Robert N. Bellah's much-discussed "Civil Religion in America" (1967), where Bellah argued for the value of an American religion that comprised the highest collective values and aspirations of this particular national collective. Bellah claimed that "there actually exists alongside of and rather clearly differentiated from the churches an elaborate and well-institutionalized civil religion in America" and he defended himself "against the accusation of supporting an idolatrous worship of the American nation."[32] This religion is distinct from Christianity, Bellah explains, but "behind the civil religion at every point lie biblical archetypes: Exodus, Chosen People, Promised Land, New Jerusalem, and Sacrificial Death [...] It has its own prophets and its own martyrs, its own sacred events and sacred places, its own solemn rituals and symbols," and like other faiths, it seeks to mold "society as perfectly in accord with the will of God" and to become "a light to all nations."[33] Though the United States may seem unique, Bellah insists that "every nation and every people come to some form of religious self-understanding," and I would add that England during the years

---

[31] Rousseau, *Social Contract*, 150–1. One of Rousseau's great anxieties is about the social discord he thinks may result from religious faith taken too seriously, and he critiques the Christianity of the Gospel for being a "saintly, sublime, genuine Religion" that "has no particular relation to the body politic" and "far from attaching the Citizens' hearts to the State, it detaches them from it as from all earthly things. I know of nothing more contrary to the social spirit" (147).

[32] Robert N. Bellah, "Civil Religion in America," in *The Robert Bellah Reader*, ed. Robert N. Bellah and Steven M. Tipton (Durham, NC: Duke University Press, 2006), 225–45. 225. Bellah affirmed the power of this alternative religion and, in the mid-1960s, expressed optimism about a US civil religion that could incorporate "vital international symbolism" as part of the "eschatological hope of American civil religion from the beginning" (245), but he would later revise his former optimism in *The Broken Covenant: American Civil Religion in Time of Trial* (Chicago: University of Chicago Press, 1975) and finally renounce the term in *Varieties of Civil Religion*, coauthored with Phillip E. Hammond (New York: Harper & Row, 1980). For more on the continued debates about whether Christians can participate fully in civil religion, see Stanley Hauerwas "On Being a Christian and an American," in *Meaning and Modernity: Religion, Polity, and Self*, eds. Richard Madsen, William M. Sullivan, Ann Swidler, and Steven M. Tipton (Berkeley: University of California Press, 2002), 224–35; and, Robert N. Bellah "God and King," in *God, Truth, and Witness: Engaging Stanley Hauerwas*, ed. L. Gregory Jones, Reinhard Hütter, and C. Rosalee Velloso Ewell (Grand Rapids, MI: Brazos, 2005), 112–30.

[33] Bellah, "Civil Religion," 245. On the use of such religious archetypes in the national imaginary, see Anthony D. Smith, *Chosen Peoples: Sacred Sources of National Identity* (Oxford: Oxford University Press, 2003) and Anthony Marx, *Faith in Nation: On the Exclusionary Origins of Nationalism* (Oxford: Oxford University Press, 2003). On the imperialist theology of divinely elected nations, see William R. Hutchison, ed., *Many Are Chosen: Divine Election and Western Nationalism* (Cambridge, MA: Harvard University Press, 1994), especially A. F. Walls, "Carrying the White Man's Burden: Some British Views of Imperial Vocation in the Imperial Era," 29–50.

of the Great War and its aftermath provides an especially clear instance of this type of religious sentiment.³⁴

The relationship between Christianity and the civil religion of the state is complex, even in a place such as England where the idea of being a "Christian nation" was largely vestigial. There is an uneasiness in the ways that traditional religious faiths sit alongside, contribute to, or sometimes contradict the enchantments of the state, and this vexed relationship has long been a part of the scholarly discourse on nationalism and religion. As the influential Catholic historian (and so-called Father of Nationalism) Carlton J. H. Hayes wrote in 1933:

> Nationalism is a religion now common to the great majority of mankind. But this is not to say that older religions have been obliterated by nationalism. [...] What is actually occurring is a new religious syncretism, by virtue of which very many persons continue nominally to adhere to the faith of their ancestors and even to practice its cult, whilst they adapt it to the exigencies of nationalist worship and discipline.³⁵

There is a fluidity between what Hayes calls the "older religions" and the new cult of "nationalist worship," and civil religion names the convergence of these ideologies within a modern political arena. The religious aura of the nation-state and its relationship with traditional religions appears in many accounts of nationalism since Hayes's pioneering work in the 1930s. Benedict Anderson influentially argued that "in Western Europe the eighteenth century marks not only the dawn of the age of nationalism but the dusk of religious modes of thought," and with the social functions of religion diminished, "what then was required was a secular transformation of fatality into continuity, contingency into meaning" and "few things were (are) better suited to this end than an idea of nation."³⁶ Anderson insists that he is not suggesting a simple replacement model where nationalism eradicates religion, only that the historic emergence of nationalist ideology and enlightenment rationalism indicates a correlation.

---

³⁴ Ibid., 225. For studies of the distinctly Christian character of Britain during this time, see John Wolffe, *God and Greater Britain: Religion and National Life in Britain and Ireland, 1843–1945* (London: Routledge, 1994); Sheridan Gilley and W. J. Sheils, eds., *A History of Religion in Britain: Practice and Belief from Pre-Roman Times to the Present* (Oxford: Blackwell, 1994); Hugh McLeod, *Religion and the People of Western Europe 1789–1989*, Second Edition (New York: Oxford University Press, 1997).
³⁵ Carlton J. H. Hayes, *Essays on Nationalism* (New York: Macmillan, 1933), 118. For another classic account of this nationalist and religious syncretism, see Salo Wittmayer Baron, *Modern Nationalism and Religion* (New York: Harper, 1947).
³⁶ Anderson, *Imagined Communities*, 11.

Subsequent scholarship has suggested a more complex relationship between religion and nationalism, relying on a less totalizing notion of secularity than Anderson, and one that registers how the interplay between faith and nation remains fraught.[37]

Though proponents of civil religion such as Rousseau and Bellah assert that this is an important, even inevitable dimension of modern political life, there are several intellectual trends in the field of political theology that have been deeply critical of this religion of the state. One of the major contentions shared by the disparate voices in this field is a challenge to the nation—especially in the ways that it consolidates power, silences individuals, and demands aggression and sacrifice. As the philosopher Alasdair MacIntyre contends:

> The modern nation-state, in whatever guise, is a dangerous and unmanageable institution, presenting itself on the one hand as a bureaucratic supplier of goods and services, which is always about to, but never actually does, give its clients value for money, and on the other as a repository of sacred values, which from time to time invites one to lay down one's life on its behalf.[38]

Such all-encompassing sacrifice is absurd, according to MacIntyre: "it is like being asked to die for the telephone company."[39] For MacIntyre and others, this alternative religion offers false promises and false theologies that contribute to wars, imperial conquest, and repressive social disciplines. Whatever hope once existed for a civil religion that calls forth the best from society, it has remained at best unfilled and at worst blatantly denied.

The English Modernist Novel as Political Theology investigates this challenge to the nation by putting modernist fiction into dialogue with numerous voices from the broad field of political theology. Even speaking of a "broad field" of political theology, however, risks oversimplifying and reducing the diversity and complexity of the many thinkers who fall under that banner. Stanley Hauerwas, a Christian ethicist and highly influential figure among political theologians,

---

[37] See, for instance, John E. Smith, *Quasi-Religions: Humanism, Marxism and Nationalism* (Houndmills: Macmillan, 1994); Peter van der Veer and Hartmut Lehmann, *Nation and Religion: Perspectives on Europe and Asia* (Princeton: Princeton University Press, 1999); Rogers Brubaker, "Religion and Nationalism: Four Approaches," *Nations and Nationalism* 18, no. 1 (2012): 2–20; Atalia Omer and Jason A. Springs, *Religious Nationalism: A Reference Handbook* (Santa Barbara, CA: ABC-CLIO, 2013); John Carter Wood, ed., *Christianity and National Identity in Twentieth-Century Europe: Conflict, Community, and the Social Order* (Bristol, CT: Vandenhoeck & Ruprecht, 2016).

[38] Alasdair MacIntyre, "A Partial Response to My Critics," in *After MacIntyre: Critical Responses on the Work of Alasdair MacIntyre*, eds. John Horton and Susan Mendus (Notre Dame: University of Notre Dame Press, 1994), 303.

[39] Ibid. For an elaboration on this claim, see William T. Cavanaugh, *Migrations of the Holy: God, State, and the Political Meaning of the Church* (Grand Rapids: Eerdmans, 2011), 7–45.

refers to the so-called field of political theology as "a mass of confusions."[40] Presumably for Hauerwas those confusions pertain to conflicting uses of the term "political theology" as well as the many unstated assumptions about political theology that occur when people from different confessional backgrounds and faith traditions argue about the role of religion in public life.[41] Hauerwas and his many allies including William T. Cavanaugh and William H. Willimon debate with reformed theologians such as James K. A. Smith and Hak Joon Lee as well as nontheist philosophers and political theorists such as Jeffrey Stout and Romand Coles.[42] Central to these disagreements is whether Christianity needs to assert its political witness as distinct from the secular nation-state or whether collaborative interaction between faith and nation can be a benefit to both church and polis. Debates such as these among theologians and scholars of religious studies run parallel to another major area of political theology comprising work by secular political theologians in the traditions of continental philosophy and theory. These writers are often nontheists who nevertheless argue that modern political life retains an aura of enchantment, and it is rare to find these two spheres of political theology interacting.[43] Major figures in this area include Giorgio Agamben, Simon Critchley, Slavoj Žižek, Clayton Crockett, and Carl A. Raschke—philosophers who disagree about many aspects of political theology

---

[40] Hauerwas, back matter, James K. A. Smith, *Awaiting the King: Reforming Public Theology* (Grand Rapids: Baker Academic, 2017). Jonathan Cole similarly writes that "political theology boasts a prolific and proliferating literature. However, little binds this literature together in terms of method, scope, and content [...] this diversity, which is a charitable way of saying incoherence, is particularly evident when one brings into focus the polar ends of the spectrum" (xxv). Cole, *Christian Political Theology in an Age of Discontent: Mediating Scripture, Doctrine, and Political Reality* (Eugene, OR: Wipf & Stock, 2019).

[41] A useful survey of these debates within confessional political theology is Elizabeth Phillips, *Political Theology: A Guide for the Perplexed* (London: T&T Clark, 2012), 31–54.

[42] See, for example, Hauerwas and William H. Willimon, *Resident Aliens: Life in the Christian Colony* (Abingdon, MD: Abingdon Press, 1989); Oliver O'Donovan, *The Desire of the Nations: Rediscovering the Roots of Political Theology* (Cambridge: Cambridge University Press, 1996); William T. Cavanaugh, *Myth of Religious Violence: Secular Ideology and the Roots of Modern Conflict* (Oxford: Oxford University Press, 2009); Hak Joon Lee, "Public Theology," in *The Cambridge Companion to Political Theology*, ed. Craig Hovey and Elizabeth Phillips (Cambridge: Cambridge University Press, 2015), 44–66; Jeffrey Stout, *Democracy and Tradition*, (Princeton: Princeton University Press, 2004); Stanley Hauerwas and Roman Coles, *Christianity, Democracy, and the Radical Ordinary: Conversations between a Radical Democrat and a Christian* (Eugene, OR: Wipf and Stock, 2008); William T. Cavanaugh, Jeffrey W. Bailey, and Craig Hovey, eds., *An Eerdmans Reader in Contemporary Political Theology* (Grand Rapids: Eerdmans, 2012); Miroslav Volf and Ryan McAnnally-Linz, *Public Faith in Action: How to Think Carefully, Engage Wisely, and Vote with Integrity* (Grand Rapids: Brazos, 2016).

[43] An important exception is the group of theologians associated with the "radical orthodoxy" movement. John Milbank, for instance, has been a collaborator and interlocutor with both Stanley Hauerwas and Slavoj Žižek. See, for instance, Slavoj Žižek, John Milbank, and Creston Davis, *The Monstrosity of Christ: Paradox or Dialectic?* (Cambridge, MA: MIT Press, 2009). See also Daniel M. Bell Jr., *Divinations: Theopolitics in an Age of Terror* (Eugene, OR: Wipf and Stock, 2017) for a student of Hauerwas who thoughtfully uses continental philosophy.

but share a set of reference points and key thinkers (Emmanuel Levinas, Jacques Lacan, etc.) in their debates about imagining public life.[44]

Essential to theopolitical reflection across its disparate subfields is Carl Schmitt's *Political Theology: Four Chapters on the Concept of Sovereignty* (1922), which for the past century has animated and provoked responses to theologies of the state.[45] Schmitt's translator George Schwab calls him "undoubtedly the most controversial German legal and political thinker of the twentieth century," a claim supported by the idiosyncrasy and influence of his theory as well as his trajectory from devout Catholic who considered the priesthood into lawyer who helped devise the Third Reich.[46] The most enduring of Schmitt's maxims is "all significant concepts of the modern theory of the state are secularized theological concepts," which he elaborates on, saying this is so: "not only because of their historical development—in which they were transferred from theology to the theory of the state, whereby, for example, the omnipotent God became the omnipotent lawgiver—but also because of their systematic structure."[47] This "systematic structure," Schmitt claims, is apparent in the way that the rise of the modern state and the rise of deism occur simultaneously within the rationalist Enlightenment tradition. Schwab summarizes Schmitt's central thesis, highlighting the damaging power of the state and a core reason for resistance to its sovereignty:

> By virtue of its possession of a monopoly on politics, the state is the only entity able to distinguish friend from enemy and thereby demand of its citizens the readiness to die. This claim on the physical life of its constituents distinguishes the state from, and elevates it above, all other organizations and associations. To

---

[44] Giorgio Agamben, *The Church and the Kingdom* (Chicago: University of Chicago Press, 2010, trans. 2012) and *Creation and Anarchy: The Work of Art and the Religion of Capitalism* (Stanford: Stanford University Press, 2019); Slavoj Žižek, Eric L. Santner, and Kenneth Reinhard, *The Neighbor: Three Inquiries in Political Theology* (Chicago: University of Chicago Press, 2006); Clayton Crockett, *Radical Political Theology: Religion and Politics after Liberalism* (New York: Columbia University Press, 2013). Carl A. Raschke, *Neoliberalism and Political Theology: From Kant to Identity Politics* (Edinburgh: Edinburgh University Press, 2021). For an invaluable compendium of this field, see Hent de Vries and Lawrence E. Sullivan, *Political Theologies: Public Religions in a Post-Secular World* (New York: Fordham University Press, 2006). See also the Columbia University Press series "Insurrections: Critical Studies in Religion, Politics, and Culture," edited by Slavoj Žižek, Clayton Crockett, Creston Davis, and Jeffrey Robbins (New York: Columbia University Press, 2008-present).

[45] Direct responses to Schmitt include Chantal Mouffe, ed., *The Challenge of Carl Schmitt* (London: Verso, 1999); Jean Bethke Elshtain, *Sovereignty: God, State, and Self* (New York: Basic, 2008); Paul W. Kahn, *Political Theology: Four New Chapters on the Concept of Sovereignty* (New York: Columbia University Press, 2011).

[46] George Schwab, introduction to *Political Theology: Four Chapters on the Concept of Sovereignty*, by Carl Schmitt, trans. George Schwab (Cambridge, MA: MIT Press, 1985), xi.

[47] Carl Schmitt, *Political Theology: Four Chapters on the Concept of Sovereignty*, trans. George Schwab (Cambridge, MA: MIT Press, 1985), 36.

maintain order, peace, and stability, the legally constituted sovereign authority is supported by an armed force and a bureaucracy operating according to rules established by legally constituted authorities.[48]

A unifying thread among the theologians, theorists, and philosophers who I marshal for dialogue with modernist fiction is their exploration of what William Cavanaugh calls a "theopolitical imagination"—that is, the development of alternative theologies to the "heretical theology of salvation through the state."[49] Cavanaugh writes from a confessional perspective as a Roman Catholic theologian, and while the theologians and literary writers I discuss in this book would not necessarily share Cavanaugh's particular dogma, there remains among these various perspectives a broad consensus about the need to challenge the nation and its destructive narratives, ideologies, and actions.

When speaking of a political theology, I mean to indicate a view of theology that is active in the world, connected to communities, publicly expressed, and historically and materially shaped. This notion of theology is distinct from expressions of faith that are only personal, private, individualistic, and "spiritual." By focusing on the "sacredness" of the nation-state, I am not attempting to point toward a "post-secular" condition that is newly aware that our seemingly secular sociopolitical arrangements are surprisingly still enchanted. Rather, I wish to claim for literary fiction an active role in critiquing the false and destructive ways that sacralized nationalism operates—its capacity to stir emotion toward ends that are violent, coercive, oppressive, and malignant.

In the following chapters, I put four modernist novelists into dialogue with more recent political theologians in an effort to show the value of reading experimental fiction alongside theopolitical philosophy. More than just a "lens" or "framework" for this fiction, however, political theology can benefit from the dialogical exchange with literary works—especially when developing the sense of a theopolitical "imagination." Though talk of new ways to imagine ourselves politically is part of theological and philosophical discourse, the contours of that expanded imagination have often remained vague. By investigating the aesthetic experiments of modernist fiction as crucial to theopolitical imagination, I contend that these literary works offer unique possibilities for refining, nurturing, and expanding political sensibilities. The demands such fiction places on its readers through experimental literary form sustain fresh imagination that is not just a matter of new worlds or alternative communities. With each

---

[48] Schwab, "Introduction," xxvi.
[49] Cavanaugh, *Theopolitical Imagination*, 5.

of the four novelists I analyze in this study, I aim to show how their unique approaches to stylistic experimentation call forth from readers an attentiveness to the destructive power of civil religion even in the mundane parts of life as well as heightening our sensitivity to alternative ways of flourishing within the nation-state. Imagination, then, is developed through modernist aesthetics that cultivate a readership more attuned to political theologies of resistance.

Modernism, Nationalism, Secularism, Religion

Scholarship on earlier literary periods has been quicker than modernist studies to embrace political theology. Within fields such as early modern literature, Shakespeare studies, and Romanticism, scholars have drawn connections between literary works and political theology to give historical and hermeneutical insight and to intervene in our current age through these resources.[50] Julia Reinhard Lupton's *Citizen-Saints: Shakespeare and Political Theology*, for instance, is an exemplary work of scholarship that recontextualizes Shakespeare within early modern religious and political history but also argues for the value of these ideas today. Lupton notes that scholarship on "the strange hybridization of religious and political thinking in the Renaissance" has too often focused on "its gallery of dead kings" rather than "the corpus of citizens implied by political theology," and her exegesis of Shakespeare's plays displaces the monarchal center with another protagonist:

> [T]he hero of this book is not the tyrant-martyr but the citizen-saint, not the two bodies of the king but the many faces of the multitude. By searching for signs of the citizen in the domain of political theology, I emphasize the always-emergent future implied by its sacred tropes of fellowship rather than the termination of its mythic past on the public stage of deposition and regicide.[51]

Lupton shows how literature can imagine alternatives to traditional sites of power and provide new possibilities for our thinking, acting, and belonging.

---

[50] See, for instance, Graham Hammill and Julia Reinhard Lupton, eds., *Political Theology and Early Modernity* (Chicago: University of Chicago Press, 2012). Jared Hickman examines romanticism in nineteenth-century US literature for the intermingling of secularization and enchantment in both literature and politics in "Political Theology," in *The Routledge Companion to Literature and Religion*, ed. Mark Knight (New York: Routledge, 2016), 124–34. See also the symposium "Literature and Political Theology: Religion and Politics in Imaginative Writing," https://politicaltheology.com/symposium/what-is-literature-and-political-theology/.

[51] Julia Reinhard Lupton, *Citizen-Saints: Shakespeare and Political Theology* (Chicago: University of Chicago Press, 2005), 5.

With a similar focus on the liberating theopolitical imagination in literature, G. A. Rosso's *The Religion of Empire: Political Theology in Blake's Prophetic Symbolism* shows how William Blake's surrealistic and gnomic texts supply a vigorous critique of Britain's religiously inspired imperialism. Rosso not only uses political theology as a framework for fresh interpretations of Blake's work and its late-eighteenth-century historical context, but he also argues for "Blake's relevance for contemporary political theology" based in a "dual critical and creative approach to the Bible and his view that the institutionalization of Christianity compromises its ability to resist state-sanctioned violence."[52] Deciphering Blake's symbolism through an anti-imperialist political theology helps clarify and interpret early Romantic literature, but Rosso also demonstrates how literature can contribute to current theopolitical debates and shape our critical imaginations today.

My argument in the following chapters seeks to join the pathway opened by Lupton, Rosso, and others by bringing modernist literature into dialogue with more recent political theology to show the mutual benefit of integrating these fields and their value for current theopolitical action. Within literary studies, there has been a growing concern for work that not only increases knowledge about history and aesthetics but also matters for our lives now. Michaela Bronstein has advocated for the potential of a "recuperative modernism" that extends Rita Felski's notion of post-critique toward even richer possibilities. Bronstein notes that while Felski and others have urged us to expand our interpretive toolbox beyond the hermeneutics of suspicion, there has all too often remained a sense that this means using literature to critique unjust social conditions.[53] As Bronstein notes, "In criticism, then, the oppositional relationship between a text and its world replaces the oppositional relationship between critic and text."[54] There is, undoubtedly, some of this kind of critique in the ways I have framed my arguments, but I am also sympathetic to Bronstein's desire for literary analysis that not only demonstrates the power of social problems but facilitates thinking about robust alternatives. For Bronstein, "Recuperative modernism suggests a different line of development, whereby the most generative gestures of some of these texts are precisely their attempts to provide a counteracting force to the destabilization and uncertainty

---

[52] G. A. Rosso, *The Religion of Empire: Political Theology in Blake's Prophetic Symbolism* (Columbus: Ohio State University Press, 2016), 48.
[53] See Rita Felski, *The Limits of Critique* (Chicago: University of Chicago Press, 2015).
[54] Michaela Bronstein, *Out of Context: The Uses of Modernist Fiction* (Oxford: Oxford University Press, 2018), 16.

they perceive" and she endorses what "the formal innovations of recuperative modernism provide: models for working through critique and coming to the value of commitment on the other side."[55]

Alongside this notion of literary "models" for political commitment, I will return to the word "resources," seeking within the novels of Woolf, Lawrence, Waugh, and Warner the resources for a theopolitical imagination. Reading literary works in this way risks contradicting some hallmark tenets of modernism, famously expressed by Virginia Woolf in her attack on Edwardian novelists who wrote fiction that she claimed was marred by "incompleteness" which resulted from its attempts at political utility: "in order to complete them it seems necessary to do something—to join a society, or, more desperately, to write a cheque."[56] Though the past two decades of the new modernist studies have paved the way such that we no longer need to make a case for modernism being politically and historically engaged, there remains a concern about turning literary works into something purely instrumental and utilitarian. This problem is inherent in the cross-disciplinary nature of this book, where a field such as political theology which is propositional and articulated from clearly named points of view and positions—Marxist, Anabaptist, anarchist, Reformed, etc.—meets with work that artistically and aesthetically renders experience without resorting to simplistic pamphleteering. My title, thus, is admittedly contentious: speaking of literature "as" political theology threatens to reduce, flatten, or sand-down the aesthetic textures of rich literary writing that contains multitudes but may appear in my accounts as a tool for theopolitical pronouncements. The analyses in the following chapters seek to show how formal experimentation is vital to the theopolitical imagination as well as elevating the very concept of "imagination" that appears in political theology but without the full sense of artistry literary studies brings to the term. The dialogue I am seeking within these pages among a variety of religious and secular theologians and a group of non-Christian English modernist novelists is not predicated on the easy integration of these voices but rather on the productive tensions that arise when people with different religious and political bases, orientations, and teleologies cooperatively share together to counteract hegemonic powers and imagine fresh possibilities—a project just as vital in the twenty-first century as it was in the early twentieth.

Attention to modernism and political theology adds to the growing scholarly interest in religion within modernist studies—work that has problematized

---

[55] Ibid., 16–17.
[56] Virginia Woolf, *The Essays of Virginia Woolf: Volume III, 1919-1924*, ed. Andrew McNeilli (San Diego, CA: HBJ, 1988), 427.

simplistic versions of the secularization thesis prominent in the sociology of religion.[57] Charles Taylor describes these reductive versions of secularization as "subtraction stories" where religion assumes a smaller and smaller role in modern life because "human beings [have] lost, or sloughed off, or liberated themselves from certain earlier, confining horizons, or illusions, or limitations of knowledge."[58] Though some form of secularization remains a hallmark of modernity, this sense of gradual subtraction offers an inadequate account of the unevenness of secularism globally. Within modernist studies there has been long-standing interest in the handful of writers who were people of faith such as T. S. Eliot, David Jones, W. H. Auden, and Graham Greene, though these are typically treated as exceptions to the generally secular culture.[59] Virginia Woolf's famous comments to her sister Vanessa about Eliot's Christian conversion are often taken as typical: "there's something obscene in a living person sitting by the fire and believing in God."[60] Secularism in early-twentieth-century Britain was not, as many scholars have shown, nearly so uniform or total.[61] Vincent P. Pecora, for example, argues in *Secularization and Cultural Criticism: Religion, Nation, and Modernity* that "the static and totalizing concept of secularism—connoting an already achieved and reliably reproducible intellectual standpoint—be supplanted with a dynamic understanding of secularization, that is, with a process that has remained [...] in some ambiguous relationship with religious tradition, neither translation and transformation, nor radical overturning and forgetting."[62] Instead of understanding the modernist period as defined by religious decline, there is a growing perception that the early twentieth century was marked by ambiguity and the uneasy, complex, and entangled relationship

---

[57] See Suzanne Hobson and Andrew D. Radford, eds., *The Edinburgh Companion to Modernism, Myth and Religion* (Edinburgh: Edinburgh University Press, 2023).

[58] Taylor, *A Secular Age*, 22.

[59] See, for example, Erik Tonning, *Modernism and Christianity* (New York: Palgrave Macmillan, 2014); Anthony Domestico, *Poetry and Theology in the Modernist Period* (Baltimore: Johns Hopkins University Press, 2017); Allan Hepburn, *A Grain of Faith: Religion in Mid-century British Literature* (Oxford: Oxford University Press, 2018).

[60] Virginia Woolf, *The Letters of Virginia Woolf, Volume III: 1923–1928*, ed. Nigel Nicholson and Joanne Trautmann (New York: HBJ, 1978), 458. As I will discuss in the following chapter, Woolf's remarks are more performative than theoretical here, writing in part to entertain her sister by voicing "shocking" opinions.

[61] Amardeep Singh, *Literary Secularism: Religion and Modernity in Twentieth-Century Fiction* (Newcastle: Cambridge Scholars, 2006); Gregory Erickson, *The Absence of God in Modernist Literature* (New York: Palgrave Macmillan, 2007); Matthew Mutter, *Restless Secularism: Modernism and the Religious Inheritance* (New Haven, CT: Yale University Press, 2017); Steve Pinkerton, *Blasphemous Modernism: The 20th-Century Word Made Flesh* (Oxford: Oxford University Press, 2017); Suzanne Hobson, *Unbelief in Interwar Literary Culture: Doubting Moderns* (Oxford: Oxford University Press, 2022).

[62] Vincent P. Pecora, *Secularization and Cultural Criticism: Religion, Nation, & Modernity* (Chicago: University of Chicago Press, 2006), 208.

between belief and unbelief, tradition and renunciation. In essence, it may now be seen as a period of "addition stories" rather than subtraction, where numerous possible modes of incomplete faith compete across a varied religious spectrum.

Perhaps the most significant challenge to the secularization thesis in modernist studies has come from scholars focusing on those "additions" through the various new, transformed versions of religion and personal faith that emerged in the early twentieth century. Theosophy, mysticism, and a host of other transcendental spiritualisms grew in popularity as traditional orthodoxies and churches began to lose sway.[63] A broad attraction to what Pericles Lewis calls "religious experience" developed among people disenchanted with historic faiths but yearning for a replacement, and, in Lewis's view, turned "the novel's sociological possibilities toward a consideration of this type of religious experience" and transformed the genre.[64] About this surprising persistence of religiosity, Lewis remarks, "If God died in the nineteenth century, he had an active afterlife in the twentieth."[65] That afterlife was sustained by a felt need for something transcendent in the modern age—a need that pure materialism and austere rationalism could not supplant. Joyce Wexler argues that the absence of religious consensus meant that "the meaning of violence could no longer be grounded in a transcendent order" and that twentieth-century writers sought innovative forms in order "to describe violent events without imposing a meaning on them," developing "strategies that make the meaning of their narratives indeterminate."[66] For Lewis, Wexler, and others, the developments in literary form through the modernist period directly relate to the changing religious landscape, the loss of traditional consensus but the expansion of more general forms of transcendence during a time of widespread political violence. Studies such as these have altered our conception of the period and its handling of religion, and my arguments in this book share their attention to ambiguous, alternative forms of faith.

Where my use of political theology shifts our angle of focus, however, is its insistence on public, collective, and material dimensions of religion rather than individual belief and doubt. The idea of a generalized "religious experience"

---

[63] Gauri Viswanathan, *Outside the Fold: Conversion, Modernity, and Belief* (Princeton: Princeton University Press, 1998), George M. Johnson, *Mourning and Mysticism in First World War Literature: Grappling with Ghosts* (New York: Palgrave Macmillan, 2015).
[64] Pericles Lewis, *Religious Experience and the Modernist Novel* (Cambridge: Cambridge University Press, 2010), 5.
[65] Ibid., 25.
[66] Joyce Wexler, *Violence without God: The Rhetorical Despair of Twentieth-Century Writers* (London: Bloomsbury, 2017), 3, 19.

is indebted to William James, who defined "religion" as "the feelings, acts, and experiences of individual men in their solitude, so far as they apprehend themselves to stand in relation to whatever they may consider the divine" and argued that from this individual basis, "theologies, philosophies, and ecclesiastical organizations may secondarily grow."[67] While this formulation no doubt describes many people's self-understanding of faith or "religious experience," it undervalues the social dynamics of religion as well as the power of ecclesiastical organizations, theologies, and philosophies to shape and determine individual lives.[68] James's sense that an individual "apprehends" for themselves a religious experience and then orients toward larger ideologies and material practices does not adequately describe the writers that I discuss in the following chapters. Woolf, Lawrence, Waugh, and Warner each had significant experiences with churches and people of faith in childhood, and their reactions against those experiences informed their mature development of alternative ideologies in adulthood. Understanding how fiction by these writers functions as political theology moves our focus away from the private, individual realm of "belief" or "relationship with the divine" and instead claims that religious and political ideologies and institutions place pressure on us regardless of our internal convictions or "experience" of faith. The resistance to oppressive social powers that I find in these novels does not come from ignoring the theologies of the state or retreating into private spirituality. It is resistance forged through conflicted efforts toward better theologies—theologies that challenge the nation's narratives of sacrifice and offer alternative means of flourishing.

---

[67] William James, *The Varieties of Religious Experience: A Study in Human Nature*. 1902 (New York: Penguin, 1982), 31. The emphasis on individual "belief" and reliance on terms established by William James appears frequently, as in Jessica R. Feldman, *Victorian Modernism: Pragmatism and the Varieties of Aesthetic Experience* (Cambridge: Cambridge University Press, 2002) and Craig Bradshaw Woelfel, *Varieties of Aesthetic Experience: Literary Modernism and the Dissociation of Belief* (Columbia, SC: University of South Carolina Press, 2018).

[68] For a nuanced appreciation of James's book, see Charles Taylor, *Varieties of Religion Today: William James Revisited* (Cambridge, MA: Harvard University Press, 2002). Taylor notes that "people have pointed out the relative narrowness of the Jamesian perspective," but he puts this perspective into an historical context during the shifting consensus about religious belief that Taylor would map more thoroughly in *A Secular Age*. Assumptions about faith as an individualistic and private matter constrain some otherwise-valuable efforts to reconcile religion with modernism. Richard Kearney's admirable attempt to bridge the distance between religious people and staunch atheists while using Woolf and Joyce as his literary allies is one such effort. Kearney seeks a third space of transcendence that can be shared by all, and in doing so under-appreciates the shaping and domineering forces of historical, material, and political institutions of church and state. See Kearney, *Anatheism: Returning to God after God* (New York: Columbia University Press, 2010) and Richard Kearney and Jens Zimmerman, eds., *Reimagining the Sacred: Richard Kearney Debates God with James Wood, Catherine Keller, Charles Taylor, Julia Kristina, Gianni Vattimo, Simon Critchley, Jean-Luc Marion, John Caputo, David Tracy, Jens Zimmerman, and Merold Westphal* (New York: Columbia University Press, 2015).

Those sacrificial narratives were especially prominent during the heights of the Great War and its aftermath—the urgency of war and the necessity of commemoration each in their own ways elevating the presence of nationalism and civil religion. But the vigorous campaigns of patriotism and public liturgies of postwar mourning are not the only ways that nationalism acts upon citizenry. Such displays are what Michael Billig refers to as "'hot' nationalist passion," the sort of demonstrations we typically think of during times of war and revolution or through imperial conquest and anti-imperial resistance.[69] Billig takes flags as emblematic of the way that nationalism operates on us, noting that "only the passionately waved flags are conventionally considered to be exemplars of nationalism. Routine flags [...] slip from the category of 'nationalism' [...] and having slipped through the categorical net, they get lost."[70] "Banal nationalism" is Billig's term for the casual presence of nationalist symbols during times of relative political calm, and he argues that "daily, the nation is indicated, or 'flagged', in the lives of its citizenry. Nationalism, far from being an intermittent mood in established nations, is the endemic condition."[71] "Banal," Billig stresses, "does not imply benign," and that among many North American and European powers, the constant presence of nationalism keeps citizens "primed" for violence and "reproducing institutions which possess vast armaments."[72] War is a significant presence in all of the novels under discussion in this book, although mostly relegated to the background of the narrative or subtly and allusively present through images of violence that encourage readers to make connections among the forces of militarism, imperialism, capitalism, nationalism, and Christianity. Across a range of narrative devices and styles, the four authors I focus on display a theopolitical imagination that contends with these forces, supplying critique but also, at times, the possibilities for better commitments.

Four Pathways for Theopolitical Fiction

Woolf, Lawrence, Waugh, and Warner can each be understood as writing fiction that presses beyond the allures of the nation and of conventional religion. Their positioning as nontheists who exhibit theopolitical reflection offers a

---

[69] Michael Billig, *Banal Nationalism* (London: Sage, 1995), 44.
[70] Ibid., 38–9.
[71] Ibid., 6.
[72] Ibid., 6–7.

fresh vantage point for examining both the literary works and political theory. Modernist fiction is especially fruitful for political theology because of its formal experimentation, the ways that literature from this period broke with the conventions of previous eras, and the following chapters examine individual writers to show how their experiments with literary form supply unique approaches to resisting the power of English civil religion.

This set of writers is by no means an exhaustive survey of the political theologies of modernism. Instead, I hope that the following chapters are productively suggestive for further study of literature as theopolitical imagination and for future critics who might find in political theology a range of resources for interpretation and cultural intervention.[73] By placing our focus on political theology, I am advocating a turn toward theological work that emphasizes community, materiality, social action, and public witness as essential to faith, not as additional benefits layered on top of an essential foundation of spirituality. Identifying the work of modern novels as "secular theology" is not meant to ferret out and expose some secret core of religious belief within the secular. I am interested in the ways that avowedly atheistic or agnostic writers end up producing works that critically explore certain forms of Christianity, revealing in the process that some kinds of public Christianity are inescapable and that disavowal of belief does not mean that one can simply choose to be rid of religion. To combat the pernicious forces of civil religion, a more robust alternative is necessary, one that is not based in single-minded rejection, avoidance, or ignorance. In a culture shot-through with Christian ideologies, as was England in the years immediately following the Great War, religion could be despised but not ignored. It is my contention that works of fiction by Woolf, Lawrence, Waugh, and Warner offer theological alternatives—not in service of orthodox Christianity but as critical rejoinders to the patriarchal/masculinist, militaristic, heteronormative, and imperialist ideologies of the sacralized nation-state. These four novelists are not uniform in their approaches or in their perceptions of the problems with civil religion, but read together they offer a range of responses

---

[73] Attention to the damaging power of the sacralized state is not the only avenue for cross-disciplinary work in political theology. Other areas include but are not limited to the work of Latin American and Black liberation theologies as well as womanist, queer, and feminist theologies and theopolitical ecology. See, for instance, Gustavo Gutiérrez, *A Theology of Liberation: History, Politics, and Salvation* (Maryknoll, NY: Orbis, 1973); James H. Cone, *A Black Theology of Liberation* (Maryknoll, NY: Orbis, 1970); M. Shawn Copeland, *Enfleshing Freedom: Body, Race, and Being* (Minneapolis: Fortress Press, 2010); Catherine Keller, *Political Theology of the Earth: Our Planetary Emergency and the Struggle for a New Public* (New York: Columbia University Press, 2018); Clayton Crockett, *Energy and Change: A New Materialist Cosmotheology* (New York: Columbia University Press, 2022); J. Kameron Carter, *The Anarchy of Black Religion: A Mystic Song* (Durham, NC: Duke University Press, 2023).

to those problems, imagining pathways for alternative visions that share with political theology the insistence that everyday practices involve liturgies that coordinate our inner lives with our public and collective energies.

Virginia Woolf, the subject of Chapter 1, was once an emblematic figure of atheistic modernism, a dissenter whose religious views were encapsulated by a few of her most famous jibes at Christian friends such as Ethel Smyth and T. S. Eliot. A rising wave of scholarship has begun to complicate this image, showing the depth of her engagement with Christianity and the influence of her family's heritage in the evangelical Clapham Sect as well as broader connections to Quakerism and Anglicanism. Very little attention, however, has been given to the religious aspects of her novel *Jacob's Room* (1922). In Chapter 1, I argue that Woolf's first fully experimental novel confronts the myriad ways civil religion shapes and deforms us through institutions such as the university and church. Even a person as aloof and seemingly disinterested as her protagonist Jacob Flanders becomes complicit in patriarchal, militaristic nationalism, ultimately finding himself ensnared by the religious aura of the state which leads to his meaningless death in the First World War. What makes the novel so compelling is not that Woolf imagines a means for escaping such ideological entrapments. Rather, by drawing on James K. A. Smith's theology of "everyday political liturgies" as well as Stanley Hauerwas and Romand Coles's work on local micro-politics and "the radical ordinary," I argue that *Jacob's Room* demonstrates in extensive detail the power of liturgy in creating collective consciousness. Woolf calls attention to the everyday rituals that conscript us into the state, but she also suggests how elegy can be a form of protest against sacrificial narratives of the nation and how attention to the "radically ordinary" parts of our lives can be an antidote to the politics of death. The novel's tragic ending casts a vision for living richly and fully while remaining "unredeemed"—a concept I borrow from the political theologian Karen Bray, who challenges political and theological narratives based in teleologies of "success." Woolf's novel draws attention to living un-conscripted by the success narratives of the church and state and seeking an alternative to those damaging institutions.

Woolf exposes the ways British social institutions harm individual lives, molding them through misogynistic, militaristic, and imperialist practices that lead toward death. In my second chapter, I turn to Lawrence's late writings which tackle even more cosmic theopolitical concerns. In this chapter, I argue that *Lady Chatterley's Lover* (1928) is deeply invested in the politics of eschatology and rich with apocalyptic imagination. Theology of the "end-times" was a preoccupation for Lawrence, who poignantly devoted his last days to a final book called *Apocalypse* (1931) wherein he applied his characteristically idiosyncratic analysis to the biblical book of Revelation. In that final book, Lawrence chastised the working-class, Congregationalist Sunday school teachers of his youth for promoting a Christianity based in class resentment and total devastation. Their delight in the apocalypse of Revelation, according to Lawrence, was characteristic of the worst parts of Christianity that emphasize spitefulness, envy, and division over unity and connectivity. Lawrence's interpretation of Revelation notably lacks any recognition of the anti-imperial politics of that biblical book, but he offers his own radical theopolitical vision by concluding with a manifesto about resurrection, rebirth, and cosmic harmony. I put Lawrence's commentary in *Apocalypse* into dialogue with Jürgen Moltmann's writings on eschatology and political theology in order to show how his idea of total cosmic renewal shares in Moltmann's theology of living eschatologically during the present time. In exploring the politics of eschatology, Lawrence anticipates the work of theologians who argue for an end-times imagination that is not other-worldly and utopian but distinctly immanent and material, giving shape to our current lives because of the imagined vision of an eschaton. This theory of political eschatology allows us to return to *Lady Chatterley's Lover* with fresh eyes. *Lady Chatterley's Lover*, captive for so long to debates about its feminism/misogyny and obscenity, offers an apocalyptic vision that is not limited to its views on sex. Like *Apocalypse*, the novel envisions the dying and rising through flames that is fundamental to Lawrence's favorite mythical figure, the phoenix. The novel ends on a note of hopefulness about the future that must necessarily be embedded in the broken, unredeemed, and unrealized present, where all that appears are ashes that promise a later union. This vision is a potential source of hope for all of us today who live within political dreams that are unfulfilled, incomplete, or even failed.

The differing ways that Woolf and Lawrence invite us to reimagine political hopes and failures lead to the third chapter which analyzes a pair of bitterly comic novels by Evelyn Waugh that expose the rotten core of all social institutions and human relationships. Waugh might at first seem out of place in a book centered on the theologies of non-Christian writers; he is, after all, a giant among Roman Catholic artists and a standard-bearer for conservative politics and traditionalist pieties. His official reception into the Roman Catholic Church, however, occurred on September 29, 1930, and before this signal event, he had published two novels that depicted Christian culture in complex and ambiguous ways. Though he always had one foot inside the church before stepping fully into its sodality, Waugh's work of the 1920s is as conflicted about Christianity as the more provocatively unorthodox Woolf and Lawrence. *Decline and Fall* (1928) and *Vile Bodies* (1930) are scathing satires that adopt a mode of cynicism which, I argue, operates as political theology by biting at the hypocrisies and absurdities of English institutions. Schools, churches, businesses, clubs, and a host of other social organizations wither under Waugh's poison pen, and this wide range of targets displays how such institutions control, confine, and destroy individuals. "Cynicism" is a term often used to describe Waugh's early works, but rarely has this word been theorized beyond its colloquial meaning. I put Waugh's fiction in dialogue with political theology by Michel Foucault, whose late work on *parrhesia* (truth-telling) and cynicism explored a political theory that endorsed early instances of radical Christianity for its revolutionary politics. Cynical political theology in Waugh's work bites at the ideologies and institutions that produce a self-stultifying middle class and fuel a vicious and senseless war, molding young people into unthinking, docile citizens and ultimately crushing them. Cynicism is a mode for speaking truthfully to power, even when Waugh's convictions were inchoate and uncertain.

In contrast to Waugh's cynical denouncements of the powerful, the fourth chapter examines a writer whose strategy for resistance to the sacralized state came from flourishing unseen, beyond state control. I analyze Sylvia Townsend Warner's first novel for its use of queer anarchism as a mode of political theology. After encountering anarchist revolutionaries in Spain, Warner wrote to a friend that "anarchism ought to be the political theory of heaven," and *Lolly Willowes* (1926) offers a surprising and fantastical exploration of the ways Christian mythologies and practices can be modified and adapted toward anarchist ends.[74] By drawing on Simon Critchley's discussion of anarchism as a secular political theology and Jack Halberstam's reclaiming of "failure" as a promising source for queer anarchy, I show how Warner's fiction explores the interstitial and illegible places where anarchism thrives beyond the control of the church and state. *Lolly Willowes* combines a realist comedy of manners with a swerve into fantasy to produce anarchism that remains imaginative, speculative, and tentative rather than programmatic and practical. The novel's theopolitical imagination promises surprising possibilities outside the gaze of the enchanted state.

Imagination is not monolithic or uniform across the four novelists I discuss in these pages and the theopolitical resources I discern from their narratives is likewise varied, but there are some shared commitments and practices made visible by reading these works side by side. Chief among these is their sense of

---

[74] Sylvia Townsend Warner, *Letters*, ed. William Maxwell (London: Chatto & Windus, 1982), 42.

political forms that are open-ended, inconclusive, tentative, and even sometimes agonized. Rather than declarative pronouncements that project certainty—and thereby draw stark lines of inclusion and exclusion as well as foreclosed political endpoints—modernist fiction models political theology that critiques injustices and strives toward better modes of individual and collective flourishing without providing definitive answers or solutions. These novels cast political visions while retaining a modernist style of inconclusiveness, multivalence, plurality, and polyvocality. From their witness, we can begin the slow work of perceiving the world more sensitively and with heightened awareness of the damaging political narratives that enthrall us. Reading modernist fiction as political theology gives depth and nuance to the vital task of improving our social imagination.

1

Virginia Woolf and Political Liturgies for the Unredeemed: *Jacob's Room*

The commemoration rituals for the Great War in Whitehall and Westminster Abbey on the second anniversary of the armistice were the products of great planning and much deliberation. But, coordinated displays of hot nationalism such as those are an acute flare-up of civil religion that is always present and subtly exerting its influence on public life. On November 11, 1918, the actual day of the armistice, without the benefit of preparation and painstaking coordination, the war's end was met with various forms of exuberance, regret, and relief that also retained a current of religious sentiment that could meet the momentous occasion with an aura of enchantment. Even in a secularizing nation such as England, the language, symbols, and rituals of Christianity promoted this aura and remained vital to the national displays of gratitude for peace in their spontaneous forms. Prime Minister David Lloyd George, for example, welcomed the news of the ceasefire by reading the Psalms in his study and then heading to the House of Commons to deliver a report followed by an impromptu "thanksgiving service" led by Archbishop Randall Davidson.[1] Nearby, the riotous celebrations in Trafalgar Square persisted for several days, but equally insistent were choruses of bells as churches made themselves heard giving thanks.[2] At Buckingham Palace, the assembled crowd shouted for King George to make an appearance, and after singing "God Save the King," they turned to other corporate songs including "Keep the Home Fires Burning," "It's a Long Way to Tipperary," national anthems of the Allied nations, and also

---

[1] Stanley Weintraub, *A Stillness Heard Round the World: The End of the Great War, November 1918* (London: Dutton, 1985), 253–4.
[2] Guy Cuthbertson, *Peace at Last: A Portrait of Armistice Day, November 11, 1918* (New Haven: Yale University Press, 2018), 1.

the Doxology—a blend of popular, patriotic, and Christian hymnody.[3] Singing together at a time such as this forms what Benedict Anderson calls "unisonance," the use of song as "the echoed physical realization of the imagined community" of the nation.[4] National imagination flourishes through unisonance, and its bonds are increased by joining with religion.[5] As a population gathers publicly to celebrate, grieve, and express relief, it enacts rituals shaped by religious practices but directed toward the supposedly secular nation-state.

This fusion is the essence of civil religion, and in the aftermath of the war, Christian churches in England contributed heartily to the nationalist effort, bestowing transcendent significance on collective grief. Guy Cuthbertson claims that the first Armistice Day "was arguably the last day in English history when the Church of England was truly a national church," a suggestion about the unifying force of Anglicanism at a time when people desperately scrambled for ways to unite.[6] The *Gazette* of the London and Northwestern Railway—not a publication typically consulted for its theological insights—declared that the celebrations at the war's end were

> of a strongly religious character, and have been directed to Him Who alone giveth the victory and from Whom must come the peace which passeth all understanding. It has been an inspiring experience to find the definite emphasis by the unanimous voice of the people, in the very dawn of their newfound gladness, that we are still a Christian nation.[7]

Similarly, when King George spoke to the roaring crowd at Buckingham Palace, he couched patriotism in prayer: "With you I rejoice and thank God for the victories which the Allied arms have won, bringing hostilities to an end and peace within sight."[8] This declaration from the monarch was followed by more corporate song that blended Christianity with patriotism—"Now Thank We All Our God" and the national anthem.[9] This collaboration between church and

---

[3] This song list was recorded by Patricia Carver and quoted in Nicholas Best, *The Greatest Day in History: How on the Eleventh Hour of the Eleventh Day of the Eleventh Month, the First World War Finally Came to an End* (New York: Public Affairs, 2008), 211.
[4] Anderson, *Imagined Communities*, 145.
[5] In describing unisonance, Anderson notes in passing that "the recitation of ceremonial poetry, such as sections of the *Book of Common Prayer*" can also produce unisonality, but his account of the nation as a modern, secular replacement for religion forecloses his investigation into how religious works such as Christian hymns or common liturgies can enhance and amplify the national imagination (*Imagined Communities*, 145).
[6] Cuthbertson, *Peace at Last*, 106.
[7] qtd. in Cuthbertson, *Peace at Last*, 106.
[8] qtd. in Best, *The Greatest Day in History*, 212.
[9] Best, *The Greatest Day in History*, 212.

state was not just an added layer of religious support for patriotic demonstration: it was the reproduction and reinforcement of an English civil religion.

These highly visible, collective expressions of civil religion can be understood as "liturgy"—that is, the "public work" of the nation operating in a manner similar to divine worship. James K. A. Smith has written extensively of such "cultural liturgies" and the powerful ways they shape and guide us, arguing that liturgies are "*rituals of ultimate concern*: rituals that are formative for identity, that inculcate particular visions of the good life, and do so in a way that means to trump other ritual formations."[10] Smith argues that too often debates in political theology have neglected this liturgical dimension of politics, remaining caught in "'spatialized' terms" where "'the political' is a kind of realm, a turf, or a territory" and competing parties focus on "boundary management and border patrols."[11] Instead of efforts to determine what "realms" of public life function as secular or religious, Smith advocates a thorough examination of the rituals and practices of politics to understand how we are formed as citizens and how we might enact liturgies that enable better possibilities for flourishing. Echoing Smith's account of political liturgy, Bob Bushaway observes that in commemorations of the First World War, "remembrance was an act rather than an object," and the physical memorials erected throughout the country were made potent by the rituals that surrounded them.[12] Public rituals of remembrance are common in many national settings, though wartime and its aftermath frequently generates greater heat than times of relative calm. By attending to this heated moment of English nationalism, we may apprehend more clearly the ways that political life always shapes and forms us, not because we intellectually assent to political "beliefs" but because of the practices and rites inherent to citizenship.

For Virginia Woolf, who was highly skeptical about both nationalism and Christianity, the Armistice Day festivities were an object for scorn. Despite her skepticism, however, her emotions were notably mixed. Her recorded comments about the day's festivities are peppered with irritation and disdain, as in a letter to her sister Vanessa describing the celebrations with their catcalls and whistles as "not in the least impressive—only unsettling."[13] The sounds in

---

[10] James K. A. Smith, *Desiring the Kingdom: Worship, Worldview, and Cultural Formation*; Volume 1 of *Cultural Liturgies* (Grand Rapids: Baker Academic, 2009), 86.
[11] James K. A. Smith, *Awaiting the King: Reforming Public Theology*; Volume 3 of *Cultural Liturgies* (Grand Rapids: Baker Academic, 2009), 8.
[12] Bob Bushaway, "Name Upon Name: The Great War and Remembrance," in *Myths of the English*, ed. Roy Porter (Cambridge: Polity, 1993), 143.
[13] Virginia Woolf, *The Letters of Virginia Woolf, Volume II: 1912-1922*, ed. Nigel Nicolson and Joanne Trautmann (New York: HBJ, 1976), 290.

the street disturbed her labors to complete her novel *Night and Day*, and the displays of hot nationalism were irksome for both their disruptiveness and their ineptitude. Woolf relates a series of observations about how the people around her were dealing with flags, the central liturgical symbols of patriotism. The servants Nelly and Lottie have become very emotional about the war's end, Woolf reports, and Nelly has four flags that she is putting in the front rooms. The taxis are honking and children are gathering around a flag, and "at this moment a harmonium is playing a hymn, and a large Union Jack has been hoisted onto a pole."[14] This holy rite of flags and hymns is conducted around and in front of Woolf by people across the generational spectrum and class hierarchy, uniting the nation in their response to the armistice. On one hand, Woolf finds all of this behavior ostentatious and irritating. On the other hand, she finds herself compelled by the national liturgies in her midst. Her narration of these events to Vanessa positions Woolf as a detached observer rather than a participant, but she comments on her conflicted feelings: "O God! What a noise they make—and I, on the whole though rather emotional (would you be, I wonder?) feel also immensely melancholy."[15] Like so many recorded moments where Woolf reacts to patriotic furor around her, there is nothing straightforward or simple in her response. She is not swept along with the national liturgy, fully and uncritically, as she perceives the servants to be, but she is also not immune to the deep emotions of the moment. The "melancholy" is especially notable, revealing that the end of combat brought feelings of loss and grief rather than satisfaction and joy. Critics have discussed the importance of melancholia in Woolf's writing as a political response to modernity.[16] The melancholia on Armistice Day, however, specifically arises from her disconnection with political liturgies, the cost of being a critical outsider at a time of national unity.

Woolf's commentary also betrays how some of her resistance to patriotism is bound up with classism.[17] Part of what makes the servants' festivities obnoxious to her is their vulgarity; the celebrations and national symbols are embraced by the masses, and disdain for patriotic devotion is colored by disdain for the masses

---

[14] Ibid.
[15] Ibid.
[16] See, for instance, Sanja Bahun, *Modernism and Melancholia: Writing as Countermourning* (Oxford: Oxford University Press, 2014) and Elsa Högberg, *Virginia Woolf and the Ethics of Intimacy* (London: Bloomsbury Academic, 2020).
[17] On this dimension Woolf's different experience from Nelly's of the war and armistice, see, Hermione Lee, *Virginia Woolf* (New York: Vintage, 1996), 353; and, Alison Light, *Mrs. Woolf and the Servants: An Intimate History of Domestic Life at Bloomsbury* (London: Bloomsbury, 2007). As Lee describes it, Woolf's "reactions to the war were a mixture of a pacifist's horror of the glorification of militarism, and alienation from the ordinary combatant or civilian's view" (339).

themselves. I mention this implication not to chastise Woolf for her unexamined prejudices but rather to highlight the connection between Woolf's conflicted feelings and what we will see in the conflicted nature of her novel *Jacob's Room*. Among the vital contributions of the novel is its capacity to make us aware of the unseen ways that civil religion conditions all of us and forms us into citizens complicit in patriarchal, militaristic nationalism. Spurning the patriotic devotion of others, however, does not exempt us from complicity in such patriotism. What *Jacob's Room* illuminates is how thoroughly the religious aura of the state can penetrate our everyday lives. Woolf's letters and diaries reveal her inner conflict about the enchantments of the state in a time of postwar celebration, and *Jacob's Room* became her first major fictional work to grapple with those conflicts by exposing the powerful allures of civil religion and the limits of personal, individual detachment.

Complicity with civil religion does not mean that there are no ways to mount forms of resistance—only that our individual detachments from religious nationalism cannot make us "pure." Woolf concludes her letter to Vanessa about Armistice Day with an anecdote about dining with her friend, the Cambridge academic H. T. J. Norton, whose presence, she writes, "solves all my religious feelings."[18] From this half-joking comment about her innate religiosity being satisfied by the aura of Cambridge, she ends with a capsule update on the Armistice Day celebrations: "We've now had marriage bells, one hymn, God save the King twice over, about a dozen separate cheers, and the old gentleman opposite has climbed to the top of a tree with an immense Union Jack."[19] The sounds outside Woolf's window are rich with the music of civil religion, where church rituals and songs freely mix with the national anthem—a hymn that famously petitions God for his blessings on the monarch. The final detail of the letter shows off Woolf's novelistic skill, using a simply described image to capture an array of feelings and to reveal the grandiose and self-serious displays of hot patriotism as self-evidently ridiculous. It is one of the letter's moments of critical resistance, deflating the patriotic scene and its civil religious liturgy by making its prevailing emblem the image of an old man scrambling with an oversized flag. The glories of war, the adventures of empire, the adoration of the monarchy, the leadership of the gentry, and the rituals of the nation all boil down to a crank in a tree. Woolf mocks the scene, but she also finds herself implicated in it, and

---

[18] Woolf, *Letters II*, 292.
[19] Ibid.

her letter-writing is a means by which she can process the range of conflicted feelings provoked by the national celebrations.

My contention in this chapter is that *Jacob's Room* explores the powerful, formative cultural practices that produce the enchanted nation-state and its militaristic and imperialist drives—but it heightens our awareness of these dangers without supplying easy ways of escape. It is a theopolitical novel, highly attuned to and critical of the presence of Christianity as a social force, but it offers fewer of the mystical comforts that give light and hope to her later fictions. As Vincent Sherry has argued, the Great War destroyed the certitude of liberal rationalism and made foolish the language of that ideology, and *Jacob's Room* is a novel of "expressive inarticulateness" where "the unspeakability of this war engages the main energy of Woolf's verbal inventiveness."[20] The novel is by no means a manifesto nor does it simply model for us any clear-cut strategies for resisting civil religion, militarism, or the demands of the state. Instead, its resources come from the ways Woolf identifies and exposes the powerful pressures of political liturgy, the limits of private, individual resistance, and the necessity for local, relational micro-politics. *Jacob's Room* ends tragically in desperation and grief, with an almost total lack of possibility for meaningful opposition to militaristic liturgies. And yet, the lack of "redemption" for its titular character may offer the novel's most significant intervention into the narratives of sacrificial nationalism that dominated the war years and the postwar celebrations and commemorations. The novel is both a tragedy and an elegy, and through its depiction of a culture damaged by militaristic institutions of church, state, and university, it enacts a creative expression of political theology.

Woolf and the Theopolitical Imagination

Virginia Woolf was once viewed as an emblem for modernist atheism, a voice of dissent during a time of relatively widespread religiosity in a nation that would experience significant religious decline in the decades following the Second

---

[20] Vincent Sherry, *The Great War and the Language of Modernism* (Oxford: Oxford University Press, 2003), 275. Sherry asserts that the "agon and pathos" of the age appears in Woolf's prose, and he says that the *Jacob's Room* has "no moralistic purpose, of the sort later critics may impute to her" (Ibid.). Sherry's caution about reading the novel didactically is important, but I would suggest that it can still be interpreted as a work of elegy, witness, and even protest without losing the sense of its conflicted, agonized style and the bleakness of its conclusion.

World War.²¹ But this image has begun to alter in recent scholarship, making her a figure of great interest for scholars focusing on modernist religion, spirituality, and complicated secularism.²² The signal feature of that interest is recognition that Woolf's critical engagement with religion and secularism did not come from a simplistic, uninformed, or unequivocal place—despite the frequently pulled quotations of her caustic remarks about Christian friends. T. S. Eliot's Anglo-Catholic conversion prompted Woolf's quip to her sister Vanessa, for instance, that "a corpse would seem to me more credible than he is."²³ What can sometimes go unrecognized in such comments is how performative and humorous they are, less a record of thoughtful critique of religion than a demonstration of Woolf's biting comedic talents in letters to a receptive audience. Her most famous barbed comments about religion are but a few instances of dismissiveness within a wealth of writing about Christianity as a spiritual, theological, social, and political force, and her record of grappling with faith has informed many scholarly reexaminations of modern secularism.

Within this growing body of scholarship on Woolf and religion, there has been a tendency to focus on mysticism, spirituality, and generalized "religious experience"—much of which centers on *To the Lighthouse* for its lyrical evocation of the numinous and mystical connections among people and nature.²⁴ Pericles Lewis argues that Woolf's fiction sought "to effect a re-enchantment of the world" and to make "a new form of spirituality independent of the Christian God and

---

[21] On Woolf's atheism, see Michael Lackey, "Atheism and Sadism: Nietzsche and Woolf on Post-God Discourse," *Philosophy and Literature* 24, no. 2 (2000): 346–63 and "Virginia Woolf and T. S. Eliot: An Atheist's Commentary on the Epistemology of Belief," *Woolf Studies Annual* 8 (2002): 62–87. For examples of the numerous responses to Lackey's arguments, see Christopher J. Knight, "'The God of Love Is Full of Tricks': Virginia Woolf's Vexed Relation to the Tradition of Christianity," *Religion and Literature* 39, no. 1 (2007): 27–46, and Mark Gaipa, "An Agnostic Daughter's Apology: Materialism, Spiritualism, and Ancestry in Virginia Woolf's *To the Lighthouse*," *Journal of Modern Literature* 26, no. 2 (2003): 1–41.

[22] Vincent Pecora describes Woolf as a crucial figure of secularization who does not show a simple absence of religion but of a Heideggerian *Verwindung* in which the "secular" is a process rather than a static place. See Pecora, *Secularization and Cultural Criticism*, 157–94. Among the many studies influenced by Pecora's work on Woolf and secularism, see Matthew Mutter, *Restless Secularism: Modernism and the Religious Inheritance* (New Haven: Yale University Press, 2017).

[23] Virginia Woolf, *The Letters of Virginia Woolf, Volume III: 1923–1928*, eds. Nigel Nicholson and Joanne Trautmann (New York: Harcourt Brace Jovanovich, 1978), 457–8.

[24] On Woolf and mysticism, see Donna Lazenby, *A Mystical Philosophy: Transcendence and Immanence in the Works of Virginia Woolf and Iris Murdoch* (New York: Bloomsbury Academic, 2014); Lara Vetter, "Journeys without Maps: Literature and Spiritual Experience," in *British Literature in Transition, 1920–1940: Futility and Anarchy*, ed. Charles Ferrall (Cambridge: Cambridge University Press, 2018), 68–83; and Kristina K. Groover, ed., *Religion, Secularism, and the Spiritual Paths of Virginia Woolf* (Cham, Switzerland: Palgrave Macmillan, 2019). Elizabeth Anderson offers one of the most sophisticated treatments of this dimension of Woolf's writing, insisting that the mystical and the material cannot be separated in her work. See Elizabeth Anderson, *Material Spirituality in Modernist Women's Writing* (London: Bloomsbury Academic, 2020).

appropriate for the twentieth century."[25] Richard Kearney similarly argues that *To the Lighthouse* produces "a Eucharist of the everyday" and "a sacrament of common 'reality,'" using Christian tropes emptied of their specific theological content and reused to build community across the theism-atheism spectrum.[26] What arguments about Woolf's "religious experience" and mysticism offer is a broad tent for accepting many kinds of transcendence as part of the complex relationship between religion and secularism in modernity. While these studies give insight into modern belief systems and Woolf's aesthetic modes, they risk occluding Woolf's theologically informed response to historically particular religious institutions, practices, and beliefs.

Supplementing these approaches are scholars who situate Woolf within a thickly described historical context of England's "Christian culture." Jane de Gay, for example, argues that Woolf recognized that Christianity was "a live social and political force to be reckoned with."[27] De Gay describes the importance of the evangelical Clapham Sect for Woolf's beliefs, aesthetics, and literary practices, shows Woolf's well-informed reactions to theological and ecclesial debates within the Anglican Church, and illuminates her productively ambivalent relationship with Quakerism.[28] Understood this way, Woolf's fiction critically interrogated her particular Christian culture and transformed it, showing that Woolf was, as Stephanie Paulsell claims, "a religious thinker who both engaged with the religion around her and moved beyond it."[29] Not merely involved in an amorphous cloud of "religious experience" or a vacillating domain of uneven secularism, Woolf grappled with specific theological claims, church practices, and Christian traditions.

Among these works on Woolf and complicated secularism, religious experience, mysticism, spirituality, and Christian culture, there has been a surprising silence about *Jacob's Room*.[30] Perhaps the mournfulness of the novel

---

[25] Lewis, *Religious Experience and the Modernist Novel*, 144.
[26] Richard Kearney, *Anatheism: Returning to God after God* (New York: Columbia University Press, 2010), 127.
[27] Jane de Gay, *Virginia Woolf and Christian Culture* (Edinburgh: Edinburgh University Press, 2018), 2.
[28] On Woolf's relationship with Quakerism via her aunt Caroline Emelia Stephen, see Jane Marcus, "The Niece of a Nun: Virginia Woolf, Caroline Stephen, and the Cloistered Imagination," in *Virginia Woolf: A Feminist Slant* (Lincoln: University of Nebraska Press, 1983), 7–36; J. Ashley Foster, "Writing in the 'White Light of Truth': History, Ethics, and Community in Virginia Woolf's *Between the Acts*," *Woolf Studies Annual* 22 (2016): 41–73; and, Kathleen A. Heininge, *Reflections: Virginia Woolf and Her Quaker Aunt, Caroline Stephen* (New York: Peter Lang, 2016).
[29] Stephanie Paulsell, *Religion around Virginia Woolf*, (University Park: Pennsylvania State University Press, 2019), 14.
[30] A telling case in point is the special issue of *The Virginia Woolf Miscellany* devoted to "Woolf and Spirituality" which features a bibliography of all scholarship relevant to the topic (see *Virginia Woolf Miscellany* 80 [2011]). Only one entry explicitly names *Jacob's Room*—Vara S. Neverow, "The Return of the Great Goddess: Immortal Virginity, Sexual Autonomy, and Lesbian Possibility in *Jacob's Room*," *Woolf Studies Annual* 10 (2004): 203–31.

and its reticence about the potential for human connections makes it less fertile for analyses of its "spirituality." Other Woolf novels such as *Mrs. Dalloway* and *To the Lighthouse* also mourn the state of the world and the militarism that has caused so much death, but the mournfulness of those books is supplemented by many numinous and transcendent elements. Trauma and suicide haunt *Mrs. Dalloway*, but there is a multitude of unseen connections that unite the characters and form a communal bond that develops through Clarissa Dalloway's party. Loss and grief pervade *To the Lighthouse*, but the titular image remains a source of inspiration, and we conclude with a small community united while an artist achieves her vision. These other novels yield more easily to attempts at finding mystical, transcendental, and "religious" dimensions of Woolf's imagination than does *Jacob's Room*. Instead of a work that promises hope or consolation in the midst of loss, *Jacob's Room* is a Holy Saturday novel that rests in the pain of death without jumping ahead to any discernible resurrection.

Because of this neglect, *Jacob's Room* is an ideal work for reevaluating in light of the turn to religion in Woolf studies, and my emphasis on the novel's political theology may point toward additional theopolitical examinations of those more heavily discussed novels in Woolf's canon. Thinking theopolitically about Woolf's fiction shifts the angle of focus away from personal, individualized belief or private, transcendental mysticism toward the ways her writing intervenes in the rituals, symbols, and narratives of the sacralized state. Reading *Jacob's Room* as a theopolitical intervention into the damaging cultural liturgies of the nation-state can reframe how we consider "the religious" in Woolf, exploring areas other than the privatized transcendence of personal, individual "spirituality" or "belief."

Scholarship on *Jacob's Room* has touched on its liturgical qualities obliquely through the frequent description of the novel as an elegy.[31] It has often been read as a mourning cry for the generation lost to war, the first venture into what Stuart N. Clarke and Susan Sellers describe as Woolf's "experimental, avant-garde elegiacs" that began with her "triptych of war elegies" and continue through her final novel *Between the Acts*.[32] Likewise, Vara Neverow succinctly

---

[31] See, for instance, Kathleen Wall, "Significant Form in *Jacob's Room*: Ekphrasis and the Elegy," *Texas Studies in Literature and Language* 44, no. 3 (2002): 302–23; Kelly S. Walsh, "The Unbearable Openness of Death: Elegies of Rilke and Woolf," *Journal of Modern Literature* 32, no. 4 (2009): 1–21; Erin Penner, *Character and Mourning: Woolf, Faulkner, and the Novel Elegy of the First World War* (Charlottesville: University of Virginia Press, 2019). Woolf herself remarked in her diary in June of 1925 that her new mode of fiction might be thought of as "elegy." Woolf, *The Diary of Virginia Woolf, Volume Three: 1925-1930*, ed. Anne Olivier Bell (New York: HBJ, 1980), 34.

[32] Stuart N. Clarke and Susan Sellers, introduction to *Jacob's Room*, by Virginia Woolf (Cambridge: Cambridge University Press, 2020), xxxviii.

and powerfully describes the novel as "an elegy for a generation and for an era; a heartfelt protest against wars past, present, and future; a stinging critique of patriarchy and gender hierarchy; an exploration of the maze of sexualities, desires, and transgression; and a lens through which the reader can glimpse the writer's own lived experience."[33] Describing the novel as an elegy captures something of its mournful tone as well as its litany of damaging forces that shape Jacob's life and the world around him.

There are two other dimensions of the elegy that I wish to emphasize in my analysis of the novel. First, I would draw attention to the ways that this elegy is not a neutral litany of mourning. Lamentation for the dead—and exposing the forces that caused this death—becomes a form of protest, acting in opposition to national liturgies of celebratory commemoration. Postwar commemoration casts death in wartime as a form of sacrifice that should be honored and celebrated rather than lamented. The nation demands fealty and devotion, and military sacrifice is one of the highest forms of worship—martyrdom for the state as tribute to its power. Woolf's fictional elegy, therefore, is not a neutral form but a pointed criticism of postwar ideologies and practices. Second, the public work of an elegy is to transform the chaos of grief into an orderly mode of expression. Meaning that could not be found in the life and death of the person themselves is now manufactured artistically to create salvation and redemption. My analysis of *Jacob's Room* focuses on Woolf's lack of redemption; the world she describes is too broken, too prone toward malformation and destruction to be salvaged by even a rich work of mourning. As Christine Froula puts it, the novel does not offer Jacob's "fate as a flame at which to warm one's shivering life but beckoning us out onto the narrow pavement over an abyss that is modern life," and as such it is a "disconnected rhapsody" that "seeks not only to re-form the novel but to orient the reader afresh" by "modeling a skeptical, critical, analytic, life-loving sensibility."[34] Reorienting readers to develop new sensibilities has political stakes as we are made more sensitive to the destructive patterns of the world and to the power of art for shaping our interpersonal relations. Jean Mills has shown how Woolf's reading of the classicist Jane Ellen Harrison facilitated her thinking about literature, politics, and ritual, and Mills argues that *Jacob's Room* "is a critique and condemnation of the individual and family structure as instruments of a militarized, war hero-worshipping state" that shares with Harrison's literary

---

[33] Vara Neverow, introduction to *Jacob's Room*, by Virginia Woolf (Orlando: Harcourt, 2008), lxxxvi.
[34] Christine Froula, *Virginia Woolf and the Bloomsbury Avant-Garde: War, Civilization, Modernity* (New York: Columbia University Press, 2005), 69, 84.

theory and analysis of *The Agamemnon* as a war text.³⁵ Jacob is "the anti-hero," Mills claims, "who is undermined by an epic wave of violence" that leaves him with a "lost thiasos"—terminology drawn from Harrison.³⁶ Harrison wrote in *Ancient Art and Ritual* (1913) that the early Greek artform that led to drama "was a choral dance, the dance of a band, a group, a church, a community, what the Greeks called a *thiasos*" which "means a *band* and *a thing of devotion*."³⁷ Furthermore, Harrison, notes: "reverence, devotion, collective emotion, is social in its very being."³⁸ Jacob is cut off from meaningful rituals and life-sustaining collective politics, and the novel enacts this separation through its depiction of rituals and its elegiac protest.

Rather than any clear path to political or religious redemption, *Jacob's Room* exposes a panoramic array of interconnected ideologies and institutions that produce the enchanted state, and in the midst of these destructive forces she offers glimpses of the politics of the "radical ordinary." I borrow this term from the political theology of Stanley Hauerwas and Romand Coles, whose effort to find common ground between Christian theology and secular political theory aligns with my attempts to read Woolf theopolitically. Though their specific practices, ranges of reference, and professed teleologies are different, Hauerwas and Coles share a profound distrust of the nation-state's "politics of death" and advocate for resources from within theology and radical democratic theory to challenge those politics. As they describe it, "The politics of death is a dense, dynamic, and finely woven mesh of destruction and fear" and their counter proposal is "an alternative politics that cares for the commonalities, differences, and emergent irregularities of life [which] must also be dense, molecular, supple, mobile, and trickster-like in its modes. It must maintain its 'heavy foot' in the complexities of the radical ordinary [...] if it is to avoid the fantasies of 'seeing like a state.'"³⁹ They emphasize the messiness and complexities of an alternative politics that can resist the death-centered state, and they contend that their commitments are revolutionary, even though they refuse large-scale political agendas in favor of "the fine grains of the politics of micro-relationships and small achievements. We yearn for radical changes to systems that are destroying the world. [...] Yet we believe that the locus of energies and intelligent visions

---

³⁵ Jean Mills, *Virginia Woolf, Jane Ellen Harrison, and the Spirit of Modernist Classicism* (Columbus, OH: Ohio State University Press, 2014), 92.
³⁶ Ibid.
³⁷ Jane Ellen Harrison, *Ancient Art and Ritual* (London: Williams and Norgate, 1913), 240.
³⁸ Ibid.
³⁹ Stanley Hauerwas and Romand Coles, *Christianity, Democracy, and the Radical Ordinary: Conversations between a Radical Democrat and a Christian* (Eugene, OR: Cascade Books, 2008), 8.

for such projects are nourished in the textures of relational care for the radical ordinary."[40] Instead of new hegemonies to counteract and overthrow the destructive powers of militarism, imperialism, capitalism, etc., Hauerwas and Coles encourage us to attend to the mundane and the micro-relational: "By radical ordinary we gesture to the ways in which the inexhaustible complexities of everyday life forever call forth new efforts of attention, nurture, and struggle that exceed the elements of blindness that accompany even our best words and deeds."[41] Though Woolf would likely have reservations about Coles's "radical democracy" and undoubtedly view Hauerwas's Christianity askance, her fiction imagines through its experimental aesthetic forms the kind of radical ordinariness that these later theologian-theorists envision. *Jacob's Room* requires of its readers an attentiveness to the mundane and micro-relational as its characters strive to understand Jacob and his actions, live out their ordinary lives, and dwell in a half-realized relationship with the natural world. So much of the novel is fixated on a politics of death, and no simple alternative erupts to overthrow the enchantments of the state, but there are subtle counterforces to those enchantments laced throughout the text.

Woolf's most forthright attack on English society's politics of death occurs in *Three Guineas*, a touchstone for comprehending her politics but not a work that is widely recognized as secular political theology. In *Three Guineas*, Woolf challenges systemic injustice by demonstrating the interrelated, interdependent forces and institutions that sustain militarism and sexism—particularly those of church and government. She communicates the "dense, dynamic, and finely woven mesh of destruction and fear" (as Hauerwas and Coles put it) by observing how "civilization" is a tapestry of places, institutions, and liturgies working in tacit collaboration to construct citizenship:

> It falls to us now to go on thinking; how are we to spend that sixpence? Think we must. Let us think in offices; in omnibuses; while we are standing in the crowd watching Coronations and Lord Mayor's Shows; let us think as we pass the Cenotaph; and in Whitehall; in the gallery of the House of Commons; in the Law Courts; let us think at baptisms and marriages and funerals. Let us never cease from thinking—what is this "civilization" in which we find ourselves? What are these ceremonies and why should we take part in them?[42]

---

[40] Ibid., 4.
[41] Ibid.
[42] Virginia Woolf, *Three Guineas*, annotated and introduced by Jane Marcus, 1938 (Orlando, FL: Harcourt, 2006), 77.

The ceremonies Woolf names are a few of the many political liturgies that create "civilized" English life—the pageantry of monarchical or mayoral ascension, the commemoration of wartime dead, the workings of government and law. Each of these displays functions as civil religion on the highest order, signifying the national community as it enacts its largest public rituals. But Woolf turns from those forms of hot nationalism to the mundane work of church rituals which she links with grander pageantry to show the complicity of everyday rites with the civic rites of the state. Her admonition that we "think" anticipates her famous comment in her diary entry from May of 1940: "the army is the body: I am the brain. Thinking is my fighting."[43] While we might readily understand why thoughtful resistance is required at coronations, the Cenotaph commemorations, and during power-brokering in Whitehall, Woolf connects these moments to the common functions of the church as practices equally in need of dissenting thought. Her charge to readers that they form an internal resistance to the pressures of civil religion is not one that her protagonist in *Jacob's Room* achieves. He is aloof and reserved rather than thoughtfully resistant, and part of his tragedy is inability to turn thinking into fighting.

Instead of an exemplary model of resistance to the allures of civil religion, Woolf portrays Jacob's life through its many failures and invites readers to witness the radical ordinariness around Jacob that he cannot access. The experimental form of *Jacob's Room*, what Clarke and Sellers call its "narrative arabesques," creates an associative style that emphasizes the radical ordinary.[44] So much of the novel is narrated through small, evocative moments or descriptions. Rather than a narrative drive where story elements propel the movement through chapters, there are movements from one impression to another. This style has been discussed as part of Woolf's developing experiments with what we understand as modernist form, but her aesthetic practices in the novel may also be taken as crucial for the theopolitical resources of her fiction. By creating a chain of associations and revealing the unseen and underlying ways that humans are interconnected, Woolf offers the opportunity for readers to become more sensitive to the connections we share and also to the institutions and ideologies that shape and define us even when we may think that we are immune to them. The project of a micro-politics that resists civil religion

---

[43] Virginia Woolf, *The Diary of Virginia Woolf: Volume Five, 1936–1941*, ed. Anne Olivier Bell and Andrew McNeillie (San Diego, CA: HBJ, 1984), 285.
[44] Clarke and Sellers, introduction to *Jacob's Room*, xxxviii.

and the theologies of the state is not conclusive, monolithic, domineering, or hegemonic. Woolf depicts political failure as much as she offers alternatives. And yet, it is through the uplifting of the ordinary and the critique of our inescapable conscription by the state that *Jacob's Room* supplies resources for a theopolitical imagination.

Civil Religion in the Streets

The world of Jacob Flanders is a nexus of interwoven forces Woolf criticized in *Three Guineas*: institutional religion, commerce, government, military, and patriarchy. Much of Jacob's life is conveyed through mundane details and activities while momentous events such as the Great War are kept to the periphery. But I wish to call attention to one of the few places in the novel where hot nationalism erupts in a civil religious demonstration that does affect the narrative, however obliquely. Guy Fawkes Day serves as an important backdrop to a series of encounters between Jacob and other characters, and though he is characteristically unresponsive to and withdrawn from the festivities, they nonetheless provide a noteworthy example of political liturgy insinuating itself into daily life.

The small final section of chapter five leaps across space from the village of Scarborough to alert us that "in London at this hour they were burning Guy Fawkes on Parliament Hill."[45] This spatial leap is significant, using a fictional device to show the connection between the rural town and the urban center where civil religion burns with literal heat. By contrast with London and its national liturgy, the town where Captain Barfoot now serves as "town councillor" is mostly asleep and silent apart from "Church bells down in the town" that "were striking eleven o'clock" (*JR*, 118). This glimpse of rural life includes an ex-sailor promoted to a role in local governance and a community sensibility created by the presence of the church—all of which is connected in parallel with the fires in London. Chapter six begins with fire—"The flames had fairly caught"—and in its light a nameless voice in the crowd exclaims, "There's St. Paul's!" (*JR*, 119). This is one of many places in the novel where St. Paul's Cathedral emerges as the emblematic figure of church and state, a reminder of the overshadowing

---

[45] Virginia Woolf, *Jacob's Room: The Cambridge Edition of the Works of Virginia Woolf*, ed. Stuart N. Clarke with David Bradshaw (Cambridge: Cambridge University Press, 2020), 118. Hereafter cited in text as *JR*.

presence of the Anglican Church and its vital role in constituting London's identity. By showing us the church alight on Guy Fawkes Day, Woolf suggests the interconnectedness of Protestantism and national politics, and she uses the fire to render the scene in a ghostly chiaroscuro. Jacob's date Florinda appears like a specter through the same fire that reveals St. Paul's. Both the young woman and the cathedral seem ethereal and mysterious in the firelight, combining symbolic church structure with the individual citizen through the ritual practice of bonfire. The image is frightening rather than rousing, evoking religious nationalism as a spectral haunting rather than a joyful celebration. Though drinking, dancing, and other revelry will be part of the Guy Fawkes festivities, Woolf's depiction of the bonfires emphasizes this holiday's association with death.

National holidays typically feature public rituals that promote unity, but Guy Fawkes Day is an especially transparent example of state politics joining a specific version of Christianity. Linda Colley has discussed how crucial Protestantism was in the formation of modern Britain, writing that "Protestantism determined how most Britons viewed their politics. And an uncompromising Protestantism was the foundation on which their state was explicitly and unapologetically based."[46] By creating a "pluralist yet aggressively Protestant polity," Britons defined themselves in part by opposing other forms of religious expression and integrating that opposition into their politicized civil religion.[47] Many national holidays mark time as a narrative of being "God's elect," what Colley describes as "a soap opera written by God, a succession of warning disasters and providential escapes which [Britons] acted out afresh every year as a way of reminding themselves who they were."[48] Within this national narrative, "5 November was doubly sacred, not just the anniversary of the landing in England in 1688 of William of Orange, come to do battle with the Catholic James II, but also the day when in 1605 Parliament and James I had been rescued from the gunpowder plotting of Guido Fawkes, yet another Roman Catholic."[49] These elements of the national story comprising rescue and escape through God's special desire for English success give weight to the looming presence of St. Paul's Cathedral in the Guy Fawkes scene in *Jacob's Room*. One of the most prominent features of the London skyline, the dome of St. Paul's, is also a towering reminder of Protestant Christianity and its vitality within English national identity. Colley notes that the official prayer supplied for Guy Fawkes Day liturgies in the Book

---

[46] Linda Colley, *Britons: Forging the Nation 1707–1837* (New Haven: Yale University Press, 1992), 18.
[47] Colley, *Britons*, 19.
[48] Ibid.
[49] Ibid., 19–20.

of Common Prayer emphasizes God's singular focus on Britain: "'From this unnatural conspiracy not our merit, but *thy* mercy; not our foresight, but *thy* providence delivered us.' God, Britons were encouraged to believe, watched over them with a particular concern. Nothing in their troubled past had escaped his notice or eluded his influence, for they were special."[50] Conceiving of England as a site of God's specific purview and an embattled outpost besieged by enemy Catholics became a narrative with immense unifying power, and the ritual enactments of this narrative on national holidays demonstrate civil religion in its hottest form. Even though the narrative does not register Jacob's acknowledgment of these forces, they loom around him nevertheless, forming him and giving shape to his world.

The remainder of the Guy Fawkes scene in *Jacob's Room* shows competing forces: the mood of jubilant national celebration maintained by the crowds and the internal resistance of Florinda and Jacob. While the celebrants gather in a hotel dining room with a "Roman bust blackened and reddened to represent Guy Fawkes" to drink wine and sing "Auld Lang Syne," Florinda hurls a glass at Jacob and declares her unhappiness (*JR*, 120). We are given little insight into the source or substance of her feelings, but they clearly run contrary to the mood of the revelers who join in national unisonance to publicly profess their joy. While Florinda's attitude is clear but unexplained, Jacob is predictably opaque: "Jacob could not dance. He stood against the wall smoking a pipe" (*JR*, 121). As is common throughout the novel, Woolf tells us nothing directly in this moment about Jacob's inner life. His actions communicate his preferred mode of aloofness, his thoughts are veiled, and his emotions hidden. And, as frequently occurs for Jacob, this mysteriousness makes him desirable to others, who sweep him into their revelry in spite of himself. Two of the dancers lure him from the wall, telling him "you are the most beautiful man we have ever seen," and then wreathing "his head with paper flowers," placing him on a "white and gilt chair," and stringing "glass grapes on his shoulders, until he looked like the figure-head of a wrecked ship" (*JR*, 121). Jacob's resistance to the festivities is shallow and easily conquered by a whiff of sexual opportunity and a social pressure that works with his inertia. Though his posture in the dining room suggests an intentional distancing from the liturgical rites of national celebration, he is easily drawn into the ritual—not as an active participant but as a passive figurehead who the narrator provocatively likens to a wrecked ship. The revelers perform the sort of national liturgy James K. A. Smith describes, where a national holiday involves

---

[50] Ibid., 20.

rituals that unite individuals with the collective story of the nation. This moment of Jacob's coronation in the dining room, of course, foreshadows the way he will similarly be lured into war and ruined, but it is more than just narrative foreshadowing. By showing a key instance of hot nationalism enacted through religious ritual and the futility of passive aloofness, Woolf offers a standout case for the formational effects of civil religion.

On the morning after Jacob's "coronation," he seeks respite from jingoistic displays through conversation with his friend Timmy Durrant with whom he can indulge a self-congratulatory and sophomoric appreciation of classical Greek literature. As if attempting to elevate himself above the masses and their political liturgies, Jacob meets his friend with a show of erudition: "it seemed to both that they had read every book in the world; known every sin, passion, and joy. Civilizations stood round them like flowers ready for picking" (*JR*, 122). Besides the self-aggrandizement of their boasts, their passion also drips with imperial possessiveness, a will to claim and own the regions they study and master. Rejecting the foolishness of the Guy Fawkes celebrations, Jacob reverts into another kind of jingoism, and his enthusiasm is ironically misunderstood by a stall-keeper who sells the young men their morning coffee, believing their talk of Greece means they are in the military. The stall-keeper misunderstands the intent of Jacob and Timmy's declarations about Greece—they are thinking literarily and philosophically—but in a way he has intuited their subtext. Pride of global ownership manifests in their fancies, and the stall-keeper recognizes in their speech the tone of military conquest. In response to the stall-keeper, "Jacob cursed the British army and praised the Duke of Wellington," a form of impotent protest that is pitched to rile up the old man but does little to separate Jacob from the imperial and militaristic ideologies that everywhere shape him (*JR*, 123). It is a subtle and unremarkable moment of daily conscription in the long foreshadowing arc where ceremony and liturgy, even when they are unwanted and casually resisted, still mold a person and portend his ceremonial death in war.

Near the end of the novel, the political liturgies of hot nationalism grow more insistent as war becomes imminent. Woolf describes "a procession with banners" in Whitehall, and the throng in her description is coded in religious and liturgical language: "elderly people were stiffly descending from between the paws of the slippery lions, where they had been testifying to their faith, singing lustily, raising their eyes from their music to look into the sky, and still their eyes were on the sky as they marched behind the gold letters of their creed" (*JR*, 280–1). There remains no scholarly consensus about the exact purpose of this procession, and speculations include a women's suffrage march or a pro-war demonstration.[51] Stuart N. Clarke and Jane Goldman observe that the procession "seems to be religious," but in the absence of a clear historical referent, it is difficult to interpret whether the religious language Woolf uses is literal or metaphorical.[52] Regardless, it is a public act in Trafalgar Square where the lions—symbols of the English nation—receive special mention and the crowd professes their convictions in the form of a "creed." Their actions are worshipful, marked as "testifying" and they sing together, forging their bond through unisonance. The procession enacts a political liturgy, and its timing is significant for being closely connected to the outbreak of war. This moment from the penultimate chapter of the novel dovetails with a paragraph that gives a global tour of international turmoil. The procession wends its way down Whitehall releasing the traffic "past Government offices and equestrian statues down Whitehall to the prickly spires, the tethered grey fleet of masonry, and the large white clock of Westminster"—a reminder of the combined forces of state and church alongside the institutions of power (JR, 281). Those ecclesial and governmental powers give rise to Woolf's litany of global unrest which is framed by how this news arrives at the Old Admiralty building through shivering wires. A survey of international politics thus originates from a military headquarters, reminding us that attention to the European community and beyond has a basis in the proliferation of arms. Winston Churchill was First Lord of the Admiralty at the time this chapter is set, and though his leadership faltered in 1915 during the Gallipoli campaign, his tenure as leader of the Navy was noted for its escalation of naval power. That sense of military escalation is pronounced through Woolf's tour of nations via the voice on Admiralty's wires which brings details from the Reichstag, Lahore, Milan, Vienna, and more where world leaders meet while ships amass near Gibraltar—the military station of the stall-keeper's son from earlier in the novel. Threats of violent conflict mount across numerous regions, notably in European metropoles and hot zones of colonization, and among the clerks working in Whitehall is Jacob's friend Timmy Durrant whose conscription into the machinery of war and empire appears as the "voice" continues, "imprinting on the faces of the clerks" while "papers accumulated, inscribed with the utterances of Kaisers, the statistics of ricefields, the growling of hundreds of work-people, plotting sedition in back streets, or

---

[51] Neverow, notes to *Jacob's Room*, 308. Sue Roe comments on the possible war rally in notes to *Jacob's Room*, 185.
[52] Clarke and Goldman, explanatory notes to *Jacob's Room*, 702.

gathering in the Calcutta bazaars, or mustering their forces in the uplands of Albania, where the hills are sand-colored, and bones lie unburied" (JR, 281–2). War and empire flow from a callous bureaucracy, and the associated elements Woolf includes show civil unrest along with violence and death. Members of the cabinet, despite their anemic appearance, wield devastating powers: "altogether they looked too red, fat, pale or lean, to be dealing, as the marble heads had dealt, with the course of history" (JR, 282). That course of history, changing hourly under the bureaucratic forces of the state, still connects with the banners and procession going down Whitehall, a recognition that the political liturgies conducted vigorously and bombastically in the public square are interconnected with the machinations of power behind closed doors. The chapter ends with a litany of global unrest and local conscription all associated with Jacob's recent international tourism.

Churchyard and Volute

Celebrations such as Guy Fawkes Day and Armistice Day are significant instances where English civil religion was hotly displayed, emblematic of broader political trends and notable for their acute demonstration of patriotism fueled by Christianity. But those times of patriotic heat can feel anomalous and exceptional, the rare surge of nationalist energy within the mundane. While the liturgies of hot nationalism contribute to a "politics of death" that is grandiose and flagrant, there are subtler, unrelenting modes by which this politics affects everyday life. What Virginia Woolf's fiction affords with such clarity, creativity, and industry is a critical rejoinder to that everyday situation, portraying and critiquing the ways that "banal nationalism," with its bellicose and religious undergirding, continues to impose itself on individual and communal life.[53] One of the tensions running through *Jacob's Room* is the persistent threat of banal nationalism versus the micro-politics of the radical ordinary, and Woolf's depiction of churches and churchyards allows a complex exploration of that tension.

Woolf's prose style, with its rich tapestry of interconnections across a vast range of ideas, images, and social forces, was integral to the genesis of *Jacob's Room*—a new direction in her fictional experimentation that was oriented, even

---

[53] Billig, *Banal Nationalism*, 2.

at its earliest stages, toward the coalescence of the natural world and the church. Woolf's first intimations of *Jacob's Room* in her diary from January 1920 focus entirely on its form and her desire to expand the style of her short fictions such as "An Unwritten Novel," "The Mark on the Wall," and "Kew Gardens" into a full-length novel—developing the style of those stories so that they will be "taking hands & dancing in unity."[54] By April of 1920, her first recorded mention of the novel's title turns from formal concerns to her effort to capture the seasonal weather. The shift from form to environment is crucial, showing how fundamental nature is to her compositional process. Just as immediate, however, is her attention to human-made elements of nature. Significantly, it is the church that appears first in her description of the season: "So I hardly notice that chestnuts are out—the little parasols spread on our window tree; & the churchyard grass running over the old tombstones like green water."[55] Initially, she depicts the tree in recognizable human terms with the blossoms appearing like parasols, but the final image is of the human-made churchyard and tombstones becoming natural through their overgrowth. This sort of interplay between the human creations and natural world persists throughout the published novel, and even at such an early point in the conception of *Jacob's Room*, there is an association with the formative dimension of churches—a vital force in making Jacob Flanders into an English citizen shaped by religious institutions.

The tension between the continuous presence of Christianity and the ordinary building blocks of social life recurs in the novel's movement between the village of Scarborough and the urban center of London as well as its other major settings in Cambridge and finally in continental Europe. The Flanders family and other inhabitants of Scarborough orient themselves around the village church, even though many of these characters seem disconnected from Christian worship or other church participation. For instance, we learn early in the novel that Seabrook Flanders's tombstone reads "Merchant of this city," a title that suggests how the liturgy of commerce has won out over the mythologies of the church or the role within his family, those other most common gravestone inscriptions (*JR*, 21). The rest of the churchyard where Seabrook's remains have "merged in the grass" include the faded detritus of Christian ritual: "the decayed wreaths, the crosses of green tin" (*JR*, 22). Betty thinks of her late husband especially when working on other household chores and hearing "the bell for

---

[54] Virginia Woolf, *The Diary of Virginia Woolf: Volume Two, 1920–1924*, ed. Anne Olivier Bell and asst. Andrew McNeillie (New York: HBJ, 1978), 14.
[55] Ibid., 29.

service or funeral" which becomes for her "Seabrook's voice—the voice of the dead" (*JR*, 22). Just as Seabrook's body has merged into the sloping landscape of the graveyard, his voice has merged into the bells of the church that signal Christian liturgy. But his distinctive identity is still that of a merchant, not a disciple or husband or father. The church's bells are not restricted to the worshipping lives of Scarborough's citizens, but instead they acquire further reach and a mystical dimension by becoming the voice of Seabrook. Betty is thus shaped by a Christian liturgy she does not actively join, but passive contact with church rites profoundly influences her. Christian liturgy insinuates itself into her life despite her lack of belief, practice, or consent. A Christian liturgy becomes a cultural liturgy where commemoration for the dead allows national citizenship to be hallowed, sanctified, and created in its intimate and local form. Betty's ruminations on the church bells are interrupted by her son Archer calling to her, "sounding at the same moment as the bell" and mixing "life and death inextricably, exhilaratingly" (*JR*, 22). The church bell unifies the memory of her husband and the presence of her child in a liturgy of commemoration that is emotionally rich. The description of Seabrook's memorial and Betty's relationship with his memory is a clear moment of elegy, foreshadowing the death and memorialization later in the novel, but it mounts little of the protest that Jacob's death elicits. Instead, Woolf establishes early in the novel how peacetime is casually (and banally) replete with the forces that produce English identity and the inescapable presence of Christian institutions and practices. Though gravemarkers and church bells do not seem as threatening as fiery celebrations or political rallies, Woolf shows how the tapestry of English life is preparing itself for the violent, militaristic, hot forms of nationalism that will later erupt.

The latent militarism in Jacob's surname has been noted by many commentators, one of the signal ways his wartime death is embedded in his character. Less often noted is how John McCrae's poem "In Flanders Fields" (1915) registers the persistence of English civil religion. The poem's famous poppies, inspiration for the red poppy campaign as a sign of military remembrance, appear "between the crosses, row on row"—a fusion of civic imagery with Christian iconography.[56] The poem's point of view, hearing the voice of "the Dead," begins with pastoral quiet but shifts into a call to action and a threat. Not merely a casual reminder of the cost of war and the peacefulness of heroic death, the poem becomes a challenge to the listener to join the bloody struggle: "Take up our quarrel with

---

[56] John McCrae, *In Flanders Fields and Other Poems* (New York: Putnam, 1919), 3.

the foe," the dead soldiers urge.⁵⁷ Not merely a poem of remembrance, "In Flanders Fields" is also a work of civil religious litany and military recruitment. Jacob is caught by the ideologies the poem promotes, but Woolf's chronicle of his life protests against the overdetermination of his name.

Other churchyards and reminders of Christian ritual reinforce Jacob's experience of the combination of Christianity, national identity, and slaughter even during supposedly peaceful times. Jacob and other children build their bug collections, poisoning and preserving stag-beetles and butterflies with camphor that evokes the toxic gases of the Western Front. "The stag-beetle dies slowly," Woolf writes, in a gesture toward the suffering of living things in conflict (JR, 33). And, she situates the deaths of the bugs near the fictional Dods Hill and actual remains from "the Roman camp"—a legacy of the region's imperial history that resounds, in Woolf's description, with "the sound of church bells" (JR, 34). The subtle insinuation of the church wafts over the Roman ruins and the waves of butterflies, the "clouded yellows" and "fritillary," that rise to meet their deaths on a Sunday afternoon (JR, 34). Jacob's childhood pleasures in the English countryside are imbued with cultural Christianity and the politics of death in their most pastoral, casual, and banal forms, all of which are punctuated by "a volley of pistol-shots suddenly in the depths of the wood" that forcefully remind us of the gunfire that will claim Jacob's life (JR, 34). *Jacob's Room* acts as political theology when it reveals the densely woven mesh of the politics of death and the political liturgies that shape characters such as Jacob even from his earliest moments of conscious memory. Woolf's prose style requires our constant attentiveness to keep track of her titular character and the people in his midst. The welter of tiny details in her descriptions produce a network of associations to show the thickly interconnected webs of civil religious life that constitute and reinforce English national identity—much of which portend the violent militarism that rages beneath the peaceable veneer.

But there is another current in the novel as well, smaller but still perceptible signs that alternatives to the culture of death exist, even if they are mostly undetected by the people who might benefit from them most. Mrs. Jarvis and Betty Flanders walk on Dods Hill to the Roman camp one evening after dinner, discussing Jacob's letters from Paris in elliptical terms that are consistent with his elusive character. In this setting, once again reminding us of Britain's Roman past, they survey the lights of Scarborough and the narrator tells us in a non-sequitur that "Neither did Mrs. Jarvis think of God" but immediately

---

⁵⁷ Ibid.

adds: "There was a church behind them, of course. The church clock struck ten. Did the strokes reach the furze bush, or did the thorn tree hear them?" (JR, 215–16). Regardless of one's consciousness of God or "religious experience," the church's clock chimes give shape and structure to the villagers' evening, an incessant presence of Christianity as a cultural force and defining feature of their society. But Woolf's inclusion of the natural world, the trees and bushes around the women, and especially her narrator's question about the effect of the church on these other elements of life, point to the alternative forms of flourishing outside the purview of banal civil religion and its liturgies. How the natural world responds to those forces is uncertain, and the uncertainty preserves a sense of the messy, unpredictable, supple, and durable modes of resistance. The remainder of the chapter has a contrapuntal structure where the persistent church clock and other signs of Christian culture alternate with natural images that thrive unchecked by the intrusions of cultural Christianity. The tolling clock bell exerts its violence into the natural flow by fracturing reality into quarterly segments. But the moors are the most significant counterpart to these intrusions, and they stay "motionless and broad-backed" as humanity's time marches on (JR, 216). The stability of the moors juxtaposes with the driving and fragmenting force of the clock. The moors are not aloof and uninvested (as Jacob is), but they are also unchanged and undiminished by the force of Christianity. They receive everything, absorbing the moonlight and brambles along with the human intrusions. And they even accept the tombstones with their vague messages from the New Testament, declarations of long dead names, and efforts to be "very proud, very emphatic, or consoling" (JR, 217). Memorials coded with Christian ideology reflect human attempts to preserve, remember, and gesture at eternity, but it is actually the moors with their constancy and acceptance that silently knit all things together, undiminished and unchanged by humanity's ideologies. The women do not seem conscious that "the moor accepted everything," but the narrator's return to variations of that phrase suggests that civic life and Christian culture cannot become all-consuming (JR, 218). Just as banal nationalism and Christianity shape the lives of the characters, so too the moor embraces and absorbs, making subtle connectivity among people, animals, and vegetation and holding fast across time. Woolf does not depict any obvious rival to the enchanted state. The English nation in its localized forms is still determined by Christian rituals and their promotion of sacrificial death. Nature cannot simply overcome. But the quiet and unseen bonds among humans and the natural world give hints of the radical ordinary and in their counterpoint to the violence of Christian nationalism supply an aesthetically rich political theology.

Nature as a crucial dimension of Woolf's political theology might seem most apt when she describes the rural areas around Scarborough, but even in her chapters on urban space we find her showing both the persistence of the church as a contributing force toward nationalism and the city as a kind of natural entity capable of forming an alternative politics. The bustling London scene in the present is, in Woolf's depiction, an extension of its rich history. Not quite the primordial durée of the moors, but an historical legacy nonetheless, the city streets contain multitudes that in modern times go unrecognized in the parade of lurching omnibuses. Woolf calls attention to individuals who form a community aboard those omnibuses: "every single person felt relief at being a little nearer to his journey's end, though some cajoled themselves past the immediate engagement by promise of indulgence beyond—steak and kidney pudding, drink, or a game of dominoes in the smokey corner of a city restaurant" (*JR*, 104). This glimpse of individuals sharing a collective experience of public transportation and similar feelings about their days is one of myriad ways Woolf shows how mundane city life is rich with communal flourishing—even if it is not consciously acknowledged. Those little moments of warm interior life shared across a public group stand in stark opposition to the grandiose narratives of sacrifice for the nation, imperial conquest, or political rallying. And even though Christianity frequently appears in *Jacob's Room* as a force that contributes to those grandiose sacrificial narratives, in Woolf's description of London, the church occupies a more ambivalent space. The narrator observes: "if there is such a thing as a shell secreted by man to fit man himself here we find it, on the banks of the Thames, where the great streets join and St. Paul's Cathedral, like the volute on the top of a snail shall, finishes it off" (*JR*, 104). Like a shell, the city offers intricate structures "secreted" for habitation and protection.[58] Humans have built a zone of security to fit themselves, and this constructed safespace appears to be natural, emerging from their bodies on a riverbank essential to the English landscape. Woolf's imagery here is ambivalent. The Thames is the natural basis for the city, the source of its historical flourishing and the lifeblood of nature that flows through its heart. Human life thrives because of that waterway, and the drive to build and create which is so vital to humanity has emerged in an imitation of the river by building "great streets" that converge around St. Paul's. The dome and spire of that classic London landmark become

---

[58] In *The Waves* Woolf writes of "a snail shell, rising in the grass like a grey cathedral," thus reversing the direction of the metaphor by making the actual shell into the figural church. See *The Waves* (San Diego: Harvest, 1959), 74.

in Woolf's description a kind of natural phenomenon like the shell on the back of a snail. This snail shell image, however, implies both natural safety and slimy sluggishness. If the London skyline with its towers and churches are a shell, then Londoners are snails: slow, soft, timid, vulnerable bodies noteworthy only for their secretions. Rather than a powerful imperial center with national status upheld by violence, Woolf's London is withdrawn into the shelter of its "great streets" topped by the "volute" of St. Paul's dome. That volute is emblematic of the interaction between nationalism and religion in Britain. The spire is an architectural marvel that calls attention to the religious institution, and yet its prominence in the London skyline diminishes the distinctly religious meaning as the cathedral becomes a sign of the city rather than uniquely, discretely signifying Christian worship. Like the Thames, St. Paul's becomes naturalized as a landmark of English nationalism, and its Christian significance transforms into civil religion. As a reminder of the church's continual social power, despite trends toward a complex and imperfect secularization, St. Paul's is a feature of banal Christian nationalism. But Woolf's association of the cityscape with the natural world—and particularly with snails, which she also made central to her stories "Kew Gardens" and "The Mark on the Wall"—creates a resonance with the rural elements of Scarborough that persist despite the pressures of civil religion. As Bonnie Kime Scott has argued in relation to Woolf's fusions of natural and human worlds, "Woolf's most memorable natural images rarely stand alone; they fuse with the identity of the animals or human beings who perceive them, or the birds and insects that move among them, with their own perceptions and uses of nature's offerings."[59]

Within the Cathedral itself, Woolf depicts another ambivalent space where civil religion and its overweening power rests uneasily along with miniature forms of resistance from people living within the radical ordinary. Jacob enters St. Paul's and witnesses the church's mixture of national and religious sacredness—a fusion that affects but does not fully constrain the people in the building's domain. Functioning as a social arbiter, a church official appears to sanction the status quo: "the verger with his rod has life ironed out beneath him [...] For ever requiem—repose" (JR, 104–5). Like the dome of St. Paul's that protrudes above the city, the church's official representative stands above the laity to authorize "the order; the discipline" (JR, 105). The verger with his iron rod seems a petty tyrant, and the limitation of his reign is exposed by Old

---

[59] Bonnie Kime Scott, *In the Hollow of the Wave: Virginia Woolf and the Modernist Uses of Nature* (Charlottesville, VA: University of Virginia Press, 2012), 213.

Spicer, the jute merchant whose office overlooks St. Paul's churchyard which, despite his proximity and fifty-year tenure, he has never entered. The church is a constant presence in Old Spicer's life, but its thrall is only slight. For other English people, St. Paul's offers comfort that the verger's dictatorial presence, the frozen statuary, and the rigid hierarchy do not extinguish. Despite his exalted position, the verger shares the cathedral with the working classes, represented by Mrs. Lidgett who, tired from cleaning offices, "which she did year in year out [...] took her seat beneath the great Duke's tomb [...] A magnificent place for an old woman to rest in, by the very side of the great Duke's bones, whose victories meant nothing to her, whose name she knows not, though she never fails to greet the little angels opposite" (JR, 105). Though her body is spent from labor for the upper classes, she has access to the repose shepherded by the verger and his rod. To be sure, this image of the cleaning woman soaking in religious mystery at the end of her hard-won life bears traces of Marx's "opium of the people," but this critique of the scene does not eliminate the sense of momentary equality that she finds in "thoughts of rest" and "sweet melodies" (JR, 105). Her ignorance of national history beside the Duke of Wellington's tomb is part shortcoming and part transcendence. She is excluded from a knowledge base that contains the narratives of English nationalism, the stories of heroes upon which the modern nation stands. But her ignorance also manages to reduce the importance of these national narratives by suggesting that the putti on Wellington's tomb are more emotionally resonant than the relic that lies inside.

St. Paul's becomes in this sense a microcosm of England, infused with the national church, class tension, and public tradition. However ironic Woolf's treatment of the scene, her choosing the interior of St. Paul's as a space of heightened national resonance indicates recognition of the church's role in producing and stimulating national imagination. The homely figure of Mrs. Lidgett finding momentary respite in St. Paul's, absorbing its pleasures while ignoring its perpetuation of mythical Englishness, becomes a woman in the liminal space between individuality and national assimilation. Her rest in the space suggests the power of the mundane and ordinary to give sustenance, and her life is elevated by the narrative style into a place of prominence above the religious and political saints hallowed inside the cathedral. The cathedral, with its tombs for military heroes and displays of ecclesial authority, is a resplendent site of banal nationalism, augustly but quietly proclaiming the enchantments of the state. But figures like Mrs. Lidgett and Old Spicer exhibit disconnection and disaffection from those enchantments. While their separation from the allures of civil religion does not form any full-blown counter narrative to the ideologies that ultimately consume Jacob and his generation, these characters still hint at micro-political alternatives to grand, sacrificial nationalisms.

"Stamped and Moulded" by the University

Seeking alternatives to the enchantments of the state is a crucial part of the theopolitical imagination, and *Jacob's Room* offers glimpses of such alternatives through Woolf's rendering of the natural world and the underlying, unseen connections among people in community across time and space—but the dominant feature of the novel's political theology is its portrayal of Jacob's formation as a subject who will die for the nation. In a famous moment from "A Sketch of the Past," Woolf reflected on the "male relations" from her youth who, much like Jacob, were educated in particular ways and set on a path toward governance.[60] Of her relative Herbert Fisher, she asked, "what would have been his shape had he not been stamped and moulded by the patriarchal machinery?"[61] This image of young men "stamped" into shapes by social machinery is crucial to Woolf's portrayal of the university in *Jacob's Room*. Woolf's writing is rich with criticisms of the current social order and the ways it is damaging to all people, but especially to women and anyone who does not conform to the patriarchal, heteronormative, capitalist, nationalistic, imperialist, and militaristic ideologies that constitute the societal mainstream. She avoids, however, any prescriptive approach to her criticisms of these powers, presenting concrete alternatives such as the famous "Outsiders Society" in *Three Guineas* only as tentative and speculative rather than programmatic or directive realities. Woolf's depiction of a young man who has been formed badly by his society does not necessarily indicate any clear alternative for better formation—at least not through any narrowly and rigidly conceived program or institution.

And yet, the manner in which Woolf exposes the systemic powers that pave the way for Jacob's death remains resonant with current religious and secular political theologies that similarly challenge the nation but have a more definitive teleology than Woolf's. As Hauerwas and Coles describe their shared project arising from their differing ideological commitments, they emphasize their

---

[60] See Alex Zwerdling, *Virginia Woolf and the Real World* (Berkeley: University of California Press, 1986), 74.
[61] Virginia Woolf, *Moments of Being: Unpublished Autobiographical Writings*, ed. and introd. Jeanne Schulkind (New York: HBJ, 1976), 132.

mutual efforts to resist the politics of death through attention to better modes of personal and communal formation: "Christianity, or at least Christianity not determined by Constantinian or capitalist desires, is training for a dying that is good. Such good dying is named in the gospel as trial, cross, and resurrection. Radical democracy names the intermittent and dispersed traditions of witnessing, resisting, and seeking alternatives to the politics of death wrought by those bent on myriad forms of immortality-as-conquest."[62] Though Woolf would (obviously) not share the Christian notions about "good dying" and (perhaps) have reservations about radical democracy, *Jacob's Room* nevertheless resounds with a critique of English society and its failure to train young men for a "dying that is good," a society that instead promotes the "immortality-as-conquest" found in imperial and military adventures sacralized by the state and hallowed by postwar memorialization. Many critics have discussed the ways that Jacob's university education led to his death, but the religious rituals in his education have been less considered.[63] Jacob's university training exhibits one of his key areas of formation, and Woolf exposes the pressures on him to embrace a false immortality through an education in civil religion at Cambridge. As is so often the case throughout *Jacob's Room*, the ideologies that claim us are shown to be inescapable and not something we can simply choose our way out of; Jacob's aloofness and disengagement appear as insufficient strategies for countering the politics of death.

The glimpse of Jacob's Cambridge education that Woolf offers is closely connected with the enchantments of civil religion. Our first images of Jacob at university begin with a contradiction to the commonly heard aphorism that the sky is the same for everyone regardless of station or location.[64] Woolf's narrator tells us that there is, in fact, a difference when at "Cambridge—anyhow above the roof of King's College Chapel" (*JR*, 48). From that hallowed spot, the sky is not like the uniform, banal certainty of everywhere else but is instead somehow brighter. The narrator, presumably echoing Jacob's feelings, asks "Is it fanciful to suppose the sky, washed into the crevices of King's College Chapel, lighter, thinner, more sparkling than the sky elsewhere? Does Cambridge burn not only into the night,

---

[62] Hauerwas and Coles, *Christianity, Democracy, and the Radical Ordinary*, 3.
[63] See, for instance, Zwerdling, *Woolf and the Real World*, 75–7; Jane de Gay, *Virginia Woolf's Novels and the Literary Past* (Edinburgh: Edinburgh University Press, 2006), 68; Megan Quigley, *Modernist Fiction and Vagueness: Philosophy, Form, and Language* (Cambridge: Cambridge University Press, 2015), 94.
[64] Sue Roe notes that Vanessa Stephen, "as a young child," asked her sister about the uniformity of the sky and that Woolf may be drawing upon that interaction from their youth. See Roe, notes to *Jacob's Room*, 161n.6.

but into the day?" (*JR*, 48). There is in this moment a strongly mystical quality that Jacob absorbs, and the hallowing of the university echoes similar imagery from Thomas Hardy's *Jude the Obscure* (as Vara Neverow has pointed out), where university life achieves an aura of sacredness and transcendence.[65] We witness, for instance, a scene in the King's College Chapel full of liturgical splendor with many robed people who become ethereal: "Look, as they pass into service, how airily the gowns blow out, as though nothing dense and corporeal were within. What sculptured faces, what certainty, authority controlled by piety, although great boots under gowns" (*JR*, 48). The processional is mystical and mysterious and curiously disembodied—far from the bodily development that Jacob will ultimately find during his school days. And, the liturgical accoutrements of the service signal the distinctly Anglican nature of the worship: "Thick wax candles stand upright; young men rise in white gowns; while the subservient eagle bears up for inspection the great white book" (*JR*, 48). Sue Roe has called attention to the fact that the King's College Chapel did not actually have an eagle on its lectern and that this detail is "another of Woolf's inventions," but the image is notable for combining university and Christian iconography.[66] Richard Taylor observes that eagles frequently appear on lecterns as a symbol for St. John the Evangelist, whose gospel "is the most mystical and spiritually revealing of the four."[67] Part of the reason for this symbol is an apocryphal belief that "an eagle was meant to be able to look unflinchingly into the eye of the sun"—soaring to great heights (and thus closer to God).[68] This lofty reaching toward the divine, signaled by the eagle and the altered sky above the chapel, is an echo of Jacob himself at this early moment in his schooling, idealizing education and the incorporeal perfecting of this body. The persistence of Christianity as a shaping force on English youth (and ultimately the English social order and its drive toward war) in *Jacob's Room* echoes Leslie Stephen's recollections of the power of Oxford and Cambridge for unifying the social order through Protestantism. In *Some Early Impressions*—written in 1903 and published by the Woolf's Hogarth Press in 1924—Stephen describes the perception of Oxford and Cambridge among critics from the left: "To the radical meanwhile the two universities represented two slightly different forms of obstructiveness. They were simply Anglican seminaries; bulwarks of the establishment which was an essential part of the

---

[65] Neverow, notes to *Jacob's Room*, 203.
[66] Roe, notes to *Jacob's Room*, 161n.8.
[67] Richard Taylor, *How to Read a Church: A Guide to Symbols and Images in Churches and Cathedrals* (London: Rider, 2003), 188.
[68] Ibid.

great conservative fortress."[69] Elite education as a religious training ground for assimilation into civil society—this is the mold where Jacob's adult self is being fashioned.

The link with militarism becomes explicit in Woolf's portrayal of the congregants within the King's College Chapel. The robed bodies seem incorporeal, much like the shadowy figures by the Guy Fawkes Day bonfires, but they are also militaristic, moving like a phalanx and docilely accepting their position in ranks and files. Citizenry are disciplined by religion and ultimately mobilized for war within the Cambridge chapel:

> As the sides of a lantern protect the flame so that it burns steady even in the wildest night—burns steady and gravely illumines the tree-trunks—so inside the Chapel all was orderly. Gravely sounded the voices; wisely the organ replied, as if buttressing human faith with the assent of the elements. The white-robed figures crossed from side to side; now mounted steps, now descended, all very orderly.
>
> (JR, 49)

These chapel scenes are both warm and sinister, giving formation to the lives of young men and conditioning them for state governance, religious devotion, and military sacrifice. The emphasis here is not on God or on a church made holy or separate; it is not a vision of the "resident alien" or of Smith's sense of overlapping allegiances; it amalgamates the church and national development, preparing the Cambridge elite for national leadership, service, and fundamentally for "order." The images of the "white-robed figures" merge with the forest beyond the chapel, the silence of which is abruptly shattered by the narrator's intrusion: "Ah, but what's that? A terrifying volley of pistol-shots rings out—cracks sharply; ripples spread—silence laps smooth over sound. A tree—a tree has fallen, a sort of death in the forest" (JR, 49). What initially sounds like gunfire—another proleptic reference to the war—is revealed to be a tree falling, but this also resonates with the culture of death. Those Cambridge congregants performing a liturgy of assimilation into the nation and production of its ruling class finds a counterpart in the natural world which proclaims the slaughter that awaits. What is especially striking about Jacob's eventually becoming a soldier is that little in his life seems to suggest patriotic or religious devotion. Not only is he far from being fanatical, he is thoroughly dispassionate, unattached, skeptical, and aloof in settings where devotion and commitment might be expected. The power in

---

[69] Leslie Stephen, *Some Early Impressions* (London: Hogarth Press, 1924), 16.

Woolf's depiction, therefore, is not that she shows a blinkered ideologue who foolishly dies for his beliefs but rather that she creates an individualistic person whose interior refusals and resistances are revealed as inadequate resources for fighting back. Jacob is bored and disconnected, and yet he still conforms to the militaristic state. His resistance is not thoughtful, communal, or sustained, and even though he seems less swayed by the liturgy than his peers, he remains captive to these forces. The civil religion of his university and the ideologies and institutions that drive toward war are not things that Jacob can simply choose to escape. Ensnared by the politics of death and blind to the resources of the radical ordinary, Jacob concludes the novel without redemption.

Unredeeming the Time in Virginia Woolf's Fiction

The final chapter of *Jacob's Room* is profoundly despairing. Jacob is dead, killed in an unnecessary war, and in her final images Woolf renders this death meaningless by refusing to give it any sort of commemorative value. We see the trivial clutter left behind in the titular room, a heartbroken friend who loved Jacob, and Jacob's mother asking this friend—the only other person around—what she should do with her son's shoes. The hopelessness and uselessness in this final image is one of the most sorrowful moments in all of Woolf's fiction. While the tone of this ending confirms the common reading of the novel as an elegy, Woolf does not supplement the sorrow with consolation or offer any memorialization. Useless shoes in a useless room with a pair of bereaved people who cannot articulate their grief or offer any comfort—these are the novel's final images, and by refusing to make Jacob's death into something meaningful such as "sacrifice," Woolf turns elegy into protest. Against the narratives of honorable sacrifice for the nation—the citizen's loftiest rite of national devotion—Woolf insists on despair. There is no redemption at the end of *Jacob's Room*, and this "unredeemed" ending completes the novel's theopolitical vision.[70]

So often we desire in our political (and theological) narratives a form of redemption, reconciliation, success, or hope—in short, a happy ending that might sustain us in the daily fight with the larger destructive forces that all too

---

[70] Madelyn Detloff powerfully argues that "the endings of Woolf's novels provide insight into eudemonia as a desirable end and a corrective to the dehumanizing instrumentalization foisted on us by the imperatives of capitalism, militarism, (hetero)sexism, and (implicit or explicit) theocratic dogmatism" (23–4). In *Jacob's Room*, the eudemonia is harder to discern than despair at this matrix of dehumanizing forces. *The Value of Virginia Woolf* (Cambridge: Cambridge University Press, 2016).

often seem to reign unchecked. Pausing in the grief rather than jumping to later conciliation is difficult, messy work that may not inspire many adherents toward a creed. And yet, the theologian Karen Bray has argued that dwelling fully and affectively in those places that seem "unredeemed" may be a vital form of resistance to the many cultural forces that urge us to acquire a uniformly optimistic attitude toward our lives and their outcome. Bray diagnoses "a soteriological and theological impulse in neoliberalism that demands we be productive, efficient, happy, and flexible in order to be of worth and therefore get saved out of the wretched existence of having been marked as worthless. The theological underpinnings of neoliberalism offer a caged freedom in the guise of opportunity."[71] Her critique of redemption narratives is spurred by her focus on affect, and particularly affective states marked as "bad" or undesirable. Her theological position seeks an open-ended, exploratory, and inconclusive posture that "asks what new questions, insights, sources, and modes of doing political theology arise when we take affects, most particularly the moods of the unredeemed, seriously."[72] Bray's specific interest is with our current neoliberal regime and the ways that going "willfully unredeemed" might create new political landscapes and solidarity with those forced out of neoliberalism's version of "success," particularly by attending faithfully to the emotions of the dispossessed.[73]

Jacob's Room becomes a valuable dialogue partner with Bray's work in this regard, appearing a century before our current neoliberal age and positioning its elusive protagonist as one who should seemingly benefit from cultural narratives of success. The glimpses of figures such as Mrs. Lidgett, the charwoman at St. Paul's Cathedral, do show connections between Bray and Woolf's interests in the affects of the underprivileged. But, as I have argued throughout this chapter, the central thrust of Woolf's novel is the myriad ways Jacob Flanders—heir to social success, elite education, economic comfort, imperial ambition, patriarchal satisfaction, and military valor—is senselessly killed by these very forces of "success." By concluding in a space where Jacob and the narrative itself are "unredeemed," Woolf offers a provocative theopolitical vision that refuses to call for any singular "solution" that might be redemptive. Our grief at the despair Jacob leaves behind is the possible source of a new politics with liturgies that do not rely on prior regimes' versions of salvation.

---

[71] Karen Bray, *Grave Attending: A Political Theology for the Unredeemed* (New York: Fordham University Press, 2019), 4.
[72] Ibid.
[73] Ibid.

Though Woolf may not have had in mind precisely the same kinds of neoliberal forces Bray is writing against a century later, the discourse on "redemption" during the First World War was being marshaled for ends that Woolf is clearly targeting in her theopolitical lament in *Jacob's Room*. In a sermon delivered in 1916, for instance, the Archbishop of Canterbury Randall Davidson expressed his belief that the current world war may be a blessing in disguise and an opportunity for living out Saint Paul's dictum from the fifth chapter of Ephesians that Christians "redeem the time" during a present evil. "Let no one," Davidson wrote, "deceive himself or herself with the thought that a mere hatred of strife can or will, by itself amend what has been amiss. A pacifism of that sort may be the very opposite to 'redeeming the time.'"[74] Instead of displaying antiwar sentiment and what the archbishop considered an impious pacifism, good Christians should experience wartime as a purgation of unrighteousness and renewal of holiness: "Out of the horrid crucible of war there must emerge, nay, there is already emerging, for those who have eyes to see, a truer knowledge of good and evil, a more keen appraising of our standards of conduct as peoples or as men and women."[75] War, though "horrid," is nonetheless able to pulverize sin, and Davidson hopes that postwar Christianity can nurture a healthy, flourishing patriotism uncorrupted by the chauvinism that led to the current crisis: "We are seeing, as some of us failed to see clearly before, how perilously easy it is for the noble plant of loyal patriotism, if it be wrongly nurtured, to degenerate into a coarse and baneful tree, and the sight of that catastrophe will put us on our guard."[76] Instead of the "baneful tree," a new growth of Christ-like, holy patriotism may emerge.[77] Davidson speaks as someone critical of the war, not blindly assuming that Christianity, the state, and militarism should collaborate. His overall posture was one of tolerant liberalism, seeking an end to conflicts local and global. (He worked strenuously to find a peaceable compromise during the General Strike of 1926, an effort that Leonard Woolf joined despite his leanings further to the political left.[78]) And yet, Davidson insists that the

---

[74] Randall Thomas Davidson, "Redeeming the Time," in *Christ: And the World at War: Sermons Preached in War-Time*, ed. Basil Matthews (Boston: Pilgrim Press, 1917), 20.
[75] Ibid.
[76] Ibid.
[77] A. J. Hoover notes that Davidson's comments are evidence that in Britain more public Christians were critical of nationalism than in Germany. That Davidson's comments here count as "critical" tells us something about the extent of the German Christian nationalism as well as the relative mildness of the British Christian critique of nationalism. See Hoover, *God, Germany, and Britain in the Great War: A Study in Clerical Nationalism* (New York: Praeger, 1989), 89.
[78] Woolf, *Letters of Virginia Woolf, Volume III*, 260.

awfulness of this war can be countered by a belief in "redemption" rather than a rejection of war itself. In 1925 Woolf remarked that she enjoyed reading classical literature (in translation) as a respite from being "sick of the vagueness, of the confusion, of the Christianity and its consolations, of our own age," and it is in redemption narratives such as Davidson's that Christian consolation strikes a particularly sinister and sickening note.[79] Woolf's "unredeemed" ending to *Jacob's Room* acts as a reinforcement of pacifism against the "caged freedoms" and devastating optimism of a theology such as Davidson's.

The caged freedom of optimism has been powerfully indicted by Judith Butler in *Frames of War* where Butler argues that the ways modern warfare is mediated through visual frames "seek[s] to institute an interdiction on mourning."[80] This interdiction has political consequences, where optimism becomes a mode for making certain lives "ungrievable," part of the acceptable cost of war or absorbed into the redemption narratives of honorable sacrifice for the nation. Challenging this enforced prohibition on mourning, Butler urges a rupturing of the frames that contain civilian experiences of war to find "the trace of lives" that are "apprehended at the margin," lives that "establish a grievable population despite a prevalent interdiction."[81] Rather than focusing on a successful assimilation of war into society—a success that cannot accept grief because grieving constitutes an acknowledgment that something is wrong—our active mourning and lamentation becomes a liturgy of protest. The grief-stricken conclusion to *Jacob's Room* asserts a lamenting, protest liturgy.

In Woolf's time, the obstacles to a flourishing life were manifest in the eruptions of global wars of increasing devastation, of an empire in decline sewing disaster in its collapse, of systemic misogyny and homophobia that made ordinary work and love a struggle, of metastasizing capitalism that threatened universal takeover and debilitating atomization—and many other interwoven and integrated forces that she chronicled throughout her fiction and in experimental treatises such as *Three Guineas*. Looking at her writing today, the resources she supplies may still speak despite another hundred years of escalation to these problems. As we face cycles of never-ending military conflict (rather than wars with declarations and peace treaties), intractable neoliberalism across many governmental, economic, and educational structures, the belligerent resentment of heterosexist and misogynist powers under threat,

---

[79] Virginia Woolf, *The Essays of Virginia Woolf: Volume IV, 1925–1928*, ed. Andrew McNeillie (Orlando, FL: Harvest, 1994), 51.
[80] Judith Butler, *Frames of War: When Is Life Grievable?* (London: Verso, 2010), xiii.
[81] Ibid., xxx.

an intensification of white supremacist energies within racially diversifying nations, and many other factors—all under the towering eventuality of total ecological cataclysm—Woolf's call to expose our destructive political liturgies and invite the mournful witness of the unredeemed may be more valuable to us now than ever. By displacing the civil religious insistence on redemption—an insistence that masks its politics of death—Woolf offers instead a lament that criticizes the false enchantments of the sacralized state and urges us into the difficult, messy, unfinished life of the radical ordinary. This is a political theology for her time and ours.

2

D. H. Lawrence's Political Eschatology: *Apocalypse* and *Lady Chatterley's Lover*

In September of 1926, D. H. Lawrence returned to his home in Eastwood, Nottinghamshire, for the last time, the place of his childhood and of deep immersion in the nonconformist Christianity that would shape his theological, political, philosophical, and aesthetic values—often through struggle, opposition, and tormented renunciation.[1] He reflected on this final visit in a posthumously published fragment where, despite his mixed feelings about his cultural inheritance, he sounds relatively optimistic about the future of English social relations. He describes property ownership as "a religious problem" but declares that "it is one we can solve" by creating "little by little a true democracy in England."[2] He predicts that "we are on the brink of a class war" but contends that "we must be prepared to have a new conception of what it means, *to live*" and that "we must be sensitive to life and to its movements. If there is power, it must be sensitive power" (*LEA*, 23). This surprisingly hopeful commentary on class war and a renewed democratization of England comes a few months after the General Strike and signals a tonal shift from the fiery rhetoric Lawrence had entertained through his "leadership novels," the last of which had been published as *The Plumed Serpent* in January of 1926.[3] Instead of blood-cults

---

[1] Stephen Kern describes "Lawrence's ambivalence about Christianity" which "alternates between biting criticism and measured praise, between deep-seated revulsion and creative reworking." Kern, *Modernism after the Death of God: Christianity, Fragmentation, and Unification* (New York: Routledge, 2017), 89.
[2] D. H. Lawrence, *Late Essays and Articles*, ed. James T. Boulton (Cambridge: Cambridge University Press, 2014), 23. Hereafter cited in text *LEA*.
[3] Paul Poplawski, however, cautions about underestimating Lawrence's continued interest in power in late works such as *Lady Chatterley*, where "even in the midst of all the talk of tenderness, there are distinct echoes of his power-mode period" (154). Paul Poplawski, *Promptings of Desire: Creativity and the Religious Impulse in the Work of D. H. Lawrence* (Westport: Greenwood, 1993). See also Stefania Michelucci, "Capsized Classes: The Aristocracy and the Annihilation of History in D. H. Lawrence's Later Works," in *The British Aristocracy in Popular Culture: Essays on 200 Years of Representations*, ed. Stefania Michelucci, Ian Duncan, and Luisa Villa (Jefferson, NC: McFarland, 2020), 140–56.

and quasi-fascist Great Men, Lawrence imagines "sensitive power" and valuing life as well as a recognition that problems of class and economy are "religious."[4] (True to form, he also includes within his optimistic predictions a eugenicist assertion that "the birth-rate should be controlled," entwining his most inspiring ideas with his most troubling in a fashion that will persist through his final books [LEA, 24].) And so, in this brief memoir, Lawrence shows his interest in several related elements that I will explore in this chapter: the political renewal of England as a religious problem, the desire for cosmic harmony, a prediction of future realities that must be lived out in the present, and a championing of imagination wherein aesthetic practices give voice to new theopolitical sensibilities.

In the previous chapter, I argued that Virginia Woolf's particular contribution to theopolitical fiction is her exposure of insidious cultural liturgies and their politics of death through an elegy of protest that elevates the unredeemed. Woolf's associative style links a series of images to highlight the subtle connections among the mundane elements of our lives as well as to reveal the densely woven mesh of ideologies that threaten to destroy us: Christian nationalism, militarism, and imperialism that constitute a social identity by crushing and ensnaring all people. Though a case could be made for focusing on nationalistic banality and political liturgy in Lawrence, as well—his images of local, menial labor in service of the national good, the mundane-yet-charged dinner conversations fraught with sexual and political energy, etc.—Lawrence differs from Woolf in his undisguised, unconstrained (and, even at times unhinged) visionary expression. His artistic vision sought a return to ancient rhythms of life that could connect all people with each other, with the earth, and with the cosmos. Embodiment was crucial to this cosmic renewal, and he challenged many aspects of modernity that prevented such restoration: technological advances, mechanization, militarism, and the political and religious ideologies that consolidate power in the wrong places. His pronouncements about the dire conditions of the modern world and the means for change are always bold and assertive, but the swirling movement of his prose gives a sinuous quality to the expression of his thought that communicates provisional speculation more than conclusive certainty. Even his propositional nonfiction glides among various thoughts to create a torrent of ideas that are sometimes inspiring, sometimes disturbing, and always fascinating.

---

[4] On Lawrence and Fascism, see Anne Fernihough, *D. H. Lawrence: Aesthetics and Ideology* (Oxford: Clarendon Press, 1993).

The visionary dimension of Lawrence's work was vital to his art and his philosophy of life.[5] Those visions, such as Ursula Brangwen's premonition of a new earthly creation at the end of *The Rainbow* (1915) or Rawdon Lilly's transfiguration into a Byzantine icon in the conclusion of *Aaron's Rod* (1922), signal how Lawrence understood his fiction as more than narrative escapism or literary experimentation. It was, as Charles Burack has argued, a "hierophantic art," in which the creator "is acting like the conductor of a religious initiation rite who leads novitiates through a series of transformative experiences designed to culminate in the awareness of or union with the divine."[6] From the mundane to the visionary with an effort at transforming his readers—these are the grand and wide-ranging goals of Lawrentian aesthetics across the many genres and media he produced. Scholarship has been very attentive to the religious quality of Lawrence's work and to his specific engagements with Christianity; these elements are virtually unavoidable due to their pervasiveness in his oeuvre.[7] But aligning him specifically with political theology—and particularly with the reflections on the end-times that were crucial to his final writings—can elicit a different set of resources from his art and politics than has often been discussed. Restoration for a damaged world was his ultimate vision, attainable through pre-Christian paganism that remained contentiously engaged with modern Christianity. This was not a nostalgic yearning for lost origins but a reclaiming of embodied human flourishing made possible through sexual and ecological communion. As a rival to the patterns of life established by industry, the state, and modern relational conventions, this regenerative vision operates theopolitically. Because they invite deep connections between individuals and the cosmos while leaving possible futures open-ended, Lawrence's late writings imagine living well in the end-times with a vigor that offers resources for our lives a century later in the Anthropocene.

Lawrence attested that he had renounced Christianity by the age of sixteen, but his art remained determinedly connected to a religious sensibility and even to the construction of his own idiosyncratic, post-Christian religion.[8] He

---

[5] See Robert E. Montgomery, *The Visionary D. H. Lawrence: Beyond Philosophy and Art* (Cambridge: Cambridge University Press, 1994).

[6] Charles Burack, *D. H. Lawrence's Language of Sacred Experience: The Transfiguration of the Reader* (New York: Palgrave Macmillan, 2005), 1–2.

[7] See Terry Eagleton, "Lawrence," in *The Prose for God: Religious and Anti-Religious Aspects of Imaginative Literature*, ed. Ian Gregor and Walter Stein (London: Sheed and Ward, 1973), 86–100; Virginia Hyde, *The Risen Adam: D. H. Lawrence's Revisionist Typology* (University Park, PA: Pennsylvania State University Press, 1992).

[8] See John Worthen, *D. H. Lawrence: The Early Years, 1885–1912* (Cambridge: Cambridge University Press, 1991), 169–83.

related that "like any other nonconformist child I had the Bible poured every day into my helpless consciousness, till there came almost a saturation point."[9] His recollection mirrors the image of Stephen Dedalus in Joyce's *A Portrait of the Artist as a Young Man* being "supersaturated" with religion that he detests, and the dying Lawrence was clearly still obsessing over and fighting with a faith that he had decidedly rejected but could not quite expel.[10] "Long before one could think or even vaguely understand, this Bible language," he wrote, "'portions' of the Bible were *douched* over the mind and consciousness, till they became soaked in" and "affected all the processes of emotion and thought"—a condition he experienced as "dislike, repulsion, and even resentment" (*A*, 59). But he would also reminisce in his late essay "Hymns in a Man's Life" that "all the lovely poems, woven deep into a man's consciousness, are still not woven so deep in me as the rather banal nonconformist hymns that penetrated through and through my childhood" (*LEA*, 130). Of the four novelists I am discussing in this book, Lawrence may be the most noticeably "supersaturated" with religion. Woolf, Waugh, and Warner also swam in the waters of a Christian culture from an early age, but of the writers in this study Lawrence was the most fully deluged by the Christian pieties of his family, chapel, and local community. That he was low-church stock was especially crucial because the nonconformist traditions staked their distinctive claim on being "personal," spiritual, and self-chosen, elements they believed distinguished themselves from the more casual associations of Anglicanism.[11] Nonconformity was also less aligned with state-sponsored nationalism than the Church of England, and Lawrence inherited that outsider's relationship to the nation and its allures.[12] What Lawrence attempted to create through his art was an alternative religious experience that discards the failed Christianity of his youth while retaining some of its hallmarks such as the appeal to transcendent realities and cosmic meaning. His religious aesthetics maintain

---

[9] D. H. Lawrence, *Apocalypse and the Writings on Revelation*, ed. Mara Kalnins (Cambridge: Cambridge University Press, 1980), 59. Hereafter cited in text as *A*.

[10] James Joyce, *A Portrait of the Artist as a Young Man* (New York: Norton, 2007), 212. There are important differences between Irish Jesuit education and English nonconformist Sunday Schools that could be developed elsewhere, but the experiences Joyce and Lawrence record about indoctrination bear striking similarities.

[11] This is not to suggest that nonconformism was apolitical. On the political character of English nonconformist churches during Lawrence's youth, see D. W. Bebbington, *The Nonconformist Conscience: Chapel and Politics, 1870-1914* (London: Allen & Unwin, 1982) and Donald Davie, *A Gathered Church: The Literature of the English Dissenting Interest, 1700-1930* (New York: Oxford University Press, 1978), 91-100.

[12] On the specific importance of Congregationalism, see Margaret J. Masson, "D. H. Lawrence's Congregational Inheritance," *D. H. Lawrence Review* 22, no. 1 (1990): 53-68 and David Newmarch, "Congregationalism in the Early Life of D. H. Lawrence: Ministers at the Eastwood Chapel," *Journal of the D. H. Lawrence Society* 5 (1990): 9-24.

a simultaneous attraction to and suspicion of nonconformist Christianity and Christian mythology more broadly.

Critical discussion on Lawrence has attended to the thoroughly religious quality of his work, though commentators often focus on a personal and private version of "religion." Luke Ferretter, for instance, in one of the most thorough examinations of Lawrence's personal religion, writes "that religion consists in emotions felt throughout the whole person, which put that person into relationship with something that transcends his or her known experience, and from which a sense of wholeness derives."[13] Ferretter draws on Lawrence's own discussions of religion, and, like many accounts of religion and modernism, associates these ideas with William James's *Varieties of Religious Experience*. The expression of deep personal feeling, transcendence, and wholeness can certainly be found in much of Lawrence's writing on religion and broader philosophizing. Lawrence's post-Christian religiosity, however, is also communal, material, and critical of the current socioeconomic order. His new religion was intended for the whole world, but as I will argue, its locus and highest expression grew from Lawrence's care for England and for renewing and revitalizing English national identity. His political theology challenged the civil religion of his place and age, and though its specific content might not be widely shared, it remains a crucial alternative to the catastrophic religious nationalisms of his context. Of particular value, I contend, are the ways Lawrence's theopolitical fiction dissents from other contemporary voices who attempted to make the catastrophe of the Great War intelligible by aligning it with Christian mythologies of the end-times, and his re-writing of that end-times imagination supplies resources for us today during our age of perpetual war and ecological crisis. The war's devastations were so vast and senseless that a narrative of cosmic destruction seemed needed to match its scale. The frequent references to the Great War as an Armageddon, for instance, or to the Four Horsemen of the Apocalypse (such as in Vicente Blasco Ibáñez's 1916 novel and its 1921 film adaptation) associate the historical war with end-times mythologies.[14] Lawrence's work has long been understood as apocalyptic, but I argue that his late writings are an idiosyncratic response to the end-times myths of the 1920s that reject teleologies of destruction and instead call for a revitalized relationship between people and the earth.[15]

---

[13] Luke Ferretter, *The Glyph and the Gramophone: D. H. Lawrence's Religion* (London: Bloomsbury, 2013), 3.
[14] See Jenkins, *Great and Holy War*, 16–20.
[15] See Helen Corke, *Lawrence and Apocalypse* (London: Heinemann, 1933); Horace Gregory, *D. H. Lawrence: Pilgrim of the Apocalypse, A Critical Study*, 1933 (New York: Grove Press, 1957); Frank Kermode, "Lawrence and the Apocalyptic Types," *Critical Quarterly* 10, no. 1–2 (1968): 14–38.

The value of Lawrence's political theology arises from its search for an eschatology of renewal and restoration to counter eschatologies of devastation and judgment. Eschatology—the theological examination of death, afterlife, and cosmic end-times—was a vibrant field of academic study in the first half of the twentieth century as well as a crucial piece of the popular imagination at the turn of the century and during the war years. Lawrence weighed in on these eschatological debates with his final completed book *Apocalypse*, written during his last winter in 1929–30. It is a commentary on the biblical book of Revelation that predominately works as a critique of the problematic philosophies Lawrence finds in Christianity, and particularly the nonconformism of his youth. The conclusion of *Apocalypse*, however, is a manifesto that reveals Lawrence's alternative philosophy and new testament, casting a vision for cosmic, universal regeneration. I situate this distinctly Lawrentian prophecy as a response to contemporary eschatologies that privilege militarism and violent upheaval, and I read Lawrence's work alongside more recent political eschatology by Jürgen Moltmann which emphasizes the importance of eschatological imagination in the present as an engine of political change rather than as a fantasy of afterlife. Catherine Keller and Clayton Crockett have argued that "political theology, inasmuch as it attends to a collective present edged with a precarious future, has always already been political eschatology," and Lawrence's writing shows his political theology most clearly through his eschatological prophecies.[16]

All of this cosmic, universal, and eschatological imagining comprises Lawrence's most magisterial and visionary thought, but it also appears productively through his fiction. Ideas such as these are particularly overt in his so-called leadership novels: *Aaron's Rod* (1922), *Kangaroo* (1923), and especially *The Plumed Serpent*. Lawrence's writings about Mexico and the American southwest are a heated stew of religious and political visions loaded with racialist bombast, revolutionary urges, psychosexual mythologizing, and spiritual-mystical philosophizing. Their exact political tenor is confusing, at times betraying some of Lawrence's worst tendencies toward fascist, racist, sexist, and eugenicist beliefs and at other times challenging settler colonialism and white supremacy.[17] Such a mixture of political ideas within creative works

---

[16] Catherine Keller and Clayton Crockett, "Introduction: Political Theology on Edge," in *Political Theology on Edge: Ruptures of Justice and Belief in the Anthropocene*, ed. Clayton Crockett and Catherine Keller (New York: Fordham University Press, 2022), 3.

[17] For works that reclaim Lawrence for anticolonial and antiracist efforts, see Mark Kinkead-Weekes, "Decolonising Imagination: Lawrence in the 1920s," in *The Cambridge Companion to D. H. Lawrence*, ed. Anne Fernihough (Cambridge: Cambridge University Press, 2001), 67–86; Ria Banerjee, "The Search for Pan: Difference and Morality in D. H. Lawrence's 'St Mawr' and 'The Woman Who Rode Away,'" *D. H. Lawrence Review* 37, no. 1 (2012): 65–89.

that refuse simplicity or closure makes Lawrence's writings a challenge to all orthodoxies, religious and political, and that challenge is not confined to his "leadership phase." According to many critics, once the extreme political theology of *The Plumed Serpent* was exorcised, Lawrence's final fictions returned to earth with less prophetic zeal.[18] Instead of writing a new global religion through fiction, such a reading claims, Lawrence shifted to the local and personal in his last years. In one prominent example of this interpretation, Anthony Burgess wrote, "With the theological politics of *The Plumed Serpent* out of his system, Lawrence was preparing to take up the implied stance of *Lady Chatterley's Lover*: that we are impotent to change the evil imposed by the mass or by the authoritarian state, and that salvation lies only in the cultivation of the personal life."[19] Lawrence's singular message, according to Burgess, is that the solution for all the world's ills is "personal tenderness."[20] My analysis of his late writings questions this turn to the personal insofar as "personal" means merely private or individual. For Lawrence, the embodied self is always inherently social, even when his interests moved away from leadership works that explored collective action.

Though *Lady Chatterley's Lover* is less international than his several previous novels, its focus on English nationalism and cosmic renewal in an age of crisis make its vision just as political. The novel has long been captive to debates about its feminism or misogyny as well as its supposed obscenity.[21] Studies that seriously consider its other political valences tend to focus on its approach to industrialization and technology, as well as its naturalism, pastoralism, and

---

[18] Luke Ferretter, for instance, claims that "after *The Plumed Serpent*, Lawrence was less interested in portraying the effect of his religious beliefs throughout society." See Luke Ferretter, "Religion," in *D. H. Lawrence in Context*, ed. Andrew Harrison (Cambridge: Cambridge University Press, 2001), 190.

[19] Anthony Burgess, *Flame into Being: The Life and Work of D. H. Lawrence* (New York: Arbor House, 1985), 216.

[20] Ibid. One of Lawrence's working titles for the novel was *Tenderness*, but its final version extends far beyond the interpersonal.

[21] See, for instance, Lydia Blanchard, "Lawrence, Foucault, and the Language of Sexuality," in *D. H. Lawrence's "Lady": A New Look at Lady Chatterley's Lover*, ed. Michael Squires and Dennis Jackson (Athens, GA: University of Georgia Press, 1985), 17–35; William K. Buckley, *Lady Chatterley's Lover: Loss and Hope* (New York: Twayne, 1993), 16–23; James J. Miracky, *Regenerating the Novel: Gender and Genre in Woolf, Forster, Sinclair, and Lawrence* (New York: Routledge, 2003); Fiona Becket, "The Law and the Profits: The Case of D. H. Lawrence's *Lady Chatterley's Lover*," in *Scandalous Fictions: The Twentieth-Century Novel in the Public Sphere*, ed. Jago Morrison and Susan Watkins (New York: Palgrave Macmillan, 2006), 70–82; Sean Matthews, "The Trial of *Lady Chatterley's Lover*: 'The most thorough and expensive seminar on Lawrence's work ever given,'" in *New D. H. Lawrence*, ed. Howard J. Booth (Manchester: Manchester University Press, 2009), 169–92.

primitivism.²² By taking seriously the cosmic elements of Lawrence's late writings, we may recognize how his fictional return to England and personal relationships engage with the sociopolitical order. My argument shows the close connection between the political eschatology of *Apocalypse* and the imaginative regeneration of *Lady Chatterley's Lover*.²³ Lawrence's prophecy of cosmic renewal begins at the most local of levels, in a relationship between two people who are synecdochic for England and, more expansively, the earth and the entire universe.²⁴ Woolf, Waugh, and Warner all give us theories about social organization and how individuals might thrive in a well-ordered world or be crushed by unjust social structures, but only Lawrence wrote explicitly about the nature of the universe and how to mend its brokenness. Though his vision does not include any sort of traditional belief in a god, it is conceived on a god-like scale that makes it unique among the novelists I am discussing. Because of this vast scope with implications for all of time and the trajectory of history as well as his hope for another epoch when the universe could be harmoniously realigned, Lawrence is an eschatological writer, attuned to the end-times as a guide for our present age. As a work of political theology, *Lady Chatterley's Lover* imagines regeneration where eschatology matters not only for a speculative future but for an embodied and material present. That combination of bold declarations about cosmic harmony and tentative gestures toward hope supplies resources for living in an age of crisis.

Apocalyptic Lawrence

Apocalypse combines biblical criticism, theology, political theory, and memoir with a resulting sense that Lawrence is both fascinated with and agonized by the book of Revelation. His commentary shows the profound impact of his childhood

---

[22] See Morag Shirach, "Work and Selfhood in *Lady Chatterley's Lover*," in *The Cambridge Companion to D. H. Lawrence*, ed. Anne Fernighough (Cambridge: Cambridge University Press, 2001), 87–102. See also Gerald Doherty, *Theorizing Lawrence: Nine Meditations on Tropological Themes* (New York: Peter Lang, 1999), 99–116; David Trotter, "Techno-primitivism: *á propos* of *Lady Chatterley's Lover*," *Modernism/modernity* 18, no. 1 (2011): 149–66; Andrew Keese, "Engineering away Humanity: Lawrence on Technology and Mental Consciousness in *Lady Chatterley's Lover* and *Pansies*," in *D. H. Lawrence, Technology, and Modernity*, ed. Idrek Männiste (London: Bloomsbury Academic, 2019), 127–36.

[23] Critics have noted correspondences between *Apocalypse* and *Lady Chatterley's Lover*, largely focusing on the typological schema for the end-times as it maps onto Connie's sexual awakening. See Frank Kermode, *Lawrence* (London: Fontana, 1973); Gerald Doherty, *Oriental Lawrence: The Quest for the Secrets of Sex* (New York: Peter Lang, 2001).

[24] Fiona Becket, for instance, argues: "Implicated in the rebirth of the self in this novel is the regeneration of England, and the engine of that regeneration is 'phallic-consciousness', evolved in Lawrence's terms out of 'blood-consciousness'" (78–9). Becket, *The Complete Critical Guide to D. H. Lawrence* (London: Routledge, 2002), 78–9.

indoctrination at Eastwood, the influence of reading Friedrich Nietzsche and later biblical scholars such as R. H. Charles, and his development of a new political theology of cosmic restoration. Like much of his writing, *Apocalypse* swerves through many pronouncements, tangents, and prophecies with gusto, weaving together a variety of political and philosophical views that upset all types of orthodoxies. Though he joins the end-times discourse of the postwar era, his approach is less deterministic or foreclosed than the theologians, preachers, or politicians whose narratives insist on final judgment, dystopia, or annihilation. Instead, Lawrence manages to cast a broad cosmic vision that is still tentative, where living for a better future must be struggled for in the present. That unity of cosmic scale and local effort makes Lawrence an apocalyptic thinker in dialogue with more recent political eschatology that reckons with our age of global crisis not by displacing hope onto an abstract future but through reorienting our lives toward present challenges while being mindful of our ultimate uncertainty.

Eschatology was personal for Lawrence since his meditation on endings occurred near the conclusion of his own life, but the years surrounding the First World War were particularly rich with eschatological thinking and end-times mythologies—many of which provide a useful contrast to Lawrence's contributions to this field. In popular consciousness, the *fin de siècle* portended epochal change and foreboding, famously expressed in Thomas Hardy's "The Darkling Thrush," also known as "Century's End, 1900," which features a bone-weary speaker describing "the Century's corpse outleant."[25] In academic theological circles, eschatology grew as an area of interest throughout the Edwardian period, producing what Mark Chapman calls "a 'crisis' theology" that "in the years before the First World War [...] was beginning to emerge as a protest against the hitherto dominant theologies of liberal synthesis."[26] Lawrence was aware of these theological currents and had immersed himself in theosophical meditations on Revelation as well as academic biblical criticism. He admired Frederick Carter's astrological work-in-progress called *The Dragon of the Apocalypse*, which despite being "confused" and "a chaos" still managed to "release my imagination and give me a whole great sky to move in" (*A*, 45).[27] He was similarly influenced by

---

[25] Thomas Hardy, *Collected Poems* (New York: Macmillan, 1958), 137.
[26] Mark D. Chapman, *The Coming Crisis: The Impact of Eschatology on Theology in Edwardian England* (Sheffield: Sheffield Academic Press, 2001), 168.
[27] Lawrence completed an "introduction" for Carter's book in January 1930, but it was published separately in *The London Mercury* largely because Carter had significantly changed his earlier manuscript so that it no longer resembled the work Lawrence had admired.

James Pryse's *The Apocalypse Unsealed* (1910), which explored the symbolism of Revelation through theosophy.[28] Within more mainstream Christian theological circles, he had read the Catholic modernist writings of Alfred Loisy, the massive two-volume commentary on Revelation by Anglican biblical scholar R. H. Charles, and had even published a short review of the Presbyterian John Oman's book on Revelation. From these sources he gathered an understanding of the complexity of Revelation as well as its competing and sometimes conflicting messages—all of which contributed to the urgency of eschatology during Lawrence's final years. The surge of end-times thinking from a range of sources secular, spiritualist, and traditionally orthodox would expand during the war years and their immediate aftermath. Wellesley Tudor Pole, voicing a common perception, wrote at the beginning of the war, "can anyone still doubt that this is the ending of the age? That the great conflict now raging is the one prophesied from time immemorial."[29] The turning century plus Edwardian social inequalities fueled a sense of breakage and ending, and viewing the First World War as crucial to this unrest and part of ancient prophecy were ways to make its chaos manageable.

For many people, managing chaos meant reaching for the biblical book of Revelation and its projection of a final war at Armageddon, describing the global conflict as an end-times crisis and fulfillment of New Testament prophecy. Edward S. Talbot, Bishop of Winchester, preached in 1917 that current events were the "fuller glory to St. John, the seer of Patmos" and his congregants are "now in the presence of Europe's Armageddon."[30] Talbot declares that the war offers an unprecedented opportunity for Christian unity and urges a hope for global missionary work, turning against the seemingly indisputable fact that the "Christian nations" of Europe have abandoned any pretense of universal faith by devolving into political chauvinism. Talbot offers a blinkered hope embedded in a biblical end-times mythology that was a template for Christian leaders throughout Europe to give meaning to otherwise meaningless displays of chaos, violence, and waste. References to the war as "Armageddon" appeared throughout the war itself and persist in current scholarship, combining the literal geographical conflict in the Middle East with the biblical narrative of

---

[28] Mara Kalnins, introduction to *Apocalypse and the Writings on Revelation*, by D. H. Lawrence (Cambridge: Cambridge University Press, 1980), 5–6.
[29] Qtd. in Jenkins, *Great and Holy War*, 152.
[30] Edward S. Talbot, "The World at the Cross-Roads," in *Christ and the World at War: Sermons Preached in War-Time*, ed. Basil Matthews (London: Clark, 1917), 33.

cataclysm.³¹ On August 3, 1914, Justin Huntley McCarthy published a poem titled "Armageddon" in the *Daily Chronicle* decrying the war and accusing "foolish prince[s]" and kings "who break an age in pieces for your play."³² McCarthy's poem is exasperated with the war and its wastefulness—already, in early August of 1914—and dumbfounded by the easy descent into Armageddon, but a raft of works would flow out during the war that reiterated this coming destruction. That history had reached a crisis point and global war was a sign of the end were beliefs that spread through popular and professional theology, journalism, and literature about the war. Lawrence also registered this sense about the war, and, as Peter Fjågesund observes, he drew "a connection between a war-ridden Europe and the apocalyptic element in his conception of history, and he ultimately came to identify the war as the manifestation of the Armageddon itself."³³ Fear of doom and ruin stalks many of Lawrence's prophecies about the war and its political ideologies.

Direct references to the First World War are few in *Apocalypse*, but end-times conflict and a sense of calamitous finality shape Lawrence's theological claims. He frequently contrasts the good version of Christianity defined by "the peace of meditation and the joy of unselfish service, the rest from ambition and the pleasure of knowledge" from the dominant strain of "the thwarted collective self" he finds in Revelation (*A*, 73). The superior version—"pure Christianity"— Lawrence claims, "*cannot* fit a nation or society at large. The Great War made it obvious. It can only fit individuals. The collective whole must have some other inspiration" (*A*, 73). Selfless love, learning, and individual security are the

---

[31] For contemporary works, see Cloudesley Brereton, *Who Is Responsible? Armageddon and After!* (New York: Putnam, 1914); Stephen Phillips, *Armageddon: A Modern Epic Drama in a Prologue Series of Scenes and an Epilogue Written Partly in Prose and Partly in Verse* (London: John Lane, 1915); Will Irwin, *A Reporter at Armageddon: Letters from the Front and Behind the Lines of the Great War* (New York: D. Appleton and Co., 1918). For later scholars who use the term, see Lyn MacDonald, *To the Last Man: Spring 1918* (New York: Carroll & Graf, 1999), 1–72; John Keegan, *The First World War* (New York: Vintage, 2000), 372–428. For works dealing with the war in the Middle East, see Arthur G. Daniels, *The World War: Its Relation to the Eastern Question and Armageddon* (Mountain View, CA: Pacific Press, 1917); Cyril Falls, *Armageddon: 1918* (New York: Lippincott, 1964); Roger Ford, *Eden to Armageddon: World War I in the Middle East* (New York: Pegasus Books, 2010).

[32] Justin Huntly McCarthy, "Armageddon," in *Songs & Sonnets for England in War Time: Being a Collection of Lyrics by Various Authors Inspired by the Great War*, ed. John Lane (London: John Lane, 1914), 3.

[33] Peter Fjågesund, *The Apocalyptic World of D. H. Lawrence* (Oslo: Norwegian University Press, 1991), 27. See also Stefania Michelucci, "The Line and the Circle: D.H. Lawrence, the First World War and Myth," in *New D. H. Lawrence*, ed. Howard J. Booth (Manchester: Manchester University Press, 2009), 117–29.

hallmarks of what Christianity at its best can offer, according to Lawrence, and the war showed that such selflessness was impossible when people choose instead to merge unthinkingly into mass ideologies such as nationalism, imperialism, and militarism. The war was an acute time of hostility that confirmed Lawrence's view of humanity at its worst and the inadequacy of Christian love to conquer such ideologies on a mass scale. His attacks on mass politics and Christian platitudes are a stark contrast with preaching like William Talbot's that find in the war an opportunity for mutual love and Christian salvation.

Lawrence criticizes mythologies and philosophies that he discerns in Revelation, but even more upsetting to him are the ways these narratives and ideas have been appropriated and disseminated. He rejects the term "eschatological" which he calls "a pet word of the scientists": "for two thousand years man has been living in a dead or dying cosmos, hoping for a heaven hereafter. And all the religions have been religions of the dead body and the postponed reward" (*A*, 96). Deadness and denial of the body are among Lawrence's foremost enemies, the fundamental forces of evil wrought by religious gnosticism. Lawrence believes that the so-called science of eschatology rests on promises of later benefits or heavenly blessings after the death of the cosmos, and he finds this narrative of doom both in Revelation and in the theological interpretations from the Congregationalist chapel of his youth. He remarks that Revelation is "a strange book" to have "inspired the colliers on the black Tuesday nights in Pentecost or Beauvale Chapel to such a queer sense of special authority and of religious cheek. Strange marvellous black nights of the north Midlands, with the gas-light hissing in the chapel, and the roaring of the strong-voiced colliers" (*A*, 64). From the intensity of his description, one can glean the powerful impression these gatherings made on the young Lawrence, how much they seem like images from a dark and mystical rite or seance rather than the boring drone of biblical literalists in a rural chapel. They make the chapel service sound magical, and they indicate how decades later Lawrence still finds them disturbing. A "thwarted collective self" expressed in the "Apocalyptic language" was foisted on a sensitive, imaginative child, "not because I spent my time reading Revelation, but because I was sent to Sunday School and to Chapel, to Band of Hope and to Christian Endeavour, and was always having the Bible read at me or to me" (*A*, 54). To the end of his life, the version of Revelation that persisted for Lawrence was that of his nonconformist youth and the para-church organizations that shaped his aesthetic and theological consciousness—theology rife with spite-filled class antagonism.

Those segues into memoir reveal the emotional impact of childhood indoctrination, but they also show Lawrence's later immersion in Nietzsche's theories of power and *ressentiment* that create a lens for his interpretation of Revelation.[34] The piety of the colliers, Lawrence claims, is not based in the loving witness of Jesus but in a self-aggrandizing power play where the triumphalism of Revelation is harnessed by working-class English people desperate to claim for themselves the power of those currently on top of the hierarchy. "There are two kinds of Christianity," he writes, "the one focussed on Jesus and the Command: Love one another!—and the other focussed, not on Paul or Peter or John the Beloved, but on the Apocalypse" which leads to "the self-glorification of the humble" (*A*, 64–5). T. R. Wright notes the similarities between these claims and Nietzsche's arguments in *The Will to Power*, where "Christianity embodies its own lust for power" and "a desire for revenge" among the weak, "weary and self-hating."[35] Throughout *Apocalypse* John of Patmos is portrayed as a corrupting influence on Christianity because his revolutionary message deviates from personal love in favor of upending hierarchies to put the lowly into seats of power. This sort of revolutionary impulse, Lawrence argues, is misguided and terrible. It is a manifestation of what Nietzsche describes in *On the Genealogy of Morals* as *ressentiment* where instead of strong acts of internal will, people adopt a "slave morality" where deeds are replaced by "imaginary revenge" that merely reacts to "a hostile external world."[36] Christianity in its earliest forms promised love and affirmation for the living body and thus had not entirely abandoned the ancient paganism Lawrence prefers, but Revelation ushers in a different gospel steeped in jealousy: "this Christianity of the Apocalypse [...] is hideous [because] self-righteousness, self-conceit, self-importance and secret *envy* underlie it all" (*A*, 144). Rather than instigating a revitalized connection between people and the earth, Revelation presents a message of curdled desire for power that Lawrence sensed among the working-class Congregationalists of his youth and more broadly within the core mythos of modern Christianity.

Lawrence's Nietzschean critique of Revelation bristles against later political theology that has shown how the book's prophetic symbolism offers a radical

---

[34] See Wright, *Lawrence and the Bible*, 239–40. For a survey of this relationship that does not mention *Apocalypse*, see Colin Milton, *Lawrence and Nietzsche: A Study of Influence* (Aberdeen: Aberdeen University Press, 1987).
[35] Wright, *Lawrence and the Bible*, 50.
[36] Friedrich Nietzsche, *On the Genealogy of Morals and Ecce Homo*, trans. and ed. Walter Kaufmann and R. J. Hollingdale (New York: Vintage, 1989), 36–7.

message of hope for a people subjugated by Roman imperialism.[37] R. H. Charles, in the introduction to his commentary on Revelation, wrote:

> [T]he object of the Apocalypse was to encourage the faithful to resist even to death the blasphemous claims of the State, and to proclaim the coming victory of the cause of God and of His Christ not only in the individual Christian, and the corporate body of such individuals, but also in the nations as such in their national and international life and relations. It lays down the only true basis for national ethics and international law.[38]

This anti-statist response to nationalism is largely dismissed by Lawrence, but it is a major area of scholarly commentary in the century since Charles's work. Jeffrey D. Meyers, for example, argues that "despite its violent language and history of being used to support violence," Revelation "can be a rich resource for learning to live faithfully in a turbulent and unjust world" by understanding it as a work of "resistance literature that engages in nonviolent methods of resisting the Roman Empire."[39] Lawrence acknowledges this revolutionary art, but he dismisses the book's context as "the rather boring process of Danielesque prophecy, concerning the Church of Christ and the fall of the various kingdoms of the earth" and concludes: "we cannot be very much interested in the prophesied collapse of Rome and the Roman Empire" (A, 129). This aspect of *Apocalypse* has been criticized for privileging mystical love over material change. J. A. Loubser, for instance, argues that Lawrence failed to grasp "the profound revolutionary irony" in "Revelation's visions of destruction" as well as the book's "consistent non-violent critique of power" and claims: "In missing this, I also think he commits the grave error of blaming the victim."[40] What Lawrence finds in the revolutionary vision of Revelation is a will-to-destroy that is envious of those who have more power and possessions rather than an outcry that denounces acquisitiveness, plutocracy, imperialism, and war. The political theology of Revelation, he writes, "shows us the Christian in his relation to the State; which the gospels and epistles avoid doing. It

---

[37] See Elisabeth Schüssler Fiorenza, *Revelation: Vision of a Just World* (Minneapolis: Fortress Press, 1991); Barbara R. Rossing, *The Rapture Exposed: The Message of Hope in the Book of Revelation* (New York: Basic Books, 2004); J. Nelson Kraybill, *Apocalypse and Allegiance: Worship, Politics, and Devotion in the Book of Revelation* (Grand Rapids: Brazos, 2010); Richard B. Hays and Stefan Alkier, eds., *Revelation and the Politics of Apocalyptic Interpretation* (Waco: Baylor University Press, 2012).

[38] R H. Charles, *A Critical and Exegetical Commentary on the Revelation of St. John* (Edinburgh: T & T Clark, 1920), xxii.

[39] Jeffrey D. Myers, *The Nonviolent Apocalypse: Revelation's Nonviolent Resistance against Rome* (Minneapolis: Fortress Press, 2021), 7, 1.

[40] J. A. Loubser, "D. H. Lawrence's Extra-Ordinary 'Ordinary Reading' of the Apocalypse," *Neotestamentica* 38, no. 2 (2004): 343. See also Donald MacKenzie, "After Apocalypse: Some Elements in Late Lawrence," in *European Literature and Theology in the Twentieth Century: Ends of Time*, ed. David Jasper and Colin Crowder (New York: St. Martin's Press, 1990), 34–55.

shows him in mad hostility to all of them, having, in the end, to will the destruction of them all" (*A*, 148). With this interpretation, Lawrence misses some of the nuance and ambiguity of the biblical text, seeing the essence of the Apocalypse as a fantasy of hostile annihilation, and he rejects the book's alternative nationalism. But, his commentary cautions against the dangers of revolutionary movements that invert hierarchies rather than fundamentally changing power structures, and he admonishes those who might embrace earthly devastation instead of restoration.

Along with this warning about new tyranny that can mount from a lower-class revolt, *Apocalypse* offers trenchant criticisms of the allures of fascism that temper Lawrence's quasi-fascist promotion of genius leaders and reflect his concern about the political forces brewing in the interwar years. He claims that while Jesus produced an ethic and way of life focused on the individual, John of Patmos, in response to the Roman state, "formulate[d] the Christian vision of the Christian State" that means "the destruction of the whole world" or "of all earthly power, and the rule of an oligarchy of martyrs (the Millennium)" (*A*, 146). This notion of an "oligarchy of martyrs," which he finds expressed in the millennialism of Revelation, is his phrase for political leaders who are willing to destroy others, themselves, and the world for the sake of revolution, and he calls their mode a "weird cold morality" (*A*, 146). Both Russia and Italy are succumbing to such "martyr-rulers," Lawrence claims, and other nations are in danger of following suit: "When every country has its martyr-ruler, either like Lenin or like Mussolini, what a strange, unthinkable world it will be! But it is coming: the Apocalypse is still a book to conjure with" (*A*, 146).[41] Revolutionary authoritarianisms brandish apocalyptic visions akin to Revelation, and mass politics involves a "conjuring" where disgruntled peoples embrace destructive fantasies of martyr-rulers. After 1930, this insight will grow more frighteningly trenchant, persisting to our current age where political figures gain mass support by trumpeting grievances, blaming scapegoats, and assuring deliverance through loyal martyrdom. Lawrence identifies in the apocalyptic politics of his time a violent core that expands through the state's theological claims about salvation. He is horrified by a vision of apocalypse that Kyle Gingerich Hiebert has argued was crucial to the political theology of Carl Schmitt: "what Schmitt leaves us with is an apocalyptically inflected aesthetics of violence, a powerful vision that [...] continues to haunt the contemporary theopolitical imagination,

---

[41] In this statement Lawrence betrays some acceptance of the political value of apocalyptic frameworks. Fjågesund notes that he "assumes the voice of a chapel preacher" and contradicts earlier rejections of the cosmic destruction in Revelation by "acknowledging the *Apocalypse* as a guide to the more far-reaching implications of contemporary politics" (*Apocalyptic World*, 173).

even and perhaps especially those who claim to have decisively broken free of the aporetics defined by Schmitt."[42] The essence of Schmitt's thought about the state revolves around the inevitability of violence, the friend–enemy dichotomy of national life, and the self-lacerations of civil war, all of which are subsumed by political organization that gravitates toward a single powerful leader who rules with force. Lawrence understands Revelation to be authorizing a similar political vision, and he seeks a pre-Christian antidote for the enchantments of apocalyptic violence.

Lawrence rejects eschatology as a story of postponed rewards and apocalyptic politics as a fascist nightmare of destruction and violent revolution led by martyr-rulers. His resistance to such ideologies puts his eschatological thinking in dialogue with Jürgen Moltmann, one of the leading theologians of the latter half of the twentieth century who has worked influentially in the fields of political theology and eschatology.[43] As Moltmann writes: "To think apocalyptically means thinking things through to their end," but he notes that too often eschatology is seen as a method of answering all the largest questions of life in search of a "final solution" to "all the insoluble problems."[44] He forcefully rejects this version of eschatology, pointedly noting that all talk of "final solutions" echoes—not coincidentally—the genocidal ambitions of the Third Reich.[45] He writes: "If eschatology were no more than religion's 'final solution' to all the questions, a solution allowing it to have the last word, it would undoubtedly be a particularly unpleasant form of theological dogmatism, if not psychological terrorism. And it has in fact been used in just this way by a number of apocalyptic arm-twisters among our contemporaries."[46] Those "arm-twisters" are theologians and other evangelizers, but present throughout his work are Moltmann's experiences under Nazism and its political narratives of destruction and finality.[47] Moltmann counters that distinctly "*Christian* eschatology has nothing to do with apocalyptic 'final solutions' of this kind,

---

[42] Kyle Gingerich Hiebert, *The Architectonics of Hope: Violence, Apocalyptic, and the Transformation of Political Theology* (Eugene, OR: Cascade Books, 2017), 16.
[43] See Richard Bauckham, ed. *God Will Be All in All: The Eschatology of Jürgen Moltmann* (Edinburgh: T&T Clark, 1999).
[44] Jürgen Moltmann, *The Coming of God: Christian Eschatology* (Minneapolis: Fortress Press, 1996), x.
[45] Moltmann, *Coming of God*, x. Moltmann challenges grand theologies of finality, such as Hans Urs von Balthasar's "theological eschatology [that] seems to present the 'Endgame' of the theodrama World History" (x). Moltmann notes that von Balthasar took this idea from Samuel Beckett but does not comment on whether Beckett's version is more palatable.
[46] Moltmann, *Coming of God*, xi.
[47] See Jürgen Moltmann, *A Broad Place: An Autobiography* (Minneapolis: Fortress Press, 2009).

for its subject is not 'the end' at all. On the contrary, what it is about is the new creation of all things."⁴⁸ Moltmann's focus on renewal rather than demolition is a valuable alternative to end-times narratives of Armageddon, and his narrative of restoration has political consequence for how we live today. He does not offer a developed program for reorganizing government or enacting polity, but rather explores a theopolitical imagination where fruition and hope guide our communities and actions.⁴⁹

Moltmann distinguishes between two types of millenarian thought that have a bearing on how we might understand Lawrence's critique of Revelation as well as his ultimate vision of hope at the end of *Apocalypse*. Moltmann theorizes a difference between "historical millenarianism," which "is the millenarian interpretation of the present in its political or ecclesiastical aspect, or in the context of universal history," and "eschatological millenarianism," which "is an expectation of the future in the eschatological context of the end, and the new creation of the world."⁵⁰ That former concept, the "historical," is "a religious theory used to legitimate political or ecclesiastical power, and is exposed to acts of messianic violence and the disappointments of history."⁵¹ It is this version of millenarianism that Lawrence identifies in the destructive wishes of his home church and in Revelation overall. For Moltmann, there is a better form of millenarian belief in the "eschatological" variety because this type provides "a necessary picture of hope in resistance, in suffering, and in the exiles of the world."⁵² From this perspective, the book of Revelation is a radical text that gives power to the disenfranchised rather than simply allowing destructive ideologies to flourish. Moltmann's explication of a political eschatology that intends to imbue our current reality with renewal rather than anticipating a cataclysmic Last Judgment has encountered criticism, especially among theologians who

---

⁴⁸ Ibid.
⁴⁹ Moltmann's political eschatology has been criticized by some theologians for being too idealistic or too invested in worldly politics rather than theological absolutes. Joseph Ratzinger, later Pope Benedict XVI, objected to Moltmann's eschatology because "the Kingdom of God, not being itself a political concept, cannot serve a political criterion by which to construct in direct fashion a program of political action." Ratzinger, *Eschatology: Death and Eternal Life* (Washington, DC: Catholic University of America Press, 1988), 58. Some of the problem seems to be in defining "political." Moltmann makes no attempt specify governmental policies based in eschatology, and Ratzinger is concerned about theology that invests in human institutions rather than divinity. Beyond the scope of my argument is an investigation of how Moltmann and Ratzinger's positions relate to both of their complicated relationships with Nazi Germany.
⁵⁰ Moltmann, *Coming of God*, 192.
⁵¹ Ibid.
⁵² Ibid.

find his arguments too radical or too utopian.[53] And yet, there is a radical vision of hope that is shared by Lawrence and Moltmann which appears as the final challenge Lawrence presents in *Apocalypse*.

After spending the majority of the book attacking the theology of John of Patmos and the interpretations of Revelation from his childhood, Lawrence turns in the last chapter to his counter-proposal and offers his own imagining of a political eschatology through a manifesto-like articulation of what he still finds valuable about "Christian fantasy" (*A*, 146). Lawrence enumerates several propositions to describe, as clearly as he ever does in *Apocalypse*, his views about religion and the state. He denies that anyone can be a "pure individual" and that we function collectively as fragmentary selves united in the state—a configuration that "cannot be Christian" because "every State is a Power" (*A*, 146). Citizenship makes a person become "a unit of worldly power," and despite the "wish to be a pure Christian and a pure individual," we are bound instead to "be a member of some political State, or Nation" (*A*, 147). Democracy, as Lawrence understands it, "is made up of millions of frictional parts all asserting their own wholeness" where "bullying inevitably takes the place of power" (*A*, 147). His preferred formation is "hierarchy" where "each part is organic and vital, as my finger is an organic and vital part of me" and he asserts that "the modern Christian State is a soul-destroying force, for it is made up of fragments which have no organic whole, only a collective whole" (*A*, 147). This denunciation of democracy in favor of hierarchy may sound like one of Lawrence's quasi-fascist pronouncements, but he expresses longing for a more genuinely collaborative and integrated social organization where coercion, dissatisfaction, and power struggles no longer dominate. Instead of suspicion and denigration on a constant quest for personal gain, Lawrence imagines a society of shared goods where individual skills are valued and supported through fairly distributed work.

His vision at the end of *Apocalypse* is far from being a detailed program for social justice, but it should not be mistaken for a small scale, meliorist, or conservative notion. Under the terms Lawrence sets, the entire cosmos needs renewing, reenergizing, and a return to synchronicity so that individuals can flourish sexually and socially. He concludes the book poetically and swooningly: "We ought to dance with rapture that we should be alive and in the flesh, and part of the living, incarnate cosmos" (*A*, 149). His sprawling vision

---

[53] See, for example, Stephen H. Webb, "Eschatology and Politics," in *The Oxford Handbook of Eschatology*, ed. Jerry L. Walls (Oxford: Oxford University Press, 2008), 500–17.

links humanity, earth, and cosmos in a spirituality that he calls organic rather than collective:

> My soul knows that I am part of the human race, my soul is an organic part of the great human soul, as my spirit is part of my nation. In my own very self, I am part of my family. There is nothing of me that is alone and absolute except my mind, and we shall find that the mind has no existence by itself, it is only the glitter of the sun on the surface of the waters. So that my individualism is really an illusion. I am part of the great whole, and I can never escape.
>
> (A, 149)

His charge to readers is a choice between the modern, technocratic, and economic forces bound into collectivity by the state versus a cosmic realignment that can change our lived relations here and now:

> I *can* deny my connections, break them, and become a fragment. Then I am wretched. What we want is to destroy our false, inorganic connections, especially those related to money, and re-establish the living organic connections, with the cosmos, the sun and earth, with mankind and nation and family. Start with the sun, and the rest will slowly, slowly happen.
>
> (A, 149)

It is a sweeping and undeniably idealistic political fantasy that David Ellis calls "a final Romantic protest against the more damaging emotional implications of the Enlightenment," but it gestures toward an eschaton emerging in the present and imagines a complete retuning of the cosmos into harmony.[54] Not a practical agenda but an aspirational and theological reimagining to counter the destructive political energies that were ascendant in Europe as he completed his final book. It is this political eschatology that we can also see him working out fictionally in his last novel.

English Regeneration versus the Spurious Religions: *Lady Chatterley* on Nation, Earth, and Cosmos

In "A Propos of 'Lady Chatterley's Lover,'" the essay Lawrence wrote in 1929 to coincide with a new authorized edition of the novel, he gives clues to the relationship between his thinking about eschatology and his revolutionary novel

---

[54] David Ellis, *D. H. Lawrence: Dying Game 1922–1930* (Cambridge: Cambridge University Press, 1998), 526.

of sexuality. "A Propos" begins as an explanation of Lawrence's effort to counter the pirated editions of the novel, turns to a philosophy of Lawrentian sexuality versus modern sexuality, and culminates in a Nietzsche-inspired discussion of renewing England by reclaiming ancient life rhythms that align humanity with the cosmos. Throughout his defense of the novel, he offers a theopolitical treatise that begins with an assertion that "love in all its manifestations" has diminished in modernity.[55] He elaborates that this means "genuine desire" and "tender love, love of one's fellow-men, and love of God: we mean love, joy, delight, hope, true indignant anger, passionate sense of justice and injustice, truth and untruth, honour and dishonour, and real belief in *anything*" ("A Propos," 312). Instead of these passions, modernity gives us "the loud and sentimental counterfeit of all such emotion" ("A Propos," 312). By linking belief, God, social justice, and a range of deeply felt emotions, Lawrence embraces political theology as a centerpiece of his critique of modern ennui and insists that the supposedly obscene elements of his novel are part of his agenda for reinvigorating pagan energies obscured and diminished by modern politics and religion.

As with much of Lawrence's philosophizing, the influence of Nietzsche can be felt in this endorsement of ecstatic paganism that is simultaneously individual and collective. Lawrence criticizes the function of the state in its ancient Roman and modern Soviet forms, instances where "the State controls every individual [...] as the great religious States such as early Egypt may have controlled ever individual [...] through priestly surveillance and ritual" ("A Propos," 321). Within such state interference, "Christianity established the little autonomy of the family," and Lawrence sees the marital relationship as an important way to resist the state's control as well as the modern drive toward isolation and individualism ("A Propos," 321). At its best, then, the church could sustain "the rhythm of life itself" which is otherwise under threat of being "cut off from the magic connection of the solstice and the equinox" ("A Propos," 322, 323). The modern church, especially in its protestant forms, has abandoned these rhythms and the connectivity they create, and Lawrence demands that we reclaim that connection through communal ritual: "It is a question, practically, of relationship. We *must* get back into relation, vivid and nourishing relation to the cosmos and the universe. [...] the ritual of the seasons, with the Drama and the Passion of the soul embodied in procession and dance, this is for the community, an act of men and women, a whole community, in togetherness"

---

[55] D. H. Lawrence, "A Propos of 'Lady Chatterley's Lover,'" in *Lady Chatterley's Lover*, ed. Michael Squires (London: Penguin, 1994), 312. Hereafter cited in text "A Propos."

("A Propos," 329). Nietzsche's famous analysis in *The Birth of Tragedy* of the "two interwoven artistic drives, *the Apolline and the Dionysiac*" undergird Lawrence's discussion of sacred rhythms achieved communally through art.[56] In "those two artistic deities of the Greeks, Apollo and Dionysos" Nietzsche found "visible representatives of two art-worlds which differ in their deepest essence and highest goals" where "Apollo stands before me as the transfiguring genius of the *principium individuationis*" contrasted with "the mystical, jubilant shout of Dionysos."[57] The individual tragic hero presents the Apolline impulse while the choric song and communal ritual of the tragedy is Dionysiac, and the two strains productively coordinate in Hellenic art. Lawrence's fiction strives for this same convergence where the individual characters of the novel are developed within a quest for communal rhythms. *Lady Chatterley's Lover* imaginatively explores Lawrence's answers to these Nietzschean questions: "The universe is dead for us, and how is it to come to life again? [...] How, out of all this, are we to get back to the grand orbs of the soul's heavens, that fill us with unspeakable joy? How are we to get back Apollo, and Attis, Demeter, Persephone, and the halls of Dis?" ("A Propos," 331).

A core problem in modernity, Lawrence argues, is the disconnection that humans have from each other and from the natural rhythms of the universe—a claim he later develops in the conclusion to *Apocalypse*. One of the places that this disconnection appears is in popular art, such as the Great War novels of the 1920s. As Lawrence describes it, humans have learned a basic mistrust of each other, and "to feel the bodily presence of any other man a menace, a menace, as it were, to their very being" ("A Propos," 332). Suspicion is "the ugly fact that underlies our civilization," and it manifests in accounts of war: "As the advertisement of one of the war-novels said, it is an epic of 'friendship and hope, mud and blood.' Which means, of course, that the friendship and hope must end in mud and blood" ("A Propos," 332). The war is not necessarily the cause of this disconnection, but it is a signal event and harbinger of the end-times sensibility and fear of Armageddon that reverberate through our modern, disconnected age. His criticism of the 1920s "war books" that poured out a decade after the armistice—or, at least, his criticism of their marketing engines—is that close kinship is inextricable from violence and despair. Scholars have frequently observed that *Women in Love* (written in 1916, published in 1920) is a war novel

---

[56] Friedrich Nietzsche, *The Birth of Tragedy and Other Writings*, ed. Raymond Geuss and Ronald Speirs, trans. Ronald Speirs (Cambridge: Cambridge University Press, 1999), 59.
[57] Nietzsche, *Birth of Tragedy*, 76.

without combat scenes, but *Lady Chatterley's Lover* is also a novel fixated on the Great War, its aftermath and its portents.[58] If war books such as Siegfried Sassoon's *Memoirs of a Fox-Hunting Man* (1928), Max Plowman's *A Subaltern on the Somme* (1928), and Robert Graves's *Good-bye To All That* (1929) end with hope and friendship ruined by mud and blood, then Lawrence responds in *Lady Chatterley* by starting with tragedy and a calling for life out of this momentous global death.[59] As Scott R. Sanders has argued, the novel responds to the war through its complex relationship with the "annihilation impulse" around which it fixates and seeks to resist.[60] Because "the war had brought the roof down over [Connie Chatterley's] head," she has embraced a philosophy that seeks the resurrected phoenix within the ashes of battle: "The cataclysm has happened, we are among the ruins, we start to build up new little habitats, to have new little hopes."[61] Connie's home is a microcosm of the war: industrialism and military violence have conspired to destroy her sexual fulfillment, her relationships with others, her connection to the earth, and her hope for a better future. But even in this despair she seeks small ways to thrive, and Lawrence's effort to show the cosmic power of local and interpersonal connectivity is the novel's imaginative challenge. It is structured in a pattern, as Charles Burack has argued, in "destructive" and "revitalization" phases that invite readers into "a sacred transformative process."[62] In eschatological terms, it begins with apocalypse as ending and destruction but moves toward revelation and the possibility of a better future.

Sexuality is integral to Lawrence's concerns about cosmic disconnection and the cataclysmic drive toward war, and national regeneration is crucial to his political philosophy.[63] He bemoans the paltry state of sexuality in modern

---

[58] On Lawrence's modernist experimentation with represented violence in *Women in Love*, see Joyce Wexler, *Violence without God*, 73–92.

[59] On *Lady Chatterley* and recovery from trauma, see Carl Krockel, *War Trauma and English Modernism: T. S. Eliot and D. H. Lawrence* (New York: Palgrave Macmillan, 2011), 150–5.

[60] Scott R. Sanders, "Lady Chatterley's Loving and the Annihilation Impulse," in *D. H. Lawrence's "Lady": A New Look at Lady Chatterley's Lover*, ed. Michael Squires and Dennis Jackson (Athens, GA: University of Georgia Press, 1985), 1.

[61] D. H. Lawrence, *Lady Chatterley's Lover*, 1928 (London: Penguin, 1994), 5. Hereafter cited in text *LCL*.

[62] Burack, *Lawrence's Language of Sacred Experience*, 9.

[63] Though Lawrence does not seem aware of the connotation, the etymology of "apocalypse" has sexual meaning, which Catherine Keller describes: "the Greek term used in the New Testament, *apokalypsis*, does not signify 'the end of the world' […] it means not to close but to *dis/close*. To *open* what is otherwise shut. Originally the word signified the sexually charged moment of an ancient bride's unveiling." Catherine Keller, *Facing Apocalypse: Climate, Democracy, and Other Last Chances* (Maryknoll, NY: Orbis, 2021), xvi.

culture, denouncing its twin poles of Puritanism among the older generations and "smart licentiousness" among the "jazzy" people "of the young world," both of which are "perversions" ("A Propos," 310). In this waste land of failed sex which lacks any harmony of mind and body, people are left with a sexuality that is "just the trimmings" ("A Propos," 315). But the problem, according to Lawrence, is not merely about physical and emotional matters or about individual or marital health. The stakes are much larger and the sexual problems he diagnoses are symptomatic of national illness. A cheap and thin sex life is troubling not only for individuals and couples but because it offers no prospects of greater restoration: "the regeneration of England with that?," Lawrence exclaims, "Good God! Poor England, she will have to regenerate the sex in her young people, before they do any regenerating of her. It isn't England that needs regenerating, it is her young" ("A Propos," 315). His belief that modern sexual lives are disordered has direct bearing on his concern about England, a nation that is susceptible to the allures of the martyr-rulers who can charm a dissatisfied populace. Representing a complicated but healthier sexuality in his novel is also an imagining of national regeneration, or at least its beginning.

The regeneration of England is central to his concerns about faulty modern sexuality, even if those broader ramifications can sometimes be obscured by his philosophizing about sex or lost as asides in the welter of his prose and denouncements of various "perversions." Lawrence's theories of national renewal, it should be noted, are inextricable from several of his worst ideological biases and prejudices. In chastising modern English culture, Lawrence frequently resorts to primitivist and racist rhetoric, inveighing against a declining civilization and accusing England of becoming "barbaric and savage" ("A Propos," 315).[64] His specific notions of robust, rightly ordered sexuality also have little space beyond the heteronormative and phallocentric, and while *Lady Chatterley's Lover* does not likely elicit today the horrors of obscenity it provoked on its initial publication, its views on sex may be objectionable for other reasons pertaining to the narrowness of its normativity. His call for more integrated lives that unify our bodies, communities, and the earth, however, remains prescient and valuable.

---

[64] On Lawrence's use of primitivism in *Lady Chatterley's Lover*, see Marianna Torgovnick, *Gone Primitive: Savage Intellects, Modern Lives* (Chicago: University of Chicago Press, 1990), 170–2; Marianna Torgovnick, *Primitive Passions: Men, Women, and the Quest for Ecstasy* (Chicago: University of Chicago Press, 1998), 52–5; Eva Yi Chen, "Primitivism, Empire, and a Personal Ideology: D. H. Lawrence's Travel Writings on the Indians of the American Southwest," *Journal of D. H. Lawrence Studies* (2000): 52–88; Judith Ruderman, *Race and Identity in D. H. Lawrence: Indians, Gypsies, and Jews* (New York: Palgrave Macmillan, 2014).

His particular emphasis on ancient, pagan ritual that can restore us to "the rhythm of the cosmos" versus the modern, industrial and Protestant Christian rituals shows concern with the cultural liturgies that we considered with Virginia Woolf's fiction in the previous chapter ("A Propos," 328). While Woolf was more explicit about the power of such liturgies for assimilating young men into war and imperialism, Lawrence expands to a broader, all-encompassing sense of human relationships with each other, the earth, and the universe. "Protestantism," Lawrence writes, "came and gave a great blow to the religious and ritualistic rhythm of the year, in human life. Nonconformity *almost* finished the deed. Now you have a poor, blind, disconnected people with nothing but politics and bank-holidays to satisfy the eternal human need of living in ritual adjustment to the cosmos in its revolutions" ("A Propos," 328). Restoring rhythms of life and relationship as a way to restore England and realign with the cosmos is not a side project developed through his nonfiction: he explicitly states that these meditations are "prolegomena" to *Lady Chatterley's Lover* ("A Propos," 328). The novel portrays the burgeoning of the "new little hopes" that it promises in its first paragraph and concludes with a tentative image of hopefulness as well. The specifics of this narrative cycle are not above reproach; the concluding image of hope is a phallocentric, heteronormative, and faintly ridiculous quotation from Connie's lover Mellors who is writing her a letter where he proclaims that "the flowers are fucked into being, between the sun and earth" and his anthropomorphized penis bids her goodnight "a little droopingly, but with a hopeful heart—" (*LCL*, 302). As a political emblem, this droopy phallus might not attract many followers. Lawrence's aspirations, however, are more promising than this specific image. What he gestures toward in the novel's conclusion is the possibility that new relational rhythms can promote community, synchronicity with the earth, and regeneration of what the state has damaged through war and modern technocracy.

It is important that he finishes the narrative without supplying a utopian vision of wholeness but rather sustains the small, minor, and tentative hope with which the novel begins. Moltmann argues that hope is essential to living eschatologically in the present because "hope's statements of promise" show that "the hidden future already announces itself and exerts its influence on the present through the hope it awakens."[65] Lawrence's fiction conveys this version of eschatological hope imaginatively: the novel's final sentence stops with an

---

[65] Jürgen Moltmann, *Theology of Hope: On the Ground and the Implications of a Christian Eschatology* (New York: Harper & Row, 1967), 17–18.

em dash rather than more conclusive punctuation. It models an inconclusive and unfinished promise, not only for the romance between Connie and Mellors but also for the grandiose promise of cosmic renewal that Lawrence projected in "A Propos" and *Apocalypse*. Much like the speculative conclusion to his manifesto in *Apocalypse* that yearns for renewal and connection throughout the universe, the renewed cosmic rhythms have only just begun with this couple. What this new connection will yield remains an open possibility—a future potential that his narrative arc and sentence structure enacts at the formal level to invite readers into this political imagination. Instead of resolution we have the brink of a dash that asks us to carry on the restorative work of developing cosmic harmony through rhythms of relationship and intimacy. Deeper bonds than those produced by the modern state and more elemental rituals than the bank-holidays of civil religion: this is the eschatological prophecy of *Lady Chatterley's Lover*.

Throughout the novel Lawrence depicts competing theopolitical currents—the pagan, natural rhythms of the lovers versus the drive toward an industrialist and militaristic modernity at odds with the earth and embodied by Clifford Chatterley. While Clifford might seem a predictable figure of detachment from the natural world through his economic privilege, bourgeois industrialism, and enmeshment in the military machine, his primary heresy appears rather as a form of gnosticism where he seeks a scientific and abstract religious philosophy removed from earthiness and embodiment. After the famous scene of Connie and Mellors's lovemaking in the rainstorm, Connie returns home to find Clifford in an activity juxtaposed with her fleshly sensuality—reading Alfred North Whitehead's "scientific-religious" philosophy (*LCL*, 233). Whitehead's Lowell Lectures, published in 1926 as *Religion in the Making*, are Clifford's companion for the evening, and in an effort to connect with his wife Clifford reads passages from the book aloud, over Connie's objections, enthusiastically praising "the great man's solemn words" (*LCL*, 234). Whitehead conceives of the universe in "two aspects": "on one side it is physically wasting, on the other side it is spiritually ascending [...] There remain the inexhaustible realm of abstract forms, and creativity, with its shifting character ever determined afresh by its own creatures, and God, upon whose wisdom all forms of order depend."[66] This account of the universe, which Clifford affirms, depicts our physical, bodily, and earthly selves wasting away so that the spirit may ascend to meet God in a higher form of

---

[66] Alfred North Whitehead, *Religion in the Making: Lowell Lectures, 1926* (New York: Macmillan, 1957), 160.

creativity—in short, it is the polar opposite of Lawrence's political eschatology. Instead of connecting with Connie, Clifford finds himself in conflict with her, arguing over the value of embodiment in their ideal future. There is, of course, some indulgence in reductive stereotyping, presenting women as essentially physical and Clifford's disability as a curse, but there is also in their exchange about Whitehead a clear sense that Connie intellectually, philosophically, and theologically objects to what she hears and that Clifford's attraction to an abstract spiritual ascension springs from his despair over the condition of his body and the mechanics of the world that brought him to this place.[67] Calling Whitehead's book "scientific-religious" is not a compliment, and the narrator tells us that Clifford "had a streak of a spurious sort of religion about him" (*LCL*, 233). The chilly, modern rationalism Lawrence detects in Whitehead's approach as well as its affirmation of a purely spiritual future seems to him philosophically and theologically bankrupt, and his novel provides a rejoinder to such philosophy through literary narrative.

Clifford's position in the novel, however, is not purely as a villain or mere symbol of modern decay. He is in many ways a symptom of the problems of modernity rather than their cause, and he is captured by a spurious religion more widespread than Whitehead's aesthetic philosophy: the combined forces of militarism and industrialism blessed by Christianity. For much of the novel, it is Clifford who stands in as the voice of conservatism, propriety, and industrial wealth, but our introduction to him reveals a more ambiguous relationship to the civil religion of his nation. As the war begins, Clifford finds all traditional sources of authority to be foolish, a stance that the narrator suggests is not truly rebellious—"perhaps rebel is too strong a word; far too strong"—but is also not blindly submissive (*LCL*, 10). Not a rebellion, but "only caught in the general, popular recoil of the young against convention and against any real sort of authority. Fathers were ridiculous [...] and armies were ridiculous [...] even the war was really ridiculous, though it did kill rather a lot of people" (*LCL*, 10). Clifford's flippant dismissal of patriarchal and military powers seems juvenile, but it culminates in a rejection that the novel does not entirely brush away.

Clifford's father, Sir Geoffrey Chatterley, is the ultimate figurehead for the kinds of authorities young Clifford recoils against, and Geoffrey's ideology becomes supremely impactful on his younger son. In the gung-ho spirit of

---

[67] Lawrence was aware of the problem of Clifford and Connie's "symbolic" functions, though in "A Propos" he explains that in the first draft of the novel this symbolism was unintentional and he decided to keep their emblematic qualities because the story seemed to demand their inevitability ("A Propos," 333).

his class and age, Geoffrey's eldest son Herbert goes to the war and is killed in 1916, leaving Clifford the unlikely heir to their ancestral home of Wragby and newly responsible for the family name. This new scenario strikes Clifford as absurd, worse than the ridiculousness that he originally felt about the war and military and all the authorities that support it. The crowning absurdity, however, is embodied by Sir Geoffrey whose bereavement leads to a doubling down of his faith in the English nation. He begins to affirm the orations of Horatio Bottomley, the *John Bull* founder who fanned the flames of anti-German sentiment. Bottomley's famous presentation "Prince of Peace" affirmed the British Empire's war effort as a holy war "along the road of human destiny" en route "to the patient figure of the Prince of Peace, pointing to the Star of Bethlehem that leads us on to God."[68] The passing reference to Bottomley as a touchstone for Sir Geoffrey's beliefs signals not only his jingoism and support for the empire but also his acceptance of English civil religion fueled by Christian mythology. His embrace of civil religion is definite: "He stood for England and Lloyd George, as his forbears had stood for England and St. George: and he never knew there was a difference. So Sir Geoffrey felled timber and stood for Lloyd George and England, England and Lloyd George" (*LCL*, 11). With a repetitious pattern that makes "England and Lloyd George" into a pulse, breath, or mantra, Lawrence renders Sir Geoffrey's grief at the loss of his son to the war machine as a litany. Rather than senseless death creating antipathy for war, it becomes meaningful as sacrifice for the nation. Nationalism thus functions, as Benedict Anderson has argued, as "a secular transformation of fatality into continuity, contingency into meaning."[69] Lawrence, who rarely missed an opportunity for attacking David Lloyd George, pointedly regards the prime minister as an ersatz leader who is a modern simulacrum for a phony saint. The ancient Christian myth of Saint George which is fundamental to English nationalism has been replaced by the mystifications of a Welsh prime minister. Sir Geoffrey's national sacrifices are exposed here as shoddy and slight, a limp substitution that leaves him "divorced from the England that was really England" (*LCL*, 11). It is uncertain exactly what this "real" England may be, but there are two clear targets of Lawrence's critique: the devolution of robust belief into manipulative, spurious civil religion and the disconnection felt among England's leadership class.

---

[68] Qtd. in Gary S. Messinger, *British Propaganda and the State in the First World War* (Manchester: Manchester University Press, 1992), 208.
[69] Anderson, *Imagined Communities*, 11.

The passing figure of Sir Geoffrey is an image of England's gentry in decline—disconnected from what matters in the world and instead immersed in civil religious ideology—but Lawrence also creates a broader sense of national decline through an apocalyptic aesthetic. Connie registers the horror in the town of Tevershall and how it is ushered in by the Chatterleys and sustained by class antagonisms Lawrence described in *Apocalypse* as the "thwarted collective self" (*A*, 73). Among "blackened miners' cottages" and "rolling country where the castles and big houses still dominated, but like ghosts," Connie sees how the landscape and the order of society have utterly changed as though industry has indeed been an Armageddon (*LCL*, 155). "One England blots out another," the narrator observes in an apocalyptic view of history: "the mines had made the halls wealthy. Now they were blotting them out, as they had already blotted out the cottages. The industrial England blots out the agricultural England. One meaning blots out another. The New England blots out the old England" (*LCL*, 156). The repetition of the word "blot" in various tenses reinforces the sense of removal, obscuring, and stain where historical development is not progress but reduction and erasure. Lawrence's desire for a regenerated cosmos is recognizable in his image of modern England where "the continuity is not organic, but mechanical" (*LCL*, 156). Mechanization is the ruling form in modern England, as witnessed in the industrialized midlands and practiced throughout the nation's families and other relationships. Tevershall and the other small towns near Wragby have experienced the blackening of coal dust and the blotting of foundries, and the lives of villagers are defined by their gloominess "as if dismalness had soaked through and through everything" and led to "the utter negation of natural beauty," "the utter absence of the instinct for shapely beauty which every bird or beast has," and "the utter death of the human intuitive faculty" (*LCL*, 152).[70] The piling up of clauses in Lawrence's sentences adds to the feeling of mechanism and the inescapable dread of these towns where even the chapel buildings succumb to oppression and the new school of "pink brick, and gravelled play-ground inside iron railings" appears "very imposing" and "mix[es] the suggestion of a chapel and a prison" (*LCL*, 152). All facets of social life and the institutions that create it, from church to work

---

[70] On the contrasting power dynamics between Wragby and Tevershall, see Hiro Tateishi, "The Hall of Inversion in *Lady Chatterley's Lover*," in *D. H. Lawrence: Literature, History, Culture*, ed. Michael Bell, Keith Cushman, Takeo Lida, and Hiro Tateishi (Tokyo: Kokusho-KankoKai Press, 2005), 454–67.

to school, are disconnected from nature and beauty and the cosmic rhythms of life Lawrence ardently prophesies. People formed by this mechanized society have become "half-corpses," Connie realizes, "with a terrible insistent consciousness in the other half" (*LCL*, 153). Importantly, it is Connie who most fully recognizes this zombification of England and thinks: "Ah God, what has man done to man? What have the leaders of men been doing to their fellow men? They have reduced them to less than humanness, and now there can be no fellowship any more! It is just a nightmare" (*LCL*, 153). Nightmarish, horrific, and apocalyptic—these are Connie's sensations at the sight and thought of modern England, and she is particularly sorrowed that even Mellors, despite his rural, working-class identity, cannot bridge the divide between the oppressive leadership class and the class of half-dead strivers. Where in *Apocalypse* Lawrence described these conditions with a critical eye toward the masses and the false promises of Revelation, *Lady Chatterley's Lover* seems more compassionate and yearning, filtered as it is through Connie's despair at England's "apartness, and hopelessness" (*LCL*, 153). England is in crisis, and all of the state apparatuses are widening the chasm rather than repairing the brokenness, deepening despair rather than fostering hope.

The intensity of Connie and Mellors's togetherness is a vital but admittedly minor and tentative effort toward counteracting the powerful forces of separation wrought by militarism, industry, and modern asceticism that distorts our relationships with each other and with the earth. For most of the novel we are closer to Connie's mind than any other character's until the final pages, which transcribe a letter from Mellors to Connie that acts as a manifesto much like the conclusion to *Apocalypse*. Concluding this way gives Mellors's voice an authority that somewhat diminishes Connie's centrality, but the vision it casts is provisional and speculative rather than conclusively asserting phallic dominance and a utopian restoration of England. He explains his situation as a laborer on the Grange Farm, working closely with animals and the land and staying in a house run by a family who "lost their only son in the war, and it's sort of knocked a hole in them" (*LCL*, 298). The aftereffects of war remain distinctly present as Mellors establishes his life by working the land while awaiting Connie's return. He tells her of the general dissatisfaction among colliers in the nearby pits and how the obvious inequity and unsustainable economic conditions cannot be fixed, even with more radical "Soviet" methods of nationalization (*LCL*, 299). Mellors, in language close to Lawrence's own voice, decries the consumption patterns of modernity and how this limited way of being has precluded far more important and healthier forms of living. The false religion that holds the masses enthralled, Mellors proclaims, is "not the devil" but rather "Mammon; which I think, after all, is only the mass-will of people, wanting money and hating life" (*LCL*, 300). Writing a century later, Eugene McCarraher argues that capitalism has mutated into the dominate religion of our age with parodic or perverse versions of sacramental theology that includes an "eschatological destiny" in "the global imperium of capital" with "incessantly expanding production, trade, and consumption."[71] Capitalism's hallmark, borrowing a phrase from Thomas Carlyle, is a "gospel of 'Mammonism,' the attribution of ontological power to money and of existential sublimity to its possessors."[72]

While McCarraher describes capitalist eschatology as a utopian myth of expansion, Lawrence in the voice of Mellors foresees calamity arising from this chasing after Mammon. This calamitous prognosis sounds much like the ravages of Armageddon that Lawrence despised in Revelation but nevertheless persist in Mellors's repeated phrase "there's a bad time coming!" as well as his declaration that if the world stays this course then "nothing lies in the future but death and destruction, for these industrial masses" (*LCL*, 300). Against this doom-laden path of Mammonism, Mellors posits the alternative life ignited with Connie—partly because of their child within her but even more significantly because of the ritual practices of their relationship that promise a new Pentecost as a "forked flame" between them (*LCL*, 301). More than just a human romance and far removed from portents of fiery apocalypse, their relationship signifies a return to Christian mythology through the fire of Pentecost, emptied of its specifically Christian content and reenacted as a mystical humanist philosophy that projects into the future but activates their lives in the present. "The old Pentecost isn't quite right," Mellors observes, undermining Christian orthodoxy as well as the personal, individualism of low church piety: "Me and God is a bit uppish, somehow" (*LCL*, 301). But the new "pentecost flame" Mellors repeatedly affirms as the force between Connie and himself is an eschatological witness to cosmic renewal. This new-fashioned Pentecost is not just an inflated rebranding of romantic love; it is Lawrence's final fictional representation of the integrated cosmos that unites all things in a regenerated creation that restores personal, national, and global relations and where the fullness of time is perceptible in the present.

---

[71] Eugene McCarraher, *The Enchantments of Mammon: How Capitalism Became the Religion of Modernity* (Cambridge, MA: Harvard University Press, 2019), 5.
[72] Ibid.

"A Grain of Hope" in the End-Times

In an essay written in February 1929, shortly after copies of *Lady Chatterley's Lover* and typescripts of his poetry collection *Pansies* had been seized by Scotland Yard, Lawrence asked "what is the matter with the English, that they are so scared of everything?" (*LEA*, 219). "They are in a state of blue funk," he explained, "and they behave like a lot of mice when somebody stamps on the floor" (*LEA*, 219). Though this essay, "The State of Funk," is largely concerned with explaining (yet again) why the portrait of sexuality in *Lady Chatterley* is wholesome and healthy rather than obscene and depraved, Lawrence contextualizes the response to his books by acknowledging that England is undergoing great changes that are understandably frightening: "They are terrified about money, finance, about ships, about war, about work, about Labour, about Bolshevism, and funniest of all, they are scared stiff of the printed word" (*LEA*, 219). Unlike the condemnatory attitude toward the masses that frequently crops up in *Apocalypse*, his essay admits that "there is, of course, a certain excuse for fear" because "we are in the throes of change, and the change will be a great one" (*LEA*, 219). "The old world of our grandfathers is disappearing like thawing snow," he writes, "and is as likely to cause a flood" (*LEA*, 220). The world is at high risk during this anxious time for turning to "bullying and repression" which brings "nothing but disastrous results" for "when the mass falls into a state of funk, and you have mass-bullying, then catastrophe is near" (*LEA*, 220). Against this danger Lawrence urges people to be courageous and compassionate with each other: "Patience, alertness, intelligence, and a human goodwill and fearlessness, that is what you want in a time of change. Not funk" (*LEA*, 220).

Though the specific conditions that Lawrence discussed a century ago have changed, his diagnosis of fear turning to bullying on a mass scale and the need for courage and patient goodwill remain urgent and timely. His image of snowmelt bringing floods was meant only metaphorically, but its unfortunate literalness grows daily in our age of undiminished climate crisis. His diagnosis of fearful societies becoming bullies would become a sickening reality shortly after Lawrence wrote those words and recur in today's nativisms, nationalisms, and border controls that brand immigrants and refugees as enemies. In "The State of Funk" he uses a metaphor of pregnancy where new life is inextricable from the "time of pain and danger ahead" but "somewhere I feel hopeful, even happy. So I must take the sour with the sweet. There is no birth without birth-pangs" (*LEA*, 219). Connie's pregnancy at the conclusion of *Lady Chatterley's*

Lover shares this sensibility, where fear, uncertainty, risk, and hope converge. Neither the novel nor the essay articulates a specific program for social change—Lawrence even admits that "as a novelist, I feel it is the change inside the individual which is my real concern. The great social change interests me and troubles me, but it is not my field" (*LEA*, 221). He says, "I know a change is coming—but I know we must have a more generous, more human system, based on the life values and not on the money values [...] But what steps to take I don't know" (*LEA*, 221). Instead, he writes fiction that explores and articulates human feelings as "a form of vital energy," giving expression to unarticulated emotions as an effort toward facing the apocalyptic changes around us (*LEA*, 221). It is in this way that Lawrence's fiction expands our theopolitical imagination, where tentative, unfinished, and partial regeneration makes future longing into present hope.

Many eschatologies, whether confessional-mythological or secular-political, focus on the importance of hope for sustaining life while facing imminent ending.[73] Such a view of hope should not be mistaken for blind optimism or wishful thinking.[74] Catherine Keller has argued that in our current moment of climate crisis and "Anthropocene Apocalypse" we must face these realities in ways that "would not mean mere recognition, submission, acquiescence" but "to confront the forces of destruction: to crack open, to disclose, a space where late chances, last chances, remain nonetheless real chances."[75] This political attitude that combines sober realism with faithful action is, to return to Lawrence's terms, a way to sustain vital energy rather than funk. As Helen Wussow describes it, "Lawrence divined the apocalyptic resurrection of the world" and imbued his prophetic works with "paschal jubilation" that rivals the predicted devastation.[76] This duality is also crucial, of course, to his favorite image of the phoenix rising reborn from its ashes, an image like his childbirth metaphor where the pain of great change also holds the potential for great newness. Writing to Hugh Meredith in 1915 at a time when despair should seemingly dominate his consciousness, Lawrence

---

[73] See, for example, Jürgen Moltmann, *The Spirit of Hope: Theology for a World in Peril* (Louisville, KY: WJK Press, 2019); Laura Duhan-Kaplan, Anne-Marie Ellithorpe, and Harry O. Maier, eds., *Visions of the End Times: Revelations of Hope and Challenge* (Eugene, OR: Wipf and Stock, 2022).

[74] Slavoj Žižek criticizes "happy, liberal-progressive" approaches to "our despair at the present deadlock" and argues that "we have to renounce the very eschatological scheme which underlies our despair" by refusing the false hope of a supposed happy ending. Žižek, *Trouble in Paradise: From the End of History to the End of Capitalism* (Brooklyn, NY: Melville House, 2014), 146. For discussion of Zizek's eschatology, see Ola Sigurdson, "A Hermeneutic of Hope: Problematising Zizek's Apocalypticism," *International Journal of Žižek Studies* 10, no. 2 (2016): 83–103.

[75] Keller, *Facing Apocalypse*, viii, xiii.

[76] Helen Wussow, *The Nightmare of History: The Fictions of Virginia Woolf and D.H. Lawrence* (London: Associated University Press, 1998), 152, 46.

spoke prophetically about global resurrection: "I believe an end is coming: the war, a plague, a fire, God knows what. But the end is taking place: the beginning of the end has set in, and the process won't be slow. I am very much frightened, but hopeful—a grain of hope yet."[77] Lawrence's apocalyptic aesthetic is not focused on violent destruction, political revolution, or promises of later goods. It is an apocalypse meant to revitalize our ways of living now—personally, relationally, and locally. The future promises, such as they exist, abide in the trust that reclaiming synchronous ways of being together as humans and in harmony with the earth might counteract the many forces that militate against such ways of life. Rampant industry, avaricious economy, imperial conquest, militaristic domination—all sanctified by religious power, martyr-rulers, and a sacralized state—have created and sustained a modern age that crushes our individual and communal flourishing and ravages our environment. Lawrence's specific remedy of sex al fresco may not be as universally liberating as *Lady Chatterley's Lover* sometimes seems to suggest, but the more general notion that embodied rituals in concert with nature may act as resistance to powerful ideologies is worthy of our attention and practice.

---

[77] D. H. Lawrence, *The Letters of D. H. Lawrence, Volume II: June 1913–October 1916*, eds. George J. Zytaruk and James T. Boulton (Cambridge: Cambridge University Press, 1981), 426.

3

Evelyn Waugh's Cynical Political Theology: *Decline and Fall* and *Vile Bodies*

In Virginia Woolf's fiction we see the inescapability of Christianity as a social force and the complex ways its institutions and cultural patterns form and construct individuals. Woolf's ambivalence about our capacity to transcend the allures of civil religion suggests resources for living "unredeemed," over and against the theologies of the state which promise a false salvation through sacrificial death. D. H. Lawrence's fiction and theology offered tentative hope through an eschatology that could reform how we live in the present time—relationally, nationally, and cosmically. From Woolf's ambivalent agnosticism and Lawrence's apostasy, we turn now to Evelyn Waugh, a writer whose faith and patriotism might seem wholly different from these other figures. Rather than having a conflicted and antagonistic relationship with Christianity and nationalism, Waugh is widely known for being "the most English of Englishmen" and for looming large in the pantheon of twentieth-century Catholic writers.[1] A great deal of his writing career was dedicated to a strain of traditionalist Catholicism that he perceived as an antidote for the evils of modernity and as a restorative force for England, and he would persistently write fiction and essays

---

[1] Martin Stannard, *Evelyn Waugh: The Early Years, 1903–1939* (New York: Norton, 1986), 140. Among critics who emphasize Waugh's distinctive "Englishness," see Christine Berberich, *The Image of the English Gentleman in Twentieth-Century Literature: Englishness and Nostalgia* (Hampshire: Ashgate, 2007), 95–134, and Leonie Wanitzek, "Englishness, Summer and the Pastoral of Country Leisure in Twentieth-Century Literature," in *Idleness, Indolence, and Leisure in English Literature*, ed. Monika Fludernik and Miriam Nandi (Houndmills, Basingstoke, Hampshire: Palgrave Macmillan, 2014), 252–72. Studies of Waugh as a "Catholic writer" include Ian Ker, *The Catholic Revival in English Literature, 1845–1961: Newman, Hopkins, Belloc, Chesterton, Greene, Waugh* (South Bend, IN: University of Notre Dame Press, 2003); Joseph Pearce, *Literary Giants, Literary Catholics* (San Francisco: Ignatius Press, 2005); Timothy J. Sutton, *Catholic Modernists, English Nationalists* (Newark, DE: University of Delaware Press, 2010); Martin Potter, *British and Catholic? National and Religious Identity in the Work of David Jones, Evelyn Waugh and Muriel Spark* (Oxford: Peter Lang, 2013); Martin Lockerd, *Decadent Catholicism and the Making of Modernism* (London: Bloomsbury Academic, 2020).

that advocated a political theology shaped by conservative social, economic, and religious values.[2] There is certainly much to investigate in Waugh's theopolitical imagination during his years as a mature writer, but my focus on his work prior to 1930 allows a different perspective on his contributions to literature as political theology. Before his official conversion, there is a messier, wider ranging, and agonized engagement with both church and state—a struggle that puts him in the company of the other novelists in this study.

Throughout much of his life before September 29, 1930, when he was formally received into the Roman Catholic Church, Waugh approached Christianity through a mixture of interest and skepticism.[3] His childhood was shaped by a family that had experienced what Martin Stannard describes as "the religious tyranny of a home dominated by the Plymouth Brethren" as well as other strains of low church Protestantism that he would eventually come to despise.[4] Waugh would later reflect on his religious upbringing:

> Like most Englishmen, I was brought up in the Church of England. By the time I was sixteen, I was convinced that if Christianity were true, then the Catholic Church was the true church. At the time, however, I rejected Christianity. When I reached twenty-six [in 1929] I came back to Christianity, and—in accordance with my original beliefs—I became a Catholic. My conversion was one from agnosticism to Christianity, really, rather than from Protestantism.[5]

In early schooling he was swept into Anglican churches he did not relish, and at university he would pass through a phase of "muscular agnosticism," showing deep attraction to a faith he could not yet abide.[6] Late in life, he would protest that while writing *Vile Bodies*, he was "as near an atheist as one could be, I think,

---

[2] On the complexity of Waugh's political and theological conservatism, see D. Marcel DeCoste, "'Tony Madly Feudal': Evelyn Waugh's *A Handful of Dust* and the Conservative Critique of Secular Conservatism," in *Literature and the Conservative Ideal*, ed. Mark Zunac (Lanham, MD: Lexington Books, 2016), 127–52.

[3] John W. Mahon observes that Waugh's diaries indicate—with "a frustrating lack of detail"—that he had been visiting the popular Oxford philosopher Father Martin D'Arcy beginning in July of 1930 and had asked his friend (and earlier object of infatuation) Olivia Plunkett Greene to help him find a Jesuit discussion partner as early as spring of that year (63). Mahon, "'A Later Development': Evelyn Waugh and Conversion," in *"A Handful of Mischief": New Essays on Evelyn Waugh*, ed. Donat Gallagher, Ann Pasternak Slater, and John Howard Wilson (Teaneck, NJ: Fairleigh Dickinson University Press, 2011).

[4] Stannard, *Waugh: The Early Years*, 8, 13.

[5] These comments are from an interview in *The Sign* in 1957, quoted in Jacqueline McDonnell, *Evelyn Waugh* (New York: St. Martin's, 1988), 9.

[6] Stannard, *Waugh: The Early Years*, 79. Selina Hastings also writes of Waugh's "aggressive brand of muscular agnosticism, always ready furiously to debate and if possible shoot down the claims of Christianity" (106). Hastings, *Evelyn Waugh: A Biography* (New York: Boston: Houghton Mifflin, 1994).

at that time," though his biographers have noted the over-simplification in that self-description.[7] His diary in June of 1921 includes Waugh announcing his break: "In the last few weeks I have ceased to be a Christian (sensation off!) I have realized that for the last two terms at least I have been an atheist in all except the courage to admit it to myself"—but he immediately adds: "I am sure it is only a phase."[8] Repulsion from and curiosity about Christian faith recur through Waugh's early life, and both of these forces emphasize his outsider's status from various forms of English Christianity—a hallmark of each of the writers in this book. Instead of a moralist on a mission, Waugh's early critical stance manifests through uncertainty and struggle, and his first efforts at literary fiction demonstrate this uncertain and skeptical condition.

His first two published novels, *Decline and Fall* (1928) and *Vile Bodies* (1930), are a pair of loosely linked absurdist comedies that target with encyclopedic thoroughness a vast range of British social institutions including schools, prisons, sporting events, and clubs, all of which constitute national identity in local forms. This satire also manifests at the formal level: *Decline and Fall* and *Vile Bodies* have episodic, seemingly haphazard plots, and they generate comedy from their absurdity and their overly rapid delivery of tragic and sensational stories. The sprawling criticism of social institutions—especially institutions created and sustained by Christianity—exhibits Waugh's assault on English civil religion. His fiction works in a comic and satirical mode that differs from Woolf and Lawrence while sharing their skepticism about the fusion of patriotism and religious faith. Much of the scholarly commentary on the religious perspectives in these early novels has turned on whether they are evidence of Waugh's immature doubt or signs of proto-Catholic belief.[9] Rather than taking for granted Waugh's eventual conversion, however, I focus on the agonistic conflict of his early, pre-conversion works to explore their thoroughgoing attacks on the myriad social institutions that construct English national identity while consolidating power and crushing

---

[7] Stannard, *Waugh: The Early Years*, 190. Hastings writes that "Evelyn had a religious temperament" and "even when going through his most atheistic period at Oxford had attended church" (*Waugh*, 228).
[8] Evelyn Waugh, *Personal Writings 1903–1921: Precocious Waughs*, ed. Alexander Waugh and Alan Bell (Oxford: Oxford University Press, 2017), 343.
[9] See, for example, John Howard Wilson, "Quantitative Judgments and Individual Salvation in Evelyn Waugh's *Sword of Honour*," *Renascence* 60, no. 4 (Summer 2008): 325–40; Frank Kermode, introduction to *Decline and Fall*, Evelyn Waugh (New York: Knopf, 1993), v–xix; Patrick Allitt, *Catholic Converts: British and American Intellectuals turn to Rome* (Ithaca, NY: Cornell University Press, 1997); David Wykes, *Evelyn Waugh: A Literary Life* (New York: St. Martin's Press, 1999); Patrick R. Query, "Catholicism and Form from Hopkins to Waugh," in *Waugh without End: New Trends in Evelyn Waugh Studies*, ed. Carlos Villar-Flor and Robert Murray Davis (Bern, Switzerland: Peter Lang, 2005), 37–44.

individual freedoms. These are works of protest with a political theology that is highly critical but not yet stable or fully formed. The works we have considered by Woolf and Lawrence were written by older people who were more advanced both in years and in their writing careers, but Waugh provides another point of view from the perspective of headstrong and dissatisfied youth. The early Waugh uses his acerbic humor and satirical force without the specific moral, theological, and political core that would define his later works, and this nascent political theology offers compelling resources for grappling with institutional power. His early fictions model a theopolitical imagination that is tentative, struggling, and uncertain while still being deeply critical of the status quo.

That deeply critical posture has been noted by many of Waugh's readers and earned him a reputation for being "cynical."[10] This cynicism is typically mentioned in passing as an obvious feature of his literary persona, but I contend that a more robust account of his cynical mode can allow us to find in these early works the resources for a radical critique of civil religion. Waugh's cynical political theology surfaces in his early fiction as radical truth-telling and protest against institutional power, even though it lacks his later, more clearly defined positions. They offer resources different from political theologies by writers with particular confessional or theoretical backgrounds. Rather than professing a totalizing moral or religious vision, Waugh satirizes institutional powers that exert discipline and exact penalties without sustaining individual or communal flourishing. Naomi Milthorpe has commented that the "satiric targets" of his early fiction "are those figures of traditional authority (the Church, the law, the aristocracy and the school system) whose abdication from responsibility results in disorder."[11] In addition to abdicating responsibility, I would argue, these institutions fail because they work to perpetuate their own power, stability, and longevity rather than serving to benefit their constituents. Church, government, the press, and schools are all portrayed as thoroughly inept and dying institutions that cling to traditional forms while consuming and destroying individuals. Waugh's cynicism attacks these powers, venting sardonic rage without supplying a clear alternative. After his conversion, Waugh would famously claim that in the present historical moment, the crucial division is not between Catholic and

---

[10] The three most common terms for Waugh's early works are satirical, anarchic, and cynical. Satire has received the most attention. On "anarchism," Malcolm Bradbury writes of Waugh's "unredeemable and anarchistic universe with no secure centres of value" (5). Bradbury, *Evelyn Waugh* (London: Oliver & Boyd, 1964). Cynicism is generally treated only in the colloquial sense where "cynical" means "snide and pessimistic" or "rudely self-centered."

[11] Naomi Milthorpe, *Evelyn Waugh's Satire: Texts and Contexts* (Teaneck, NJ: Fairleigh Dickinson University Press, 2016), 20.

Protestant "but between Christianity and Chaos"—an assertion that pits his newly declared Christian commitments against the absurdity of the modern world.[12] His early creative works, however, dwell in the chaos rather than the order that religious faith supposedly establishes.

Dwelling in chaos rather than dogmatic certainty accords with Waugh's later theorizing of the relationship between political convictions and aesthetic practices. In a review of Arthur Calder-Marshall's *A Date with a Duchess* (1937), he noted his wariness about the book because of its author's avowed Marxism which Waugh presumed would make the fiction into something more ideological and less artistic. Pleasantly surprising, however, was Calder-Marshall's literary craft that Waugh argues has transcended politics and manifested as "anarchist" rather than dogmatically Marxist. According to Waugh, "anarchy is the nearer to right order, for something that has not developed may reach the right end, while something which has fully developed wrongly cannot."[13] And, in a statement that echoes the theopolitical vision of his own early works, Waugh insists, "A robust discontent, whether it be with joint stock banking or the World, Flesh and Devil, is good for a writer."[14] In its inchoate form, Waugh's cynical theology offers this "robust discontent," voicing critique but little resolution in a posture that remains valuable for all of us today living bound by institutional constraints that cannot simply or easily be overthrown. Questioning, challenging, and laughing at these institutions is Waugh's mode, and his youthful energy is a model for political resistance and protest.

"Without Being Cheaply So"

Shaping my view that Waugh enacts a cynical political theology are Michel Foucault's late lectures that sought to reclaim ancient cynicism for the modern age. Louisa Shea has shown that the cynical tradition centered around Diogenes of Sinope had a surprising afterlife, emerging with renewed vigor in eighteenth-century Europe among figures such as Diderot, Rousseau, and Sade and also in the early 1980s with Peter Sloterdijk and Michel Foucault each turning independently to cynicism for intellectual and political support. The youthful

---

[12] Evelyn Waugh, *Essays, Articles, and Reviews 1922-1934: The Complete Works of Evelyn Waugh 26*, ed. Donat Gallagher (Oxford: Oxford University Press, 2018), 367. Hereafter cited *EAR 1922-1934*.
[13] Evelyn Waugh, *The Essays, Articles, and Reviews of Evelyn Waugh*, ed. Donat Gallagher (London: Methuen, 1984), 206.
[14] Ibid.

Waugh also found the eighteenth century to be a source of intellectual delight, and he recorded in his diary that studying the machinations of "influential priest and statesman"[15] Cardinal Giulio Alberoni enlivened the drone of "battles and colonies" because: "I love all the corrupt politics and diplomacy [...] It is so healthily cynical."[16] Waugh at the age of sixteen was not, of course, thinking of "cynicism" with quite the level of historical depth and philosophical rigor of Shea's account, but his use of the word does signal one of the many instances in his juvenilia where we find him entertaining the role of the cynic as social commentator rather than isolated pessimist. Beginning in January 1915, Waugh and his friend Derek Hooper began a short-lived paper called *The Cynic* which bore the subhead:

> CYNICAL WITHOUT BEING CHEAPLY SO
> PIQUANT IN MODERATION
> RACY IN EXCESS[17]

Though this bit of juvenilia is not a career-determining manifesto or sustained philosophical treatise, it does indicate the importance of cynicism for Waugh's approach to the world. That qualification—"without being cheaply so"—reflects Waugh's concern that "mere" cynicism of the standard variety would be cheap. By desiring to avoid cheapness, Waugh suggests that cynicism is not a flippant posture or knee-jerk reaction but rather resembles a worldview.

That "worldview" version of cynicism is especially pronounced in the early roots of the word. Shea explains that "the name Cynic [...] claims two roots, one in *Kynosarges*, the name of an ancient Greek gymnasium where Antisthenes is said to have held his lessons, and the other in the Greek *kyon*, 'dog.'"[18] This twofold etymology elevated Cynicism "to the status of a school on a par with the Academy and the Lyceum" while simultaneously reclaiming an insult by embracing the word *kyon* and seeing dogs as creatures attuned to simple living and fierce guardianship.[19] Shea also notes that Heinrich Niehues-Pröbsting suggests another meaning of *kyon* "to designate all authors of satires (those whose writings 'bite')."[20] Thus, Shea writes, "the literary aspect of Cynicism

---

[15] Waugh, *Personal Writings 1903–1921*, 253 n3.
[16] Ibid., 253.
[17] Ibid., 91 n1. See also Naomi Milthorpe's comments about reading *The Cynic* at the Huntington Library, including a reproduction of the header in its original form: https://staffblogs.le.ac.uk/waughandwords/2016/01/27/evelyn-waugh-cynic/
[18] Louisa Shea, *The Cynic Enlightenment: Diogenes in the Salon* (Baltimore: Johns Hopkins University Press, 2010), 7.
[19] Ibid.
[20] Shea, *Cynic Enlightenment*, 8.

would thereby be inscribed in its very name" and its etymologies frame Cynics as "serious philosophers, as scurrilous public denouncers of social vices, and as authors of satires."[21] That complex mixture of philosophical heft, public witness, and literary activism is modeled by the early novels of Evelyn Waugh, extending his juvenile commitment to cynical art that was not merely cheap.

Shea examines the surprising afterlives of classical Cynicism, culminating with Foucault's last lectures at the Collège de France which argue for Cynicism's value in modern life. Shea's analysis does not emphasize, however, the extent to which Foucault discussed Cynicism as it relates to Christianity. Foucault found in the cynical tradition a mode of opposition to repressive political power, and his integrated analysis of Christianity, social order, and cynical resistance becomes a political theology. Of particular relevance for Waugh's early fiction is Foucault's exploration of Cynicism as a type of "free-spokenness (*francparler*)" or "*parrhēsia* as [a] modality of truth-telling."[22] Foucault champions parrhesiastic truth-telling as discourse that not only talks back to power and models resistant ways of living but also constitutes the subject. To be a parrhesiast differs from roles such as the "prophet" who only speaks as an intermediary on behalf of God or another power, the "sage" who dispenses wisdom but gathers learning only for its own sake, or the "professor" or "technician [teacher]" who conveys knowledge.[23] In Cynicism Foucault finds a particularly valuable model of *parrhēsia*, and he affirms Epictetus's metaphor of cynics as scouts for the advanced guard:

> The Cynic's function [will be to locate] the enemy armies and where we might find, where we might meet with points of support or aid which will benefit us in our struggle. [...] the Cynic, sent ahead as a scout, will not be able to have a shelter, a home, or even a country. [...] He will return to announce the truth [...] without being paralyzed by fear.[24]

An avant-garde for truth-telling that risks homelessness and ostracism aligns with Waugh's criticism of all parties, beliefs, and institutions in his early work. Ric Hudgens, in an echo of Foucault's account of cynicism, describes the thoroughness of cynical questioning: "The cynic questions not only the bare assertions that are being made, but also the underlying assumptions that support

---

[21] Ibid.
[22] Michel Foucault, *The Courage of Truth (The Government of Self and Others II): Lectures at The Collège de France, 1983–1984*, ed. Frédéric Gros, trans. Graham Burchell (New York: Palgrave Macmillan, 2011), 2.
[23] Ibid., 15–19.
[24] Ibid., 167.

them. [...] The cynic is seen as a threat to the conversation that the naive and the skeptical are trying to maintain."[25] There is a constant challenge and protest in the cynical mode, but Waugh also shows how thoughtfulness is required to keep this posture from being merely "cheap."

Foucault's account of cynics displays an interest in political theology, particularly when he identifies historical outgrowths of ancient Cynicism in later social and religious movements. He notes that early Christianity was shaped by cynicism—especially with regard to asceticism and other parrhesiastic practices—and that Christian history offers numerous instances where Cynicism was revived as a corrective to the ossified, institutional Church.[26] Foucault's discussion of revolutionary theology within Christianity segues directly into the cynical modes of politics found in "revolutionary movements"—many of which "borrowed a lot from the different, orthodox and other forms of Christian spirituality. Cynicism, the idea of a mode of life as the irruptive, violent, scandalous manifestation of the truth is and was part of the revolutionary practice and forms taken by revolutionary movements throughout the nineteenth century."[27] And so, in Foucault's meandering and suggestive lectures on the afterlives of cynicism, he associates the anti-institutional, provocatively revolutionary elements of Christianity with the "scandalous" political revolutions of modernity. That conjoining of separatist, outsider, reformist factions of Christianity and radical alternatives to the political status quo is the essence of a theopolitical imagination.

To be clear, I am not suggesting that early Waugh exhibits anything as fully formed and programmatic as revolutionary collective politics or that his own life was a model of asceticism and truth-telling through embodied practices. Rather, it is the works themselves that evince a theopolitical cynicism through the ways they confront all the institutions of British society that form individuals growing into maturity. Foucault argues that "art has been the vehicle of Cynicism in the modern world," and though his examples are predominately drawn from nineteenth-century French artists such as Baudelaire, Flaubert, and Manet, his description of the strategy of modern art resonates with Waugh's early satires: "art itself, whether it is literature, painting, or music, must establish a relation to reality which is no longer one of ornamentation, or imitation, but one of laying

---

[25] Ric Hudgens, "Three Cheers for Cynicism," in *Cynicism and Hope: Reclaiming Discipleship in a Postdemocratic Society*, ed. Meg E. Cox (Eugene, OR: Cascade Books, 2009), 13.
[26] Foucault, *The Courage of Truth*, 182. He notes, for instance, that the Dominicans claimed the term "*Domini canes* (the Lord's dogs)" in possible homage to Cynics.
[27] Ibid.

bare, exposure, stripping, excavation, and violent reduction of existence to its basics."[28] While this kind of "violent reduction" may apply most obviously to a writer like Beckett, who honed his craft continuously toward minimalism, it is also possible to read Waugh's early fiction as works of exposure and excavation, the stripping bare of modest protagonists such as Paul Pennyfeather and Adam Fenwick-Symes and the thorough demolition of all institutional structures that govern young people. As Foucault puts it, "Modern art is Cynicism in culture; the cynicism of culture turned against itself."[29] In his comic assaults on English civil society, Waugh exposes a culture turned against itself, and his cynicism, even when it does not promise a viable alternative, manifests a politics of critique.

Bloody Saint Bartholomew's Day and the Fate of a Nation: *The Scarlet Woman*

That cynical posture was a work in progress, maintained throughout Waugh's career with the raciness, piquancy, and resistance to cheapness that he postulated as a teenager but developed into a sophisticated comedic aesthetic. The world Waugh portrays in these novels is full of brutality, chaos, and arbitrary cruelty suffused with gallows humor that passes as whimsical levity—a worldview that finds one of its earliest, important but neglected expressions in the film he made as an undergraduate at Oxford. When he was not yet twenty-one years old, Waugh along with a crew that included his brother Alec and Terence Greenidge serving as producer and director created a short film called *The Scarlet Woman* (1924).[30] With a story by Waugh and featuring Alec plus Evelyn in two roles, the film's legacy today is primarily as a curio of Waugh juvenilia rather than as an important artwork. It merits a significant footnote in film history for the casting of their friend Elsa Lanchester in the title role, a screen debut whose campy enthusiasm anticipates her iconic performance with a fright wig as James Wale's *Bride of Frankenstein* (1935).[31] But apart from remarking on the film's goofy exuberance and intriguing visual record of the

---

[28] Ibid., 188.
[29] Ibid., 189.
[30] Waugh worked with Greenidge on two additional films—*Mummers* and *666*. See Jeffrey Manley, "Terence Greenidge and Degenerate Oxford?" https://evelynwaughsociety.org/2018/terence-greenidge-and-degenerate-oxford/ For more on Greenidge's relationship with the Waugh family, see Waugh, *EAR 1922–1934*, 208–10.
[31] In an essay from 1930 on the appeal of certain film stars, Waugh would write of having "a feeling of personal pride" about Lanchester's career since he had provided her debut (EAR 1922–1934, 229).

youthful Waugh at play, commentators usually treat *The Scarlet Woman* as a minor curiosity or callow lark.[32]

Though this film is unlikely to be regarded as a major contribution to the classical era of silent cinema or even as an essential part of Waugh's oeuvre, I would argue that it is more significant than its few commenters have allowed: it is Waugh's first sustained effort to contend with the combined forces of Christianity and nationalism through his art. Its blithe surreality and irreverent tone are consistent with *Decline and Fall* and *Vile Bodies*, and it wields the cynical humor Waugh brandished more confidently and completely in those later fictions. Rather than viewing the film as merely sophomoric and prankish, I see it as an extension of Waugh's mission to be cynical but "not cheaply so." Its tone and technique may be rougher hewn than his first two novels, but *The Scarlet Woman* supplies good evidence for his development of a theopolitical imagination that cynically confronts the politics of civil religion.

The premise of the film plays as a ribald joke that targets Christian institutions and religious leaders grasping at national power (while also grasping at women's bodies). *The Scarlet Woman*'s haphazardly executed plot unfolds from a scheme devised by the Pope, who guzzles wine in a garden in Rome and deviously plans what the inter-title calls "a gigantic attempt at the conversion of England"—an anti-Catholic portrait that delights in profanity while registering outrage at the ways churches define the nation. While strolling in his garden, crozier in hand, the Pope leers at an elderly woman called Chiara—Alec Waugh in drag—who happens to be the mother of a devilishly ambitious cardinal with the cheap gag name "Montefiasco." The Pope and Chiara, each half-soused, commend Montefiasco on his Italian invasion where his first contact is the Dean of Balliol played by a smirking Evelyn Waugh in a wig that the BFI jokingly describes as seemingly borrowed from Andy Warhol.[33] (Robert Murray Davis likewise

---

[32] Robert Murray Davis claims: "The film reveals little except that the penchant for anarchic Oxonian nonsense did not begin with the Monty Python group." Davis, *Evelyn Waugh, Writer* (Norman, OK: Pilgrim Press, 1981), 31. George McCartney is similarly dismissive, referring only to the film's "bizarre plot" and the benefit of casting Lanchester (101). See McCartney, *Evelyn Waugh and the Modernist Tradition* (New Brunswick, NJ: Transaction, 1987; 2004). Cara L. Lewis is a significant counter-example, arguing that this film and much of Waugh's film writing shows a "bad formalism" where "guilt and disgust with the cinema" manifest in chaotic, modernist narrative forms. See Lewis, *Dynamic Form: How Intermediality Made Modernism* (Ithaca, NY: Cornell University Press, 2020), 137.

[33] https://player.bfi.org.uk/free/film/watch-the-scarlet-woman-1924-online; For a complete description of the film, see Charles E. Linck Jr., "Waugh—Greenidge Film—*The Scarlet Woman*," *Evelyn Waugh Newsletter* 3, no. 2 (Autumn 1969): 1–7.

muses on the similarity between the wigs of Waugh and Harpo Marx.[34]) The Dean of Balliol is described as the "leading Catholic layman" who is luring the Prince of Wales into his thrall and away from His Majesty the King, "defender of the faith"—a battlefield drawn across religiously defined political boundaries. The dean and cardinal enlist a local Jesuit priest Father Murphy to aid them in their conversion plot, seeking to corrupt the prince by ensnaring him in a honey trap with a "cabaret-queen" Beatrice de Carolle—the titular woman, played by Lanchester, who is introduced in her "bohemian flat" luxuriating on a wing chair, taking snuff, smoking a pipe, and contemplating suicide rather than paying her outstanding debts. Beatrice assents to the scheme, which involves an attempted seduction of the prince that is deliberately thwarted by planting on her jewels stolen from the king. In remorse over his entrapment by a "scarlet woman" and supposed thief, the prince turns to the Dean of Balliol and his Catholic community for support and repentance—one of the film's many silly narrative twists—and Catholicism seems to have gained a foothold.

The film changes focus at this point, away from the main conversion plot and toward Beatrice's persecution during a hostile religious coup. Logical progression and seamless editing are not the film's strong suits, but it nonetheless exploits fears about violent religious nationalism. The church's effort to convert the English to Rome is, apparently, not going well enough, and Catholic extremists plot to reenact the Saint Bartholomew Day Massacre of 1572 by killing all "the leading Protestants of the country" and Beatrice along with them. Invoking this massacre and the broader phenomenon of the French religious wars highlights Waugh's cynicism about all forms of Christianity. Instead of charity, compassion, and goodwill, the church's public presence is marked by murderous sectarianism and political striving. Father Murphy, despite his best intentions, falls in love with Beatrice and tells her of the assassination plot. A vigorously edited chase montage ensues, begun with the title card: "The fate of a nation was running that night." In the end, Beatrice implores the king to "prevent a bloody Saint Bartholomew," and the king responds in haste, ordering the Earl of Botley to deal with the Catholic leaders as he once dealt with communists. These leaders, including the Dean of Balliol, are lured by a promise of a conciliation talk, but their celebratory refreshments are poisoned by Lord Botley's emissary.

---

[34] Davis, *Evelyn Waugh, Writer*, 31. Terence Greenidge later reported that they "did not know of the Marx brothers ... but by telepathy Evelyn drew enormously on Harpo Marx" (qtd. in Cooke 98). Barbara Cooke, *Evelyn Waugh's Oxford, 1922–1966* (Oxford: Bodleian Library, 2018).

The Pope, his "gigantic attempt at conversion" thwarted, sits in his garden dejected, staring down at his "consolation philosophica"—a child's ball-in-maze game. Mother Chiara returns to her drink. And, Father Murphy, in an oddly lyrical and emotive ending to such a wildly farcical film, walks gently among a group of smiling, laughing children.

Little in the film's production suggests that it was approached with high seriousness—the ill-fitting wigs and half-in-character mugging make it look knowingly slapdash and amateurish. But the premise and sources of humor entertain, nonetheless, a political theology. The film's subtitle is "An Ecclesiastical Melodrama," and the portrayal of both Roman Catholic and Protestant Churches emphasizes their political character. There is no suggestion of private religious belief or spiritual pieties; every character is a Christian, but Christianity is fundamentally a matter of power and conflict among competing groups. The Catholic–Protestant divide is also clearly coded as a matter of national difference, with the former being unequivocally Italian and the latter English. Converting England to Catholicism, Waugh implies, is also an effort to colonize the English by Rome. Beatrice's heroic run to spread word of the coming massacre is not just a matter of saving Protestants; she is, after all, the "fate of a nation." Waugh's contemptuous take on the Dean of Balliol suggests that deep in the heart of Oxford there resides a traitor to the faith and to Englishness, disguising itself in a foppish hairdo. Terence Greenidge, the film's director and producer, later published a "critical study" of his time at Oxford, including a chapter called "Church and State" that sought to catalog and humorously critique the varieties of Christianity and political affiliations of his university peers.[35] Writing in 1930, the same year Waugh would publish *Vile Bodies*, Greenidge described the tenor of Roman Catholicism at Oxford in milder terms than the exaggerated form depicted in his film. Greenidge describes the "most common and most characteristic brand of Papist born and bred" as a person who "in no field of conduct, public or private, will you find him holding those extremist views which weigh so heavily on the possessor of them that he must needs hurl them off on all around him. [...] Especially is he eager not to appear a fanatic."[36] Greenidge's

---

[35] Terence Greenidge, *Degenerate Oxford?: A Critical Study of Modern University Life* (London: Chapman & Hall, 1930). Waugh gave a mixed review of the book, declaring that "the chapter on Church and State is interesting but not of direct practical application to university problems" (*EAR 1922–1934*, 209).

[36] Greenidge, *Degenerate Oxford?*, 144, 145–6.

perspective of Catholics at Oxford, at least as captured by his slightly older self in the more measured genre of the "critical" memoir, shows little of the extremism portrayed in *The Scarlet Woman*, and his portrait of the cradle Catholics "on an average Sunday morning at Oxford" is composed of men in "exquisitely cut [...] plus-four suits" sitting with "that expression of modified hauteur which one has learnt to associate with the conception of an English country gentleman."[37] Rather than this genteel and distinctly English character, Catholicism at Oxford is portrayed in the film as a fanatical, alien, and bloodthirsty cabal. Waugh's portrayal of the dean exacts artistic revenge with several turns of the knife—making him foolish, conniving, impious, and un-English.

The Scarlet Woman also depicts Christianity as always expressing nationalist politics. Having a crucial part of the film orient around a repetition of the Saint Bartholomew's Day Massacre may seem a sophomoric jibe, displaying cursory knowledge of European history and flouting good taste by making light of sectarian violence. But, the warring forces in the film are competing visions of civil religious dominance with English Protestantism battling Italian Catholicism for control of the nation. The film's portrait of civil religion as corrupt and swirling in a haze of sex and drink aligns its worldview with Waugh's first two novels. While certain elements of *The Scarlet Woman* could be accused of being "cheap," the cynicism it maintains for all forms of Christian nationalism give it a theopolitical heft greater than its rudimentary form. And, while not excelling at cinematic craft, the disjointed plotting, panoply of grotesques, and acerbic biting at all peoples, institutions, and ideologies anticipate the later novels—even in their cinematic style of "cutting" between events rather than fluidly cohering. Waugh expanded his vision and improved his craft, but he retained *The Scarlet Woman*'s conviction that English society is undergirded by religious power and violence, that institutions uniformly fail to support and sustain individuals, and that most people are motivated by selfishness, greed, spite, and malice. Skewering institutional power and individual failings preoccupies his early fiction where the parrhesiastic truth-telling would grow more incisive. *The Scarlet Woman* is an early salvo in his war against damaging institutions and their ways of producing a hostile state, shots that would find more targets in *Decline and Fall* and become concentrated on modernity's drive toward war in *Vile Bodies*.

---

[37] Ibid., 143.

Godless "in the Soup" and "The Making of an Englishman": *Decline and Fall*

The structure of Waugh's first novel functions as an arch-joke and manifestation of cynicism through narrative form. Rather than the comforting narrative arc of the conventional Bildungsroman, where the protagonist rises to maturity through a series of educational experiences, *Decline and Fall* is built of conspicuously meaningless circularity and happenstance. While some readers have perceived this apparent meaninglessness as springing from Waugh's underdeveloped sense of empathy—what Alain Blayac calls the "callous, careless impertinence of [*Decline and Fall*] and the first half of [*Vile Bodies*]"—I suggest this tone may be interpreted as cynical outrage at the failures of the social order.[38] The universe of Waugh's debut novel is capricious and amoral, and his satire of institutions is encyclopedic. Woven throughout this comprehensive portrait of institutional failure is Christianity which adds to the problems of the modern nation-state. Waugh's first novels offer resources for a cynical political theology that challenges national identity.

Framed by a mordant view of university life, the narrative of *Decline and Fall* propels its nominal protagonist Paul Pennyfeather through three major sections where he is battered by public school teaching in Wales, a romance with the destructive society woman Margot Beste-Chetwynde (whose finances are bolstered by sex trafficking and enslavement), and imprisonment for Margot's crimes. In a metafictional aside halfway through the novel, the narrator tells us that "the whole of this book is really an account of the mysterious disappearance of Paul Pennyfeather."[39] Self-consciously undermining the protagonist and his heroic status turns the novel into a perverse and corrupted Bildungsroman in a modernist style.[40] Playfulness with form, however, was also crucial to Waugh's exploration of national identity. As Ashley Maher argues, Waugh's satirical take on the problems with modern architecture mixes aesthetic tastes with nationalism, particularly evident in the destruction of the ancestral estate King's Thursday and its reimagining by the modernist architect Otto Friedrich Silenus: "Now that the generation that embraced modernism has a taste for the second-rate, they are fodder for manipulation by any new agenda. Silenus's creation

---

[38] Alain Blayac, "Evelyn Waugh and Humour," in *Evelyn Waugh: New Directions*, ed. Alain Blayac (New York: St. Martin's, 1991), 115.
[39] Evelyn Waugh, *Decline and Fall* (New York: Little, Brown, 2012), 168. Hereafter cited in text as *DF*.
[40] As Ashley Maher notes, "Pennyfeather marks a new novelistic protagonist: ineffective, static, depthless, and shaped *by* his environment." Maher, *Reconstructing Modernism: British Literature, Modern Architecture, and the State* (Oxford: Oxford University Press, 2020), 33.

thus embodies the political and aesthetic misdirection of the nation, a failed modernity as well as a failed modernism."[41] The association of artistic style, modernism, and national identity operates diegetically within the narrative, but it is also pertinent to *Decline and Fall*'s entire project. For a time, Waugh called the novel "Picaresque, or The Making of an Englishman"—indicating that it was as much a journey narrative as a novel of education—but also suggesting that the central character's Englishness was essential.[42] While the young hero of a Dickens novel might go through trials that lead to maturity, sadder but wiser and equipped for full participation in liberal society, Waugh's Englishman suffers extraordinarily but only reaches complete mediocrity. Signs of his mediocre ascendency to the middle class are a tony education, anemic political affiliation, and training for the Anglican priesthood.

While many critics view this narrative as Waugh's condemnation of individual waywardness, I argue that the novel's cynicism about institutions is even more important than its skepticism about modern individualism.[43] The world Waugh depicts is not a place where institutional support is available to characters who choose selfishness and sentiment over life-giving forms of community. Rather, the institutions such as schools, churches, governments, and the arts are just as likely to damage and corrupt the individual. In his notes for an Oxford Union debate he observed about the value of public schools, Waugh wrote affirmatively of a statement by one of the debaters, Ronald de Couves Matthews, a speaker whose "really good oratory and really good satire" were a staple.[44] Matthews, in Waugh's report, stated "that the worst characteristic of Englishmen was their facility for tolerating bad institutions as good jokes," and Waugh added: "I thought that amusing."[45] In his art, Waugh would turn that "good joke" into an attack on the bad institutions that elicited this response. The cynical critique is not exclusively pointed at individuals but weighs heavily on institutions that ought to provide life-sustaining resources. No clear alternative to this unjust world system is indicated by the novel; struggle, irritation, and sarcasm are the

---

[41] Maher, *Reconstructing Modernism*, 71.
[42] qtd. in Douglas Lane Patey, *The Life of Evelyn Waugh: A Critical Biography* (London: Wiley-Blackwell, 2001), 25.
[43] Patey describes the characters as "cut off from saving tradition, unable to realize themselves fully," which puts the onus on individuals' failure to self-realize through redemptive institutions, rather than on the failures of those institutions to provide salvation (*Life of Evelyn Waugh*, 57). See also George McCartney's claim that "the ease with which savagery supplants civilization in Waugh's twentieth century is largely due to a general abdication of authority. It seems that those putatively in charge lack the will to impose the order they represent" (*Evelyn Waugh and the Modernist Tradition*, 11).
[44] Waugh, *EAR 1922–1934*, 65.
[45] Ibid.

hallmarks of Waugh's alternative theology rather than any specific salvation story. But that cynical mode, even without a clearly defined agenda or political theory, enacts *parrhēsia*—the truth-telling that bites at all of the corrupt and corrupting power structures that damage us.

The process by which our main character becomes a representative Englishman includes full conscription into British civil religion, beginning and ending with his commitment to anodyne political and religious enterprises. Our introduction to Paul is a quasi-cinematic moment of parallel editing. While the rest of Scone College, Oxford is in a frenzy of celebratory destruction by revelers from the annual dinner of the Bollinger Club, Paul is alone and unaware of the riotous celebrations, riding his bicycle while "happily [returning] from a meeting of the League of Nations Union" (*DF*, 7). We quickly learn Paul's backstory: he is at Scone College on scholarship, is a fastidious person of moderate habits, and his course of study is "reading for the Church" (*DF*, 6). So, while exuberant chaos reigns over Scone College for the evening, a pious and restrained young man has been soaking in a variety of bland liberal orthodoxies.[46] Paul's foundational commitments to church bureaucracy and liberal internationalism are two sides of the same coin. As a student, Paul is only tangential to the central goings-on of the college—just as his Christianity is tangential to the life of the church and his politics are tangential to the heart of diplomacy and realpolitik. Throughout the narrative the League of Nations recurs as a sign of liberalism without consequence, and Paul's journey signifies that inconsequential political organizing.[47] The novel has a circular structure, returning in the epilogue to a scene very similar to that of the prelude, with the exception that Paul is now three years into a successful education at Scone College (albeit enrolled under a pseudonym) and has become impervious to the destructions of the Bollinger Club. The "confused roaring" that led to his misadventures has returned with equal force, but its ravages do not touch him (*DF*, 3, 297). Paul is once again reading theology and preparing for the priesthood. His training for professional Christianity confirms his return to mainstream, platitudinous respectability, and it is matched by his recommitment to "the League of Nations Union and the

---

[46] Though in the novel the LNU signifies clubby political idealism, Waugh's own university experience included an affirmation of the potential for the League as articulated by one of its architects, Lord Robert Cecil, whose Oxford Union debate performance Waugh rated approvingly (*EAR 1922-1934*, 13).

[47] Maher notes the importance of Paul's friend Potts for the satire of the League of Nations. Potts is employed by the League, and Maher shows how "Potts's enthusiasm for postwar internationalism matches his enthrallment with the aesthetically new"—associating internationalist politics with modernism that casts both in unfavorable light (*Reconstructing Modernism*, 65).

O.S.C.U. [Oxford Student Christian Union]" (*DF*, 294). The League of Nations Union (LNU), supported by leading intellectuals such as H. G. Wells, George Bernard Shaw, and Leonard Woolf, sought a fairly radical agenda of antiwar internationalism and supranational law enforcement on terms that would appeal to moderates. In the 1930s, it would mobilize the so-called Peace Ballot, a large-scale survey that showed enormous support for international arbitration rather than war. But in the 1920s the LNU had a reputation for fanciful idealism and fashionable cosmopolitanism.[48] Waugh repeats this stereotypical view of the LNU, insinuating that being "made" into an Englishman involves a heavy helping of weak sauce. The Oxford Student Christian Union, during Waugh's time, was an emblem of Christianity as social club and campus activism.[49] Paul's renewed acceptance into organizations of clubby faith and insipid politics signal his "resurrection" and absolution, but they also mark him as a milquetoast liberal whose Christian and political convictions stand no chance of ruffling the status quo or of quelling modernity's "confused roaring" through either activism or orthodoxy.

This conclusion is a mild triumph for our protagonist, but the cynical undercurrent prevents complete satisfaction. Circularity in this novel, as Jerome Meckier argues, is absurd and pessimistic rather than meaningful.[50] Instead of renewal, growth, rebirth, or even the "resurrection" proclaimed in the novel's seventh chapter title (*DF*, 287), we find a "fruitless circularity."[51] With a formal structure that seemingly signals completion, wholeness, or victory in the mode of the Victorian novel, Waugh lures us into Paul's complacency as an envoy of civil religious virtue. He has gone from hapless undergraduate to globetrotting pariah to respectable citizen, training for the religious managerial

---

[48] Helen McCarthy documents this public perception: "LNU rhetoric might trumpet the League's transformative potential, but its two major leaders, the Conservative aristocrat Robert Cecil and Oxford classicist Gilbert Murray, peddled a version of international co-operation which was fatally stunted from birth, promising 'all the advantages of revolution without its troubles'" (2). See McCarthy, *British People and League of Nations: Democracy, Citizenship and Internationalism, C. 1918–48* (Manchester: Manchester University Press, 2011). See also Charles Andrews, "Calling All Armed and Fanatical Pacifists: Collective Security, the League of Nations, and Bernard Shaw's *Saint Joan*," *The Space Between Journal* 15 (2019). https://scalar.usc.edu/works/the-space-between-literature-and-culture-1914-1945/vol15_2019_andrews.

[49] Terence Greenidge recalled: "The Oscu became a great force in my own college of Hertford. Once it even succeeded in electing one of its leading spirits to the secretaryship of the J.C.R. Over the head of the nominee of the Athletes. The student of Oxford politics must realise that this is almost as if an Independent Christian Party suddenly arose in England, secured a Parliamentary majority and had the Archbishop of Canterbury appointed Premier. Hertford became an hierarchical state" (*Degenerate Oxford?*, 125–6).

[50] Jerome Meckier, "Cycle, Symbol, and Parody: in Evelyn Waugh's *Decline and Fall*," *Contemporary Literature* 20, no. 1 (1979): 51.

[51] Meckier, "Cycle, Symbol, and Parody," 52.

class. Becoming an Anglican clergyman with an Oxford education in theology is a route toward maintaining the social order that fundamentally failed to support Paul when he was an outcast.[52] The church throughout *Decline and Fall* is a bastion of respectability and temperance that covers up and excuses its wayward, incompetent, and sometimes even villainous members in order to preserve its own institutional power. Like every institution in the novel, the church is portrayed as self-perpetuating rather than seeking any individual or common good.

After being sent down from Scone College, Paul stumbles his way into a remarkably bad post at a boys' school in Wales where he encounters a cavalcade of foolish and pernicious types who create a tableaux for Paul's continued immersion in civil religious formation. The school where Paul ends up teaching is a training ground for young gentlemen and is replete with the sort of faults that Peter Parker described in *The Old Lie: The Great War and the Public School Ethos*—Christianity is central to the boys' education and assimilation into gentrified society, and it molds them through moralism, classism, and militarism. Parker argues that while many citizens felt unprepared for the Great War, "there is no doubt that one section of the community was ready to meet the challenge: the English Public Schools."[53] That readiness for war came from being "educated in a gentlemanly tradition of loyalty, honour, chivalry, Christianity, patriotism, sportsmanship and leadership" so that "public-school boys could be regarded as suitable officer material in any war."[54] Though Waugh presents a low-rated Welsh school, the ideological matrix at Llanaba matches Parker's account of the public school ethos. In a chapter with the coincidentally Foucauldian title of "Discipline," we learn that education at Llanaba Castle includes regular indoctrination where the headmaster Dr. Fagan leads morning prayers and Bible reading—rituals of social order rather than spiritual practice. To start, "the Doctor advanced to the table at the end of the room, picked up a Bible, and opening it at random, read a chapter of blood-curdling military history without any evident relish" (*DF*, 46). Among the jokes here is the reminder that the Bible is filled with "blood-curdling" violence that can randomly be flung at youth with a vague intention of moral enrichment. Not only is there comedy in the

---

[52] Milthorpe argues that *Decline and Fall* satirizes "the figures in traditional positions of power" and "Paul, representative of the moral protectorate of England (the middle class) is directly implicated in this failure and satirically punished" (*Evelyn Waugh's Satire*, 30). Paul's "implication" in the failed structures is another way of naming how institutions rather than individuals are the essential problem.

[53] Peter Parker, *The Old Lie: The Great War and the Public-School Ethos* (London: Constable, 1987), 17.

[54] Ibid.

lackadaisical reading of obscene stories in front of children, but there is a harsher strain of critique in Waugh's reminder that the public school is where militaristic, sacrificial nationalist ideologies are imparted to youth who may soon become combatants. Indoctrination continues from Dr. Fagan's blasé reading to the next piece of liturgy, where boys recite an Our Father along with the intonations of Prendergast, the school's Chaplain: "From that [Fagan] plunged into the Lord's Prayer, which the boys took up in a quiet chatter. Mr. Prendergast's voice led them in tones that testified to his ecclesiastical past" (*DF*, 46). Much of this scene gets comic traction from juxtaposing the public pieties of Dr. Fagan with the *sotto voce* ribaldry of Grimes, one of the teachers who has been drinking all night before chapel and is responsible for some of the boys' misbehavior. By showing the boys taking up the "quiet chatter" of the Lord's Prayer, Waugh indicates the disciplinary force of liturgical acts, where even the intrusions of Grimes cannot overmatch the unifying energy of corporate prayers.

This fictional chapel scene offers a significant contrast from Waugh's nonfiction on the same themes, a difference that highlights the importance of imaginative creation in producing a political theology that differs from propositional statements about institutions and politics. In his essay "The War and the Younger Generation" published in *The Spectator* in April 1929, Waugh blamed public schools for indulging their students with the fashionable modern notion of "think[ing] for themselves."[55] This mistaken pedagogy, where students' "crude little opinions were treated with respect," Waugh contends, has led to the current predicament where the youth are "Bolshevik at eighteen and bored at twenty."[56] In this declension narrative, the lack of structure and discipline in school leads first to trendy, revolutionary leftist politics and then to ennui—a view of youth culture that reinforces Waugh's persona as a conservative scold. As Donat Gallagher observes, there is a "conservative cast of mind" apparent in Waugh's writings on generational division: "it is one thing to demand that Youth be recognized, another to demand that the old 'grow up' and enforce the values passed on to them."[57] "Preachers in the school chapel," Waugh suggests in further evidence of educational disarray, "week after week entrusted the future to [the students'] hands."[58] These preachers and schoolmasters returned from the Great War having lost faith in the traditional ways of life that produced them, and Waugh laments this cultural change and the way it has produced a postwar

---

[55] Waugh, *EAR 1922–1934*, 185.
[56] Ibid.
[57] Ibid., 127.
[58] Ibid., 185.

"younger generation" that is unmoored and rudderless.[59] While *Decline and Fall* does cast a vision of youth without bearings, and *Vile Bodies* extends this view further, the problem does not seem to lie solely with a war generation that has lost its faith in tradition. It is a more chaotic portrait where institutions are irredeemable, the war generation is corrupt, wanton violence can erupt at any moment, and the nation is constituted and reproduced by civil religious practices combined with militarism. Whatever anxieties Waugh felt about the laxity of public schools, his literary depiction suggests that corruption and violence are the likely outcomes of their failures rather than socialism and disaffectedness.

Prendergast's prominent role in the morning prayer, despite his not presiding over its liturgies, reinforces his role as the novel's most important figurehead of civil religion. Though Fagan fulfills the headmaster's duties of leading the chapel service, it is Prendergast's voice that resounds, giving weight to the liturgy through his vocal tone and association with the institutional church. Church and school fuse during this service, and both institutions are revealed to be merely husks of the values they purport to uphold. Prendergast leads the boys in an empty ritual, and his personal piety is also magnificently hollow. He explains to Paul that "severe" tribulations that have burdened him since leaving ministry—most recently that his bathing schedule must be disrupted because Paul, like Prendergast, prefers to take morning baths. Prendergast attributes hardships such as these to his fall from grace: "If things had happened a little differently I should be a rector with my own house and bathroom. I might even have been a rural dean" (*DF*, 40). The cause, Prendergast confides, is that "I had *Doubts*"—most significantly: "*I couldn't understand why God had made the world at all*" (*DF*, 40, 42). He waves away the "ordinary sort of Doubt" that comes from biblical inconsistency or arcana of church politics because his education has given him all the answers to such classic puzzlers. Prendergast has not come to disbelieve in God's existence but more nihilistically to wonder why God bothered with creation. He retains his theism but begins, in essence, to disbelieve in the world. He is not perplexed by more typical concerns such as why there is suffering if God is omniscient, omnipotent, and all-loving, but rather by a more materialist problem: why did God waste time making the world? There is an arch-joke in this concern where Prendergast thinks he is facing the most fundamental questions about God and Christian faith while in fact he is facing a

---

[59] Maher shows how this essay establishes a link between the failure of the war generation to restore civilization and the development of modernist styles that Waugh rejected (*Reconstructing Modernism*, 63).

more materialist, philosophical, and—indeed—cynical question. The cynicism also appears in his bishop's reply that total disbelief would not matter "as far as my practical duties as a parish priest were concerned" (*DF*, 43). Muddling through institutional obligations is enough of a task, the bishop suggests, because building the parish and reinforcing its civic role are plenty to occupy the dutiful priest. Asking questions that could potentially disrupt the institution and its unthinking self-perpetuation is going much too far, and it is that kind of penetrating question that defines the intellectual project of the cynic—especially when it challenges institutional structures that propagate themselves rather than working for a common good.

A self-propagating institutional church emerges as the real problem rather than any individual tyrant. The bishop who counsels Prendergast is blithely unhelpful rather than deliberately evil, and bland tyrannies that perpetuate flawed institutions recur throughout the novel. The Welsh setting of Llanaba Castle affords recurrent commentary about the outer reaches of Britain, especially from Dr. Fagan, whose persistent discussion of the differences between Wales and England explicitly defines Englishness by opposing it to the non-English other. While explaining the school to Paul, Dr. Fagan launches into a disquisition on the "Welsh character" which he attests "is an interesting study" about which he has "often considered writing a little monograph" (*DF*, 87). He unspools an elaborate thesis for this imaginary monograph, arguing that Wales is not a Celtic nation but is rather filled with Iberian people, "the aboriginal inhabitants of Europe who survive only in Portugal and the Basque district" (*DF*, 87).[60] Once Fagan confirms that Paul has no Welsh ancestry, he takes his dissection of Wales further, beyond its racist and imperialist overtones and into the problems the Welsh have caused for the English. His litany of sins fuses the church and nation, perfectly encapsulating the essence of civil religion and echoing the disparaging wit of *The Scarlet Woman*:

> [W]e can trace almost all the disasters of English history to the influence of Wales. Think of Edward of Carnarvon, the first Prince of Wales, a perverse life, Pennyfeather, and an unseemly death, then the Tudors and the dissolution of the Church, then Lloyd George, the temperance movement, Nonconformity and lust stalking hand in hand through the country, wasting and ravaging.
>
> (*DF*, 88)

---

[60] Krishan Kumar describes Wales as the original English colony, the first acquisition of the British empire and its oldest legacy, Fagan's commentary embraces this legacy with imperialist and racialist pride. Krishan Kumar, *The Making of English National Identity* (Cambridge: Cambridge University Press, 2003), 71–4.

The "disasters" wrought upon England by Wales include the queer monarchy of Edward II and the rise of the Tudors alongside the "dissolution of the Church" and the leadership of the Welsh Prime Minister David Lloyd George. England has been assaulted, in Fagan's dour history, by the twin engines of Welsh Nonconformity and lust, curses that erupt from the exotic and primitive backwaters of this semi-colonial nation. Thus, Fagan appears not as a tyrant but as a prejudicial, Christian defender of the borders of Englishness.

Counterpointed to both Prendergast and Fagan is Captain Edgar Grimes, whose equal parts banality and evil emphasize the sinister amorality of the novel's universe. While Prendergast struggles with his disbelief and his anguish over the lack of moral certainty, Grimes admits that he is unbothered by such thoughts: "I don't pretend to be a particularly pious sort of chap, but I've never had any Doubts" (*DF*, 45). His reason for being without "Doubts" is a perverse faith sustained by his experiences where no punishment corresponds to his crimes. Grimes is frequently involved in drunken misadventures and in one of Waugh's most acidic subplots, we learn that he is a sexual predator among the boys in his charge. Grimes's theology, however, arises from his consistent success despite his recognition that judgment ought to befall him:

> When you've been in the soup as often as I have, it gives you a sort of feeling that everything's for the best, really. You know, God's in His heaven; all's right with the world. I can't quite explain it, but I don't believe one can ever be unhappy for long provided one does just exactly what one wants to and when one wants to.
>
> (*DF*, 45–6)

Untrammeled hedonism and rampant selfishness motivate Grimes, and his constant rewards indicate to him the presence of a benevolent God. What Waugh suggests, however, may be the opposite; when the good are punished and evil are rewarded, the universe is tuned to a god of malevolence, or simply to no god at all. Were it only Grimes for whom this theology worked, we might be able to chalk it up to an individual character or a particular object of satire, but the entire structure of the novel seems to support Grimes's theological claims. Characters who fight the tide of sin and evil, or who simply strive for moral honesty, such as Prendergast, are crushed by the world's systems. Paul's eventual success involves submitting to the capriciousness of the world, where the tumultuous path to being "made" an Englishman arises from handling life "in the soup." Grimes philosophizes that "there's a blessed equity in the English social system" because attending public school and going "through four or five years of perfect hell at an age when life is bound to be hell anyway" ensures that "after that the social system never lets one down" (*DF*, 35). Privilege reinforces privilege, even if Grimes, as he later admits, did not last those requisite five years of hell. Simply being in the orbit of privilege sustains unjust thriving.

Grimes's constant falling into and swimming out of "the soup" has origins in his military service during the Great War where his atrocious conduct in France required a court-martial—a subtext of militaristic failure that pervades his numerous blunders and crimes. A rapid series of falls and rises bounces him successfully from the army, and public school rescues him to ensure his vices will continue undeterred. His regiment decides that his suicide would be preferable to the disgrace of a military trial, but instead of shooting himself he gets drunk and goes to trial after all, only to have the judge remark that despite his crimes "it's out of the question to shoot an old Harrovian" and send him instead to Ireland where "you can't get into the soup" no matter what you do (*DF*, 37). The English public school system thus perpetuates itself, and the British Isles beyond England are again mocked as vicious and backward. Paul later declares that Grimes "was of the immortals. He was a life force [...] he would rise again somewhere at some time, shaking from his limbs the musty integuments of the tomb" (*DF*, 276). Grimes is like a deity capable of bodily resurrection whose viciousness is too pedestrian and petty to rise to the level of an anti-Christ. No full-blown goodness or evil prevails in Waugh's cynical portrait of postwar schoolteachers. Declining, falling, and rising again does not imply the existence of a compassionate divinity or rewards for personal industry and righteousness; it is a form for both the narrative and life that indicates the amorality and thoroughgoing injustice of the universe. It is cynicism as a formal device and theological claim.

A sign of the world's full-tilt absurdity is that meaningless war can erupt at any moment—a threat fully realized in *Vile Bodies* but also intimated in *Decline and Fall*. There is a day of sporting events at Llanaba Castle where boys compete and spectators—comprising military, religious, and aristocratic leaders—reveal how institutions they represent are undergirded by violence. Lord Circumference, a jokily named parent of a Llanaba student, asks Paul "very earnestly" whether he thinks that sports are good for the boys, and Paul responds affirmatively, adding that they are "so useful in case of a war or anything" (*DF*, 90). At first Lord Circumference is taken aback and asks Paul whether he thinks there really will be another war. Paul, perhaps recalling his LNU experience, assures the Lord of a future war, and Circumference replies: "I'm sure of it too. And that awful bread, and people coming on to one's own land and telling one what one's to do with one's own butter and milk, and commandeering one's horses! [...] My wife shot her hunters rather than let them go to the army. And girls in breeches on all the farms! All over again!" (*DF*, 90–1). The afflictions he dreads include loss of control over food and livestock and the inconvenience of having to kill gamekeepers while putting up with unseemly women's fashion. This is comic irony, but its serious side reveals the gentry dismayed by preparations for war not because of the impending devastation and loss of life but because of the diminishment of social norms and privileges.

Following this exchange about the problem of war, there are several bitterly comic moments involving Prendergast that associate the militarism of sport with the church's blind endorsement of the status quo. Prendergast has a prominent role at the games, but these duties stymie him due to being, as Grimes puts it, "tight as a lord, whisky" (*DF*, 94). In this condition, Prendergast is "flushed and unusually vivacious" while conversing with the vicar who is among the spectators (*DF*, 93). The vicar later describes this interaction with Prendergast to Colonel Sidebotham: "He was talking very excitedly to me […] about some apparatus for warming a church in Worthing and about the Apostolic Claims of the Church of Abyssinia. I confess I could not follow him clearly. He seems deeply interested in Church matters. Are you quite sure he is right in the head?" (*DF*, 95–6). Church and military are essential to the school and the boys' formation. The vicar, with great irony, reveals his distrust of anyone passionately devoted to the church: "I have noticed again and again since I have been in the Church that lay interest in ecclesiastical matters is often a prelude to insanity" (*DF*, 96). Being a professional churchman involves building and sustaining the ecclesial institution out of duty and obligation, but interest and devotion among laity is suspicious, and this commentary on the church joins with military violence. But Prendergast, at the nadir of his competence, signals the beginning of a quarter-mile race for under-sixteens by firing his starting pistol into a boy's foot. Among the jokes is that no one suspects Tangent, the injured boy, to run well anyway—Lady Circumference remarks that "the boy can't run an inch" (*DF*, 93). But the crowd around him becomes sympathetic, tends to his grazed heel by giving him cake, and decides "to remove the pistol from that old man before he does anything serious" (*DF*, 94). With his mouth full, Tangent asks "Am I going to die?," and the intoxicated Prendergast "gleefully" exclaims "First blood to me!" (*DF*, 94). Nasty hilarity arises from the incompetence and callousness of schoolteachers as well as the aristocratic families that indulge this mode of education, but there is also *parrhēsia* in the reminder that these games are conditioning for later bloodshed. Indeed, what appears first as a joke about an over-privileged child receiving a minor injury and wondering if he will die becomes a bleaker comic subplot as little Tangent eventually requires an amputation and ultimately succumbs to his wound. In the running gag of health updates on Tangent, there is the serious core that the small and presumably innocuous practices of the school can snowball into violent death. Normalizing the institutional linkage among school, military, and church while also breezily accepting pain and drunken malfeasance is how the social order produces national citizens who will drift into global war.

The novel's cynical response to civil religion also directly engages imperialism and racism, notably through the difficult character of "Chokey." Disentangling Waugh's politics with this character can be challenging, because even though the novel clearly presents the racism of the other characters as a target for derision, it also seems to indulge in racist stereotypes for some of its laughs. Sebastian Cholmondley, called "Chokey," is the Black American companion to Margot Beste-Chetwynde who arrives with her on the sports day at Llanaba Castle and announces his interest in English art and culture, particularly England's cathedrals. His enthusiasm for an English culture constructed from Shakespeare and church architecture supplies a throughline of civil religious conversation that is counterpointed by a torrent of racist comments from the other guests. This comic structure pairs hifalutin artistic and religious sentiment with white supremacy to suggest that among the English elite, these are inseparable values. In a telling moment, Colonel Sidebotham excuses himself, describing to the vicar in a barrage of racial slurs that he wishes to depart from Chokey due to his military experience "in the Soudan" where he found Africans to be "devilish good enemy and devilish bad friend" (*DF*, 105). The vicar offers no response, but church and military remain united in viewing people of color exclusively through the prism of imperialist violence. Chokey gives a heartfelt speech about enslavement that Waugh crafts in a self-consciously maudlin style for comic effect, announcing that "you folks think the colored man hasn't got a soul. [...] Beat him; put him in chains; load him with burdens" (*DF*, 107). This litany of abuse elicits "a responsive glitter in Lady Circumference's eye," as though the mere thought of slavery gives her a sadistic thrill, and several other guests vocally respond with stories about murderous and lascivious Black people (*DF*, 107). Waugh's portrayal of Chokey as emotional, amorous, and casually violent (Margot admits that he "shot a man at a party the other night") invokes stereotypes that perpetuate rather than undercut the novel's racism (*DF*, 107). But, he also unquestionably loads the surrounding white characters with intensely racist, imperialist, and uniformly prejudicial views that show how the essence of English upper-class society is animated by these convictions. Church and empire consolidate with art and culture in the creation of Englishness, and the boundaries of this English identity are strictly policed along racial lines.

By calling attention to the coalescence of church, state, school, military, empire, and class hierarchies, the caustic vivacity of Waugh's set pieces is theological, challenging the awfulness and absurdity of these institutions and their ultimate claims on citizens' lives. Tangent's mildly injured foot turning black and leading to his death is only one of the many caustic gags that run through the novel, reminding us of the painful costs of unjust institutions that are simply accepted by people within them. The cynical critique of this world does not carry with it a clear alternative—Waugh's novel is far from proposing any new sociopolitical or religious order that could replace the oppressive structures currently in power. Indeed, there is great relish and delight as Waugh savors the nastiness of his fictional world. But the novel's outrage works alongside its *schadenfreude* to challenge these structures and how they engulf individuals.

Acting "Super-Religious" in "The Jaws of Destruction": *Vile Bodies*

Decline and Fall is a circular picaresque that cynically mocks the Bildungsroman through its encyclopedic catalogue of failed institutions—institutions that "make" and support the mildly patriotic Christian Englishman. Waugh's second published novel, *Vile Bodies*, extends his cynical political theology by attacking a variety of Christian expressions and the collusion of nationalism, religion, shallow fashion, and incompetence in the creation of a pointless war. Many of the novel's critics have understandably focused on its portrait of Jazz Age debauchery and the satirical-yet-stylish depiction of the Bright Young People that made the book such a sensation in its own time.[61] *Vile Bodies* can be enjoyably read as a distorted F. Scott Fitzgerald novel in which Waugh has replaced Fitzgerald's luscious poetry with prickly comedy and given us grotesques instead of characters. (Jonathan Greenberg similarly notes that *Vile Bodies* is like "an English equivalent of *The Sun Also Rises*."[62]) But Waugh's snapping at the Bright Young People is not, I would argue, limited to cynicism about their

---

[61] D. J. Taylor notes that the novel "is always taken as the definitive exposé of this reckless, rackety Mayfair world." See Taylor, *Bright Young People: The Lost Generation of London's Jazz Age* (New York: FSG, 2007), 7.

[62] Jonathan Greenberg, *Modernism, Satire, and the Novel* (Cambridge: Cambridge University Press, 2011), 48.

(mis)behavior. Rather, much like *Decline and Fall*, Waugh's cynical art functions as truth-telling about the failure of every social institution—especially those that manufacture national consciousness infused with Christianity. The novel's culmination in a world war is an essential part of its theopolitical vision, offering a powerful critique of the consequences of destructive institutions.[63] In *Vile Bodies*, there is no salvation, and the hedonistic culture of youth that fumbles its way through the novel culminates in a war of vicious exploitation and senseless devastation.[64]

Vile Bodies was written at a breakneck pace, became an emblem for youth culture in the Jazz Age, propelled its author into fame and notoriety, and marks a vital turning point from juvenilia and early fiction to his "mature" satires of the 1930s. In the "preface" to *Vile Bodies* that Waugh appended in 1964, he brushed off his sophomore effort as being "totally unplanned" and the product of a twenty-five-year-old self who could "set a few characters on the move, write 3,000 words a day, and note with surprise what happened."[65] In this self-reflection of an older man there is, of course, some continued myth-making and persona-building that contributes to critical perceptions that Waugh's first two novels are less serious in their intent or merely the products of immaturity and self-deluded youthful confidence. (The older Waugh also seems keenly aware that the public's interest in his novel was misguided, viewing him as a representative voice of a generation rather than its critic, and skeptical of his popularity—a similar reaction to his experience with the success of *Brideshead Revisited*.) There is a clue, however, in the preface to the novel's most noticeable structural and tonal shift—"from gaiety to bitterness," as Waugh puts it (*VB*, vii). Waugh suggests that the calamities in his personal life—including his brief first marriage—are the source of this mood. Though the preface helps frame the novel autobiographically or historically, it gives little sense about how valuable the novel is as a work of theopolitical fiction.

---

[63] My argument thus differs from critics who read the novel as ambivalent about the source of war. Greenberg, for instance, claims that "the novel seems stubbornly to refrain from answering the question of whether the connection between large-scale political instability and small-scale social anarchy is causal or coincidental" (*Modernism, Satire, and the Novel*, 48). Though I do not claim that the war is caused by the debauchery of the younger generation, I do see a causal chain from the brokenness of social institutions to the eruption of total war.

[64] Lara Ehrenfried observes that Waugh's cynicism appears in meaningless babble: "the novel takes its place amid the clamor and cacophony of the late twenties, and the cynic Waugh might have agreed that *Vile Bodies* makes the form of the novel speak for its time: it is all sound and no meaning" (443). I contend that this senselessness is cynical truth-telling about the path toward violence that the world is taking. See Ehrenfried, "'There's a Song There, Really': Evelyn Waugh's *Vile Bodies*, the Musical Revue, and Early Sound Film," *Modern Fiction Studies* 66, no. 3 (2020): 423–49.

[65] Evelyn Waugh, *Vile Bodies: The Complete Works of Evelyn Waugh, Volume 2*, ed. Martin Stannard (Oxford: Oxford University Press, 2017), vii. Hereafter cited in text as *VB*.

Waugh creates a link between his first two novels and *The Scarlet Woman* through the character of Father Rothschild, S. J. He would later regret his portrayal of the priest, but this character supplies a consistent undercurrent of institutional Christianity as social cohesion. Rothschild talks with the protagonist Adam Fenwick-Symes about their prior acquaintance "at Oxford five years ago at luncheon with the Dean of Balliol" (who appeared in *The Scarlet Woman* as an insurgent Catholic radical) and their upcoming appointment "at Lady Metroland's on the twelfth" (the married name of Margot Beste-Chetwynde from *Decline and Fall*) (*VB*, 4). These works share a universe and a stylistic similarity in their haphazard movements from event to event. *Vile Bodies* also contains a subplot involving the production of a flagrantly amateurish film reminiscent of *The Scarlet Woman*. Like those prior works, *Vile Bodies* lacks any defined alternative to the social systems it satirizes, but it restlessly critiques several forms of Christianity, the power of the church, the failures of government, the wastefulness of the young, the mediocrity of the press, and many other shortcomings of postwar modernity. Its most significant contribution, however, is the way it aligns these institutional failures with global war, concluding with a thoroughly cynical vision where social dysfunction leads to total catastrophe. This cynical political theology highlights the violence inherent in institutional power and the fragility of our social structures, how their enchantments are more than just irritants or inconveniences but rather lead to cataclysmic violence.

That apocalyptic conclusion is foreshadowed by the chaotic opening chapter aboard a ship making a stomach-churning crossing—a scene of tumult and nausea across the English channel that Martin Stannard provocatively reads as Waugh's "metaphors for an unstable Ship of State."[66] Stannard notes that the novel "is littered with half-buried references to actual people, places, and events" including politicians and celebrities such as William Joynson-Hicks and Aimee Semple McPherson whose Christianity fueled their public crusades.[67] The tumultuous ship of state is laced with religiously determined politics and fears about problems such as drug use among the youth. Queasiness about a nation drifting from conservative Christian values thus reflects civil religion in *Vile Bodies*, and the later descent into militarism and chaos grows from the shallowness and hypocrisy of this religious nationalism.

---

[66] Martin Stannard, introduction to *Vile Bodies*, by Evelyn Waugh (Oxford: Oxford University Press, 2017), lx.
[67] Ibid.

A flurry of religious types populates the beginning of *Vile Bodies* and functions as a parallel to the "confused roaring" at Scone College that begins *Decline and Fall* (*DF*, 3). There is a changing landscape of religious diversity in England in the modern age, but Waugh perceives this religiosity as a symptom of shallow convictions and casual tolerance rather than inclusivity.[68] Mockery of modern religious fashion occurs throughout *Vile Bodies*, but Waugh's Christian figures also expose the social and institutional power of religion where phoniness and duplicity thrives and helps cultivate English social order. Three types of Christianity are derisively portrayed: the American evangelicalism of Mrs. Melrose Ape, the Roman Catholicism of the Jesuit Father Rothschild, and the historical Wesleyanism of Colonel Blount. The range of these traditions reveals the complexity in Waugh's satire of civil religious discourse and offers resources for cynical political theology by suggesting myriad ways that public forms of institutional Christianity can support destructive ideologies and practices that crush and exploit individuals.

A troupe of American evangelicals functions similarly to dynamics from *The Scarlet Woman*, suggesting that evangelical missions are an invading force and national danger. Mrs. Melrose Ape appears like an angel of doom, her automobile cinematically framed above the head of Father Rothschild, a "travel-worn Packard car, bearing the dust of three continents, against the darkening sky" (*VB*, 1). Melrose Ape is a globetrotting American evangelist with an entourage of "angels," nubile female assistants whose presence serves as allurement and chastisement for potential converts. Prudery and prurience are the sickly conjoined twins of American sexual discourse proffered by evangelical Christianity and exported. Crass Americanism is its own sort of civil religion with an imperialist impulse and puritanical obsession with sex that parallels the marriage plot between Adam and Nina. Evangelical Americanism is likewise a Christian nationalist force that is self-evidently ridiculous and serves to highlight social decline in the Jazz Age. The angels have all been given names of virtues—Faith, Charity, Fortitude, Chastity, etc.—and throughout the novel Waugh returns to this gimmick for ironic humor.[69] He devises these characters

---

[68] In 1922 Waugh wrote to Dudley Carew about an eclectic gathering at Oxford with various religious types including "a well bred Roman Catholic and a few deep-thinking, pipe-sucking Christians" that seems like a draft tableaux of religious shallowness from his fiction (11). Evelyn Waugh, *The Letters of Evelyn Waugh*, ed. Mark Amory (New York: Ticknor & Fields, 1980), 11.

[69] Stannard notes that the actual Semple McPherson did not have such an entourage and are thus Waugh's own invention ("introduction to *Vile Bodies*," lx).

for their comic portraiture of the age, where Bright Young People conspicuously indulge every imaginable vice while evangelical Christian missionaries flaunt their virtue. Much has been made of Waugh's approach to the Jazz Age through the vicious characters, but the virtuous have been far less discussed. Melrose Ape and her troop represent an invasion, an infiltration of England by an American-style evangelicalism.[70] Like *The Scarlet Woman*, a religious sect attempts conversion not merely to affect the "spirituality" or piety of a populace but to overtake a nation. The Angels and Ape are humorously distasteful because the piety they espouse is manifestly public and driven to change outward appearances by cultivating "holy" celebrity. It is a stereotypically American version of Christian evangelism: brash, loud, optimistic, and performatively "humble" while actually being self-aggrandizing. Semple McPherson notoriously staged her own kidnapping in 1926 to raise funds for her Christian crusade—an event one wishes Waugh had found space to incorporate into *Vile Bodies*—but her fraudulent self-promotion still presents itself as Melrose Ape lures audiences by parading desirable girls while giving them monikers such as "Chastity." Melrose Ape mounts an invasion to convert English people; she is not just a missionary force but a threat to national identity. If the Bright Young People are evidence of the nation decaying from within as its youth culture spirals into addiction, corruption, and death, the Angels are evidence of the nation being converted from without, a turn toward phony public morality in what Lauren Berlant has called an "intimate public sphere."[71] By the novel's conclusion, Lady Metroland has lured Melrose Ape's proselytes into becoming sex workers entrapped by the military machine, an image of defeat for virtue and an acidic joke about the easy alliance between religion, war, and abuse.

The Roman Catholicism of *Vile Bodies* is portrayed through a curious mixture of satire and fascination that jabs at Father Rothschild's pretensions and fakeries while still allowing his philosopher-critic posturing to voice cynical truth-telling. At first Rothschild seems to be another of Waugh's religious grotesques, with a valise of "imitation crocodile hide" containing "a false beard" (*VB*, 1). These signs of duplicity are matched by the detail that the case is not even his own but was borrowed from his hotel's *valet-de-chambre*. His appearance, the narrator

---

[70] In 1922 Waugh went "to hear an American revivalist of great transatlantic fame," and he joked that "I thought he was dangerously near converting me to righteousness but like Pharoah [sic], I steeled my heart" (*Letters*, 11).

[71] Berlant describes late-twentieth-century American politics as a time where the nation has "collaps[ed] the political and the personal into a world of public intimacy." Lauren Berlant, *The Queen of America Goes to Washington City: Essays on Sex and Citizenship* (Durham, NC: Duke University Press, 1997), 1.

snidely observes, has "a peculiar resemblance to those plaster reproductions of the gargoyles of Notre Dame which may be seen in the shop windows of artists' colormen tinted the color of 'Old Ivory'" (*VB*, 1). Rothschild is a collection of quirky details rather than a person, and his multiple layers of facsimile suggest that he is a simulacrum rather than a man of integrity.[72] Although he never fully sheds those suspicious qualities, he is not simply villainous.

The satire of Roman Catholic power and falsehood persists, but Rothschild gradually emerges as a voice of reason and *parrhēsia*. In one of the many party scenes, revelers gossip about the debauched behavior of the younger generation—those titular vile bodies—but their discussion exposes how leaders of church and state fail to comprehend the youth, the postwar condition, and their own complicity in social breakdown due to their myopia and incompetence. Prime Minister Outrage, for instance, is a prominent figurehead for an institution that perpetuates itself without any concern for the people he supposedly serves, and he adopts an attitude of comical self-absorption and self-pity: "Poor Mr. Outrage, thought Mr. Outrage; poor, poor old Outrage, always just on the verge of revelation, of some sublime and transfiguring experience; always frustrated … Just Prime Minister, nothing more, bullied by his colleagues, a source of income to low caricaturists" (*VB*, 87). Sadly carrying the weight of power and leadership while burdened by mockery in the press—this is Outrage's cross to bear, and he consoles himself: "He sipped his champagne, fingered his ribbon of the Order of Merit, and resigned himself to the dust" (*VB*, 87). Forced into the difficult labor of drinking champagne at upper-crust parties, Outrage bemoans the failures of the "younger generation" who, in his opinion, have squandered the opportunity given them by the Great War. There is no respect for his office or for government itself, and he complains to Lord Metroland and Father Rothschild, "They had a chance after the war that no generation has ever had. There was a whole civilization to be saved and remade—and all they seem to do is to play the fool" (*VB*, 87). The debauchery of the Bright Young People is more than just youthful recklessness or experiments in vice; it is a sign of generational breakdown where civilization is ruined by lack of respect for offices and institutions. What exactly Outrage thinks the new, postwar civilization requires is unclear—he has little vision or insight himself. But his generalized fear and concern—and, indeed, his

---

[72] Greenberg notes that Rothschild is "a conspiracy-theorist's fantasy come to life" in being "the fusion of two great institutions: with his Jewish surname he embodies the wealth of European banks, while with his title Father he carries the religious authority of the Catholic Church" (*Modernism, Satire, and the Novel*, 68). Waugh's satire of corrosive institutions thus carries a whiff of antisemitism along with distrust of economic systems.

outrage—at the inability to rule Britain because young citizens do not care about the nation is one of Waugh's sharp commentaries on the generational divide.[73] Though Waugh would later become convinced of the need for strong conservative government, his portrait in *Vile Bodies* is of governors who deserve no respect or honor and governments whose inadequacy gives license for self-destruction. Lord Metroland responds to Mr. Outrage by saying that he understands the reluctance of youth to deal with "all this business of government" because "As far as I'm concerned it stands for a damned lot of hard work and precious little in return. If those young people can find a way to get on without it, good luck to them" (*VB*, 87). Father Rothschild concurs and adds a religious dimension to this claim, merging the political and the theological in an explicitly theopolitical account of the Bright Young People. The situation, Rothschild suggests in one of his most sagacious moments, "is in some way historical," and he proclaims: "I don't think people ever *want* to lose their faith either in religion or anything else. I know very few young people, but it seems to me that they are all possessed by an almost fatal hunger for permanence" (*VB*, 88). Rothschild says that the old adage "if a thing's worth doing at all, it's worth doing well" has been taught by his church for centuries, but he acknowledges that the young people may be right in reversing the saying (*VB*, 88). "If a thing's not worth doing well," they feel, then "it's not worth doing at all," and thus they recuse themselves from broken institutions like church, state, school, news media, and the like (*VB*, 88). If there is a moral center to the novel's satire and cynicism, it may be this moment, expressed in a tentative theory by a priest whose church is as much a part of the problem as the other social structures the "younger generation" have renounced. This cynical political theology retains Waugh's youthful uncertainty while explaining the postwar generation's physical excesses and unwillingness to conform to the broken systems of their elders.

A gathering at the Metroland's estate offers one of the most explicit moments of religious nationalism in all of *Vile Bodies* as Father Rothschild and Prime Minister Outrage enthusiastically conspire in Lord Metroland's study while the Lord himself distractedly lusts after the girls in Mrs. Ape's troupe. Thinking a spy

---

[73] Alice Reeve-Tucker and Nathan Waddell note that Outrage's "name equivocally suggests both being in a state of annoyance and being its cause" and "that the defiance of the younger generation is at least in part a corollary of his own generation's prejudices." This satire of the prime minister, I would argue, is not just about personal foibles and generational disfunction but about the failures of an entire era and the governmental structures intended to benefit constituents. See Alice Reeve-Tucker and Nathan Waddell, "Wyndham Lewis, Evelyn Waugh and Inter-war British Youth: Conflict and Infantilism," in *Wyndham Lewis and the Cultures of Modernity*, ed. Andrzej Gąsiorek, Alice Reeve-Tucker, and Nathan Waddell (Burlington, VT: Ashgate, 2011), 167.

has disrupted their meeting, the men hide behind curtains as a man in a false beard attempts a phone call. When they reveal themselves to apprehend the spy, the narrator reports that "this concurrence of Church and State, coming so unexpectedly after an evening of prolonged embarrassment, was too much for Simon" (*VB*, 67). Not a political spy after all, but only a member of the gossip press sneaking into the fête in hopes of a juicy report for the "Mr. Chatterbox" column in the *Daily Excess*. This "concurrence," then, explicitly unites the religious and political with sexual scandal and the shabby mediocrities of the tabloid press. Instead of interest in the nationally significant scheming of power brokers, the pressman is disappointed by an inability to deliver scandal, and Waugh amplifies the comedy by depicting the prime minister as ignorant of the gossip columns: "It was like one of those Cabinet meetings, when they all talked about something he didn't understand and paid no attention to him. Father Rothschild led him away, and attempted with almost humiliating patience and tact to make clear to him some of the complexities of modern journalism" (*VB*, 67). Simon Balcairn, the erstwhile Mr. Chatterbox, files his report on the evening in a string of libelous falsehoods centered around an imaginary religious revival that featured Mrs. Melrose Ape, Margot Metroland, the countess of Throbbing, and the archbishop of Canterbury in the throes of a spiritual ecstasy that leads to raucous public confessions of misdeeds, dalliances, and escapades guaranteed to shock all hearers and to demolish the confessors' reputations. The final comic flourish on Balcairn's un-illustrious life is a quick, parenthetical survey of his family history. Simon is "the last Earl of Balcairn" in a long lineage that because of "the eccentricities of British Foreign policy"—that is, because of their imperial enterprises—has meant that Balcairns have "fallen in many lands" (*VB*, 69). The ignominious and tawdry death of Simon Balcairn shows a slow decline from forefathers who died "in glory" at Agincourt to the shame-filled suicide of an Earl reduced to rumor-mongering with a scandal-rag press. Military and imperial adventures among the aristocracy thus devolve into disgrace, connecting the goings-on of "church and state" with a fourth estate in shambles.

One of the last set-pieces in the novel before its wartime conclusion is Colonel Blount's effort to screen his film about the life of John Wesley for the local rector on Christmas Eve—another instance of Christianity helping create an English national identity. A series of comic mishaps culminate in a power outage after the first reel, and Waugh's droll humor about the shoddiness of the film peppers his description—even though much of the film's style recalls Waugh's own contribution to cinematic art.[74] The scene is also a tour de force evisceration of civil religion as produced through mass entertainment. The Colonel summarizes the importance of his film not just as an artwork but as gospel ministry and missionary export for British culture. "It is the most important all-talkie super-religious film to be produced solely in this country by British artists and management and by British capital," the Colonel announces, and supervisors include "a staff of expert historians and theologians" who contribute to "the life of that great social and religious reformer John Wesley" which is "for the first time portrayed to a British public in all its humanity and tragedy" (*VB*, 150). Waugh's cynical wit operates on several levels throughout the filmmaking subplot. Colonel Blount, the quintessence of blinkered self-importance born of wealth and military command, believes himself to be on a nation-improving mission. Through a popular artform, the Colonel intends to bestow Christian values beneficial for the moral core and fortitude of the nation. The "all-talkie" and "super-religious" film will be thoroughly British from both the creative and business sides of the project, combining religious education and national pride and uniting artists with historians and theologians to generate popular appeal, scholarly accuracy, and religious indoctrination. The historical and theological dimensions are subsidiary to the commercial elements, made especially comic by Waugh's description of the Hollywood genres Colonel Blount pilfers to keep his picture buoyant. To remain engrossing, there are scenes such as "Wesley in America [...] being rescued from Red Indians by Lady Huntingdon disguised as a cowboy"—a trope cribbed from movie Westerns and tacked onto the biopic to supplement tedious scenes such as Wesley "uninterruptedly composing a pamphlet for four and a half minutes" (*VB*, 144). Waugh attacks Hollywood conventions as well as inept and earnest "passion projects" from vain movie producers, but his cinema criticism also punctures civil religion. The title cards for Colonel Blount's film announce that "THE WONDERFILM COMPANY OF GREAT BRITAIN PRESENTS [...] EFFIE LA TOUCHE IN [...] A BRAND FROM THE BURNING, A FILM BASED ON THE LIFE OF JOHN WESLEY"—a list of credits that emphasize the film's national origin and religious intention (*VB*, 144). One of the intertitles locates a scene in "EPWORTH RECTORY, LINCOLNSHIRE (ENG.)" which the Colonel explains is "in case it's taken up in the States [...] I don't believe that there is a Lincolnshire over there, but it's

---

[74] Barbara Cooke notes the connection between *Vile Bodies* and *The Scarlet Woman* and suggests that the similarities between Colonel Blount and Waugh's father Arthur "may have made uncomfortable reading" (Cooke, *Evelyn Waugh's Oxford*, 83).

always courteous to put that in case" (*VB*, 144). Not only will the film be morally improving and promotional for the nation, it can serve as an exportable product of English cultural heritage in a reversal of the evangelizing missions of Melrose Ape and the Angels.

All of the cultural production and other markers of civilization established throughout the novel collapses into wide-scale war, an extreme and absurd conclusion subtly prepared for by the conditions left in the previous world war—a trajectory explicitly acknowledged by Father Rothschild. In one of his crucial statements of *parrhēsia*, Rothschild matter-of-factly asserts that the Bright Young People's decadence is motivated by their tacit acceptance that another war is coming. *Vile Bodies* is a significant example of interwar fiction that predicts the Second World War, but rather than the tension and anxiety that so often accompanied such predictions, Waugh gives us resignation to this fate in a tone of deeply felt cynicism. That resignation may still signal what Paul K. Saint-Amour has described as the "proleptic mass traumatization" and "*pre-traumatic stress syndrome whose symptoms arose in response to a potentially oncoming rather than an already-realized catastrophe*," but for Waugh the anxiety and fear are subsumed in dour acceptance of the catastrophic future.[75] Father Rothschild's often-quoted claim that youth have a "fatal hunger for permanence" within their disappointing world is poignant during this time of inevitable war (*VB*, 88). He explains: "Wars don't start nowadays because people want them. We long for peace, and fill our newspapers with conferences about disarmament and arbitration, but there is a radical instability in our whole world order, and soon we shall all be walking into the jaws of destruction again, protesting our pacific intentions" (*VB*, 88–9). This statement is a stinging indictment of peace work in the 1920s and gives grounding for the absurdism in Waugh's early works. Rothschild's comments hearken back to *Decline and Fall* with its recurring bit about Paul Pennyfeather's involvement with the LNU where "pacific intentions" and liberal internationalism are impotent compared with global militarism. Antiwar activism cannot deter international belligerence, and throughout *Vile Bodies* war is fueled by broken social institutions, religious and imperialist ideologies, and collective ennui.

The novel's final chapter, entitled "Happy Ending" in a gesture of flagrant irony, depicts full-blown entrance into the predicted "jaws of destruction." Though not as self-consciously eschatological as Lawrence's late works, *Vile*

---

[75] Paul K. Saint-Amour, *Tense Future: Modernism, Total War, Encyclopedic Form* (Oxford: Oxford University Press, 2015), 7–8.

Bodies is apocalyptic and suggests never-ending total war with aerial combat above "a great expanse of mud in which every visible object was burned or broken" and "sounds of firing thundered beyond the horizon" (*VB*, 152). War machines and wreckage are all that remain of modern "civilization," and the chapter begins "on a splintered tree stump in the biggest battlefield in the history of the world" where Adam finds momentary respite from the endemic combat (*VB*, 151). After the zany adventures with wild parties, scandalous media, and fractured romantic comedy, the conclusion surges with violence, devastation, and despair. Unlike the archly comic circularity of *Decline and Fall* which emphasizes the blind amorality of the universe and the perpetual motion of blithely oppressive social institutions, the ending of *Vile Bodies* emphasizes rupture and destruction caused by human ineptitude and the sinister results of institutions such as church, government, military, and press when their worst energies are unleashed. The deliberately inapt title "Happy Ending" rubs our faces in the squalor and the consequences of all the failed institutions and movements that followed the Great War—a "scene," Adam notices, that is "one of unrelieved desolation" (*VB*, 151–2).

Adam reads a letter from Nina that serves as a window to the fractured world remaining beyond the battlefield, a space less flagrantly violent but nonetheless completely remade by war. Journalism is just as unreliable and fictitious as it was during Adam's time as a gossip columnist, but now the lies are vital to war propaganda, and a fabricated story about Adam's supposed valor is leading to a groundswell campaign for him to receive the Victoria Cross.[76] False reporting compounds with military pomp in the construction of a narrative about the condition of the world—heroism and adulation cling to a military system that perpetuates global havoc. Nina's husband Ginger is also snared by this web of obfuscation, working "a job in an office in Whitehall" while "wear[ing] a very grand sort of uniform" and forgiving Nina for her affair with Adam because "in war time one lets bygones be bygones" (*VB*, 151). Nina is pregnant with Adam's child, but Ginger makes up his mind that the baby is his, as if his governmental role and costume can absorb all facts that contradict his status as a civil servant and leader during a time of national need. The institutions of marriage and family are a sham. The sacrificial, national war narrative is the only story permitted and all contradictions are consumed by its force.

---

[76] Amanda K. Greene argues that the ending connects tabloid misrepresentation with the public's refusal to face combatant injury. See Greene, "The Passing Hour: 1930s Real-Time, *Vile Bodies*, and the Ethics of Reading," *Configurations* 29 (2021): 119–54.

Civilian and combatant life have merged as culture and art are transformed by the war machine. Nina reports that the familial estate is now a hospital, her father "shows his film to the wounded and they adore it," and Adam's former publisher Mr. Benfleet complains "how awful it was when one had given all one's life in the cause of culture to see everything one's stood for swept away" (*VB*, 151). On the bright side, though, Benfleet is "doing very well with his 'Sword Unsheathed' series of war poets" (*VB*, 151). The cultured world that enabled artistic production is utterly ruined, but injured veterans need hospital entertainment and the cycle of recruitment needs propagandist poetry. A war-shaped culture has replaced the shallow modern world of parties and arts, and that former "high life" now seems a pathway to this bellicose fate. The government orders everyone to wear gas masks, blurring the line between combatants and civilians. Such erasure would come to define the real-world war that erupted a decade after Waugh's novel, but *Vile Bodies* already envisions that there is nothing "civilian" left. Unending chaos is the result of institutional failures, and those institutions still fight to perpetuate their own existence at the cost of individual worth.

Nothing much is directly said about institutional Christianity in this "Happy Ending," a striking absence given the novel's opening survey of religious types. All that remains is the failed vestige of Melrose Ape's troupe, one "woebegone fragment of womanhood": a sex worker whose former name was "Chastity" (*VB*, 153). Like the chapter title itself, her name has become gruesomely inapt through her exploitation across numerous international forces in the war, and her appearance in the novel's final pages is a queasy-making joke about the ravages of war on the most vulnerable. We return to the running gag of the "drunk Major" to whom Adam loaned money and who accidentally won a fortune at the races—a runner that paralleled Adam's rising and falling fortunes in his romance with Nina. Now promoted to a general but still exhibiting his over-fondness for drink, the former major discovers Adam and offers to share a case of champagne and the girl he has found by the roadside. Adam and the drunk Major initially meet with their weapons drawn, the major holding a flamethrower and Adam a (fictional) "Huxdane-Halley bomb (for the dissemination of leprosy germs)" (*VB*, 152). Whatever "civilized" practices once governed warfare are now clearly forsaken as one man wields the latest in grisly technology intent on burning another man alive while his opponent uses biological weaponry. Hardly a duel for skilled warriors, this scene evokes the devolution of military etiquette resulting from the evolution of technology. Once they discover each other's identity, the general invites Adam to his broken-down car for a drink—a fractured echo of the motor car races from earlier in the novel. The general remembers the money he owes to Adam, but the ruined economy makes currency worthless, undermining all the farcical efforts to gain a sustainable living and marry Nina. The former Angel "Chastity" tells her story of abuse from being trafficked by Lady Metroland up to the present through an array of maltreatments among every combatant nation. With a grimly comic understatement, she concludes her story: "*My*, isn't war awful?" (*VB*, 153). The General becomes one more exploiter, and the "sounds of battle" finish the novel "like a circling typhoon" (*VB*, 289). As Reeve-Tucker and Waddell observe, "the 'circling typhoon' imagery of the chaos by which the two figures are surrounded evinces the circuitousness and meaninglessness of the Establishment's justifications of the First World War."[77] Circularity has turned from arch-joke about the amorality of a god-abandoned universe in *Decline and Fall* to the more pointed satirical barb that total war must always return when social institutions are built for destruction. We end on the storm of war with the image of circularity once again, but rather than an ironic restoration of the status quo, this circularity is a windstorm of annihilation. Adam's tiny relief in the eye of this storm is exhausted sleep while the drunk General turns leering attention to "Chastity." Such is the endpoint for Christian evangelism and the promotion of virtues: trading sexual favors for survival in the midst of an all-encompassing and utterly meaningless war as the church fully recedes under the looming power of the military, the only institution still desperately persisting while the world burns. It is a striking condemnation of war and the institutions that produce and sustain global violence as well as the capacity for militarism to infect the personal, private, and intimate spheres of individual life. No glory, no "good" sacrifice, and no real "victory" seem possible. Only cataclysm persists, and Waugh's cynicism, like the war he imagines, is total.

Imagining Cynicism as Protest

Decline and Fall and *Vile Bodies* are, for the most part, hopeless novels. Despair is not their overriding tone—their wicked comic flair prevents anything maudlin or even truly mournful from creeping in. But both novels cast hermetic visions of a world without an escape from systemic injustice and unrelenting violence. In the absence of any clear alternatives to this world or any obvious ways to combat its predations, Waugh's novels turn toward cynical humor that draws attention to the myriad failures of the social order and ruefully laughs at their dire

---

[77] Reeve-Tucker and Waddell, "Wyndham Lewis, Evelyn Waugh, and Inter-war British Youth," 169.

consequences. It is a frequently noted irony that Waugh, who would become so widely known for conservatism and promotion of a Catholic moral order, would in his early works satirize all social institutions with such gleeful abandon. David Bradshaw describes *Decline and Fall*, for instance, as "hilariously anarchic," and notes that "Waugh, an author who would soon become synonymous with political reaction, Establishment values and customary forms, could not have written a debut novel in which bad form, irregularity, irrationalism, social flux, moral chaos, and the undermining of time-honoured conventions and ancient institutions are handled more delightfully."[78] That "delightful" undermining of ancient institutions is, as I have argued throughout this chapter, a key component of Waugh's cynicism, where the humor provides a method for the satirical "bite" and the underlying seriousness of his protest keeps the cynical from becoming cheap. Because there appears to be no solution to the problems created by such institutions and no simple restoration for the chaos, we must embrace the uncertainty. Keeping a cynical edge and knowing how to bite back when societal forces threaten to overwhelm and crush us is a value of reading early Waugh.

If *The Scarlet Woman* is Waugh's first significant work of cynical theopolitical imagination, then his travelogue published the same year as *Vile Bodies* may be the final such work of his restless youth. *Labels: A Mediterranean Journal* (1930)—entitled in the US edition *A Bachelor Abroad*—was written after Waugh's divorce but before his conversion, a personal situation he disclaims in his Author's Note: "So far as this book contains any serious opinions, they are those of the dates with which it deals, eighteen months ago. Since then my views on several subjects, and particularly on Roman Catholicism, have developed and changed in many ways."[79] The book forms a fitting capstone to the early, pre-Christian phase of Waugh's youth, and it retains traces of the inchoate cynical theology he explored in his first two novels. As Patrick R. Query observes:

> *Vile Bodies* had made Waugh's reputation as a novelist in the same year, and *Labels* established him as a travel writer of real talent. [...] the Catholicism that would later come to sharpen certain of his perceptions abroad but to dull others is not yet present. He is happy to keep his distance from all orthodoxies and thus to find more fun in them.[80]

---

[78] David Bradshaw, introduction to *Decline and Fall*, by Evelyn Waugh (New York: Penguin, 2001), xiii.
[79] Evelyn Waugh, *Labels: A Mediterranean Journal*, 1930. (London: Penguin Classics, 2011), ix. Hereafter cited in text as *L*.
[80] Patrick R. Query, introduction to *A Tourist in Africa*, by Evelyn Waugh, ed. Patrick R. Query (Oxford: Oxford University Press, 2021), lv–lvi.

The moments of detached scorn for Roman Catholicism that occur periodically through the travelogue create some of its piquant humor and also show the persistent association between Christianity and national identity. Early in his narrative, Waugh amusingly recounts the perils and discomforts of aeroplane travel, flying from London to Paris in February of 1929. Amid the nerve-wracking, stomach-churning lurches of the flight (an echo of the nauseating rough crossing at the start of *Vile Bodies*), he observes an earnest travel companion—"President of the Union, logical, matter-of-fact in disposition, inclined towards beer and Ye Olde Merrie Englande, with a marked suspicion and hostility towards modern invention"—a man who persistently mutters: "Oh, my God, oh, Christ, oh, my God" (*L*, 7). "Two days later," Waugh tells us, "without a word to anyone, he was received into the Roman Church," and he concludes this episode with a jibe at such pieties and their institutional sanction:

> [D]uring this aeroplane's brief visit to Oxford, three cases of conversion occurred in precisely similar circumstances. I will not say that this aeronaut was directly employed by Campion House, but certainly, when a little later, he came down in flames, the Jesuits lost a good ally, and to some people it seemed as if the Protestant God had asserted supremacy in a fine Old Testament manner.
>
> (*L*, 7–8)

This glimpse of a Jesuit conspiracy to convert hearty Englishmen sounds like a cast-off episode from *Vile Bodies*, presented with amused disdain for and suspicion of the Society of Jesus.

This short aeroplane episode that references both Catholicism and Englishness reflects Waugh's distance at the time from personal religious conviction. Later in the travelogue, however, his experience of places remote from his English home inspires him to adopt a persona of religious and nationalistic chauvinism. He comments on an Arab art museum in Cairo that he "was moved by something of the Crusader's zeal for cross against crescent" and is struck that the time of "Arab supremacy in Egypt coincides almost exactly with the dominion of Latin Christianity in England" (*L*, 140). He concludes: "It seems to me that there is no single aspect of Mohammedan art, history, scholarship, or social, religious, or political organisation, to which we, as Christians, cannot look with unshaken pride of race" (*L*, 140). Moments like these have understandably drawn censure from readers critical of Waugh's persona—the *faux-naïf* traveler merged with the dogmatic jingoist, exercising a seemingly willful lack of perception, historical sense, and charity. In Waugh's claims about aesthetic superiority among the "race" of English Christians over Egyptian Muslims, he betrays interwoven threads of race, empire, nationality, religion, and cultural production that construct civil religious discourse.[81] Waugh's personal prejudices cannot be fully extricated from his astute perceptions, but across his many genres and modes of creativity there is valuable attention to the interweaving of these forces and a thoroughgoing questioning of their power over us.

Waugh's cynical position ultimately leaves him isolated with a sense of the homelessness Foucault theorized as essential to cynicism. The religious and political uncertainty of *The Scarlet Woman* along with the more sophisticated aesthetic development of that doubt in his first two novels provides imaginative resources even without the stability of community or of robust ideological conviction that would come to define his later thought. The role of cynic as expressed in his early works is lonely, speaking hard truths about the wide-scale failure of the many institutions we rely on for sustenance in the modern, "civilized" world. The world's condition is thoroughly chaotic, but no single watchword such as "Christianity" can be supplied as a counter because Christian institutions and expressions are as susceptible to chaos as all others.

Though no single alternative to the chaos can be found in these works, what they offer nonetheless is a powerful expression of protest. Cynicism bites at the status quo and challenges the assumptions that sustain it, calling out the falsity and failures that may go unnamed and demanding that we no longer blindly and docilely accept these givens—especially when they are leading us toward devastation. Waugh's pre-conversion works show the imbrication of Christianity and the state and call us to question these alliances. His satire gives cynicism a consistently humorous edge, inviting bitter laughs at absurdity, outrageousness, and foolish optimism. By protesting oppressive institutional power through marshaling cynical laughter at what is otherwise too painful to bear, Waugh's fiction enacts a theopolitical imagination rich with *parrhēsia*—truth-telling that makes cynicism far from cheap.

---

[81] Nicholas Shakespeare writes: "if one wishes to discover Waugh's creed in Waugh's words, whether it be his opinions on politics, religion, architecture, journalism, novel writing, or simply what constitutes his notion of Englishness, one has to turn to his travel writing." See, Shakespeare, introduction to *Waugh Abroad: The Collected Travel Writing*, by Evelyn Waugh (New York: Knopf, 2003), x.

4

Sylvia Townsend Warner's Queer Anarchist Theology: *Lolly Willowes*

Sylvia Townsend Warner's ambivalence toward Christianity was a consistent part of her life. She was baptized at St. Paul's Church, Newton Abbot by her grandfather, and though she was not steeped in piety like, for instance, the young D. H. Lawrence, her youth was continually inflected by the social functions of the church. In an interview Warner gave in 1975, she was asked whether she considered herself to be a Christian, a question prompted by her extensive work in the Tudor Church Music project as well as her medieval religious orders novel *The Corner That Held Them* (1948). "Oh no! I couldn't possibly do that," was her emphatic response, and she recalled asking her mother about a cantankerous old churchwoman: "I said to my mother in confidence, 'Are all Christians cross?' She replied, with great justice, 'Not *all* of them.'"[1] Her biographer Claire Harman explains that while Warner was a child, a pious and threatening nurse attempted to coerce her into moral behavior by telling her a goblin would attack if she misbehaved.[2] Warner reacted to her nurse's threats by becoming, as she put it, "an agnostic," which Harman observes "was more of a definition than a decision, as she had never had a great deal of Christianity thrust upon her, though she had had, in the usual course of things, a great deal of Church."[3]

That "great deal of Church" provided a lifelong source of conflicted feelings, arising with particular force during her four decades of partnership with Valentine Ackland, whose spiritualism, religiosity, and eventual commitment to Roman

---

[1] Michael Schmidt and Val Warner, "Sylvia Townsend Warner in Conversation," *PN Review* 23 8, no. 3 (January–February 1982): 36. See also, Warner, *With the Hunted: Selected Writings*, ed. Peter Tolhurst (Norwich: Black Dog Books, 2012), 399–407.
[2] Claire Harman, *Sylvia Townsend Warner: A Biography* 1989 (London: Penguin, 2015), 12.
[3] Harman, *Warner*, 12.

Catholicism and the Society of Friends was a sore spot in their relationship.[4] Ackland wrote in 1952 that Warner "is to a great extent 'allergic' to each & every form of religion ... She has a positive horror of any form of religion, which she believes to be immeasurably dangerous and destructive."[5] And yet, Warner would frequently write about Christian themes, depict Christian characters, and examine with great imaginative curiosity the effects of Christianity on English culture. In an analysis of the thirty or so religious poems Warner wrote, Pauline Matarasso argues that there is much more on display than simple satire, and that her so-called Christian poems show her "divided mind": "if we read her, not as the 'great religious poet' she once flippantly envisaged being, but as the writer of some fine religious poems, we shall be entirely justified, and she, if she knew, would laugh, half mocking, half delighted."[6]

It is this image of the half-mocking, half-delighted Warner that inspires my argument through this chapter, placing her alongside Woolf, Lawrence, and Waugh as a significant English novelist whose immersion in Christian culture and deep ambivalence toward all religious faith gave leverage for a theopolitical imagination. Though a few critics have carefully considered Warner's relationship with Christianity, and many have mentioned the satirical and critical attitude toward religion in her novels, little has been written about the political dimension to her handling of Christianity. Maroula Joannou, for example, aptly characterizes the ambivalence in Warner's prose while implying its half-hearted religiosity: "The characters in Townsend Warner's novels are expert in the vertiginous break with convention, the wildly improbable liaison, and the nonsensical or whimsical fancy, pursuing the Keatsian 'holiness of the heart's affections'—a term that this most anti-clerical of writers would certainly have resisted."[7] In Joannou's account, a clarifying reference to Keats on "holiness" swerves to reassure us of Warner's "anti-clericalism" and her writing as resistance. This flourish qualifies what at first might look like a critical overstatement, and it subtly reinforces Joannou's claim about the

---

[4] Warner reflected in 1956 that "It was a pin-prick in a wound [...] that my anti-clericalism had no weight with [Ackland] [...] Alternatively, slighting or magnifying my distress, I asked no questions because I dreaded the answers. As my father said 'Church' to forbid his following spaniel, she would say 'Church' to me. 'Church' would impend over every conversation, qualify our trust in each other." Warner, *I'll Stand by You: Selected Letters of Sylvia Townsend Warner and Valentine Ackland with Narrative by Sylvia Townsend Warner*, ed. Susanna Pinney, (London: Pimlico, 1998), 328.
[5] Qtd. in Harman, *Warner*, 249.
[6] Pauline Matarasso, "A Recurrent Modulation: Religious Themes in the Poetry of Sylvia Townsend Warner," *The Journal of the Sylvia Townsend Warner Society* 2016, no. 1 (2017): 61.
[7] Maroula Joannou, "Preface," in *Critical Essays on Sylvia Townsend Warner, English Novelist 1893-1978*, eds. Gill Davies, David Malcolm, and John Simons (Lewiston: Edwin Mellen, 2006), ii.

vertigo induced by Warner's breaks with convention. Just when it seems that "holiness" is a useful term for Warner's passions, the heightened emotion becomes too high, and the critic undercuts the claim to more accurately reflect the sort of undercutting Warner herself employs. Vertigo may indeed be the feeling induced by the in-between, uneasy, elated-yet-ironic tone in Warner's best books. It is that ill-at-ease, hard to pin down, twixt-between space that I seek to explore in this chapter as I argue that this liminality expresses an alternative political theology which feints toward religiosity but develops through sympathies with anarchism.

Anarchism is another of the ambivalent associations in Warner's life, most fully arousing her interest while working in Spain during the civil war of the mid-1930s. Her longest official political affiliation was with the British Communist Party, but experiences with Spanish anarchists sparked an attraction she would ruminate on with fascination and whimsy for many years. "I always find anarchists very easy to get on with," Warner related near the end of her life:

> I think that's because, if the English turn to the left at all, they are natural anarchists. They are not orderly enough to be good Communists and they're too refractory to be good Communists. I became a Communist simply because I was agin [sic] the Government but that of course is not a suitable frame of mind for a Communist for very long. But you can go on being an anarchist for the rest of your life, as far as I can see, and doing very well. You've always got something to be anarchic about—your life is one long excitement.[8]

"And," she concluded, "anarchists are the most *charming* people!"[9] This self-professed affinity with anarchism, despite no formal commitments with anarchist groups, has been echoed by scholars who identify her outsider's status as a chief characteristic of her persona. As Wendy Mulford describes her, "Warner never had any time for the 'respectables'; she was a natural anarchist."[10] Beginning in September of 1936, Warner and Ackland made the first of several visits to Spain as part of their long campaign to support the Spanish people and the antifascist efforts to resist Franco's coup and dictatorship. Though ostensibly traveling on behalf of the British Communist Party, Warner would confess to Elizabeth Wade White her infatuation with the forthrightness of Spanish anarchists over and

---

[8] Schmidt and Warner, "Warner in Conversation," 35.
[9] Ibid.
[10] Wendy Mulford, introduction to *After the Death of Don Juan*, by Sylvia Townsend Warner (London: Virago, 1989), xvi.

against the timidity of the English.¹¹ "And you cannot imagine," Warner writes, "after this mealy-mouthed country, the pleasure of seeing an office with a large painted sign, Organisation for the Persecution of Fascists. [...] That beautiful directness is typical of anarchism, a most engaging type of thought, though I do not want to be an anarchist myself."¹² It is clear from this letter that Warner's hesitation about becoming an anarchist was not because of a political objection or any particular conviction about the superiority of communism. Rather, it was a matter of her practicality quashing her idealism; she concludes her letter with a grace note lauding anarchism: "The world is not yet worthy of it, but it ought to be the political theory of heaven."¹³

This small rhetorical flourish is not, I admit, a developed political theology, but it does signal the way that in her casual speech, "heaven" functions as a term for the unreal, fantastical, but still desirable future. Her fiction so often dances in that same sort of fantastical space, a space that is not blindly utopian but cautiously and melancholically imaginative. That she regards anarchism as a "theory of heaven" gives it a vaguely religious aura, and her warm prose lights on a political faith she associates with an aspirational future that is not entirely believable. The connection with Christianity that I investigate in Warner's fiction is closely related to the anarchy she entertains: she does not really believe in heaven or in practical anarchism, but she dwells in the possibilities of political alternatives to the given state of things. The attraction to anarchism Warner expressed in her letters from the 1930s is, on its surface, a playful and only semi-serious flirtation with a political vision that captured her imagination at the height of her involvement with the Spanish Civil War, but her exploration of alternative, liminal spaces was a preoccupation from her earliest fiction.

Her first novel, *Lolly Willowes; Or, The Loving Huntsman* (1926), predates by a decade Warner's Spanish Civil War experiences, but its intersection of Christianity, the state, and heteronormative marriage strictures aligns with many of the concerns of prominent anarchist voices of the early twentieth century.

---

[11] Janine Utell discusses the importance of this letter—the only time in Warner's collected letters that White is mentioned by name. See Utell, *Literary Couples and 20th-Century Life Writing: Narrative and Intimacy* (London: Bloomsbury Academic, 2020), 100. White was an American writer and Spanish Civil War activist who later had a relationship with Ackland. See Valentine Ackland, *For Sylvia: An Honest Account* (London: Chatto & Windus, 1985), 134; and, Peter Haring Judd, *The Akeing Heart: Passionate Attachments and Their Aftermath—Sylvia Townsend Warner, Valentine Ackland, Elizabeth Wade White* (New York: CreateSpace, 2013).
[12] Sylvia Townsend Warner, *Letters*, ed. William Maxwell (London: Chatto & Windus, 1982), 42.
[13] Ibid. Warner also adds in a postscript that the newspaper accounts of the war are misleading because journalists cannot tell the difference between communists and anarchists. Warner insists that the Spanish "are nearly all anarchists" (42).

Emma Goldman bulks large in this context, and her writings on church, state, and marriage forge a constellation of anarchist thought that resonates with Warner's interests.[14] Drawing on Mikhail Bakunin's *God and the State*—first published in 1882 but brought to prominence through Goldman's Mother Earth Publishing Association in 1916—Goldman wrote forcefully of the destructiveness of Christianity, particularly when it allied with state governance. "Anarchism is the only philosophy which brings to [humanity] the consciousness of [itself]; which maintains that God, the State, and society are non-existent, that their promises are null and void, since they can be fulfilled only through [humanity's] subordination," Goldman wrote, in "Anarchism: What It Really Stands For" (1911), adding a particularly vociferous denouncement of religious faith:

> Religion! How it dominates [humanity's] mind, how it humiliates and degrades [one's] soul. God is everything, man is nothing, says religion. But out of that nothing God has created a kingdom so despotic, so tyrannical, so cruel, so terribly exacting that naught but gloom and tears and blood have ruled the world since gods began. Anarchism rouses [us] to rebellion against this black monster. Break your mental fetters, says Anarchism.[15]

Enslavement to religion and bondage to the state manifests through many social contracts, but Goldman's ire was raised with special force by what she identified as the shackles of marriage: "soul-poverty and sordidness are the elements inherent in the marriage institution. The State and the Church approve of no other ideal, simply because it is the one that necessitates the State and Church control of men and women."[16] Goldman's critique of the church and state for colluding in the repression of individual liberties and human flourishing was central to her anarchism, and her extensive writings on marriage and what she called "the sex question" demonstrate the interconnectedness of state, church, and marital relationships in governing and disciplining society. As we will see throughout this chapter, *Lolly Willowes* exhibits very similar concerns, but Warner adds a queer dimension

---

[14] On Goldman's influence, see Shawn P. Wilbur, "'Let Us Not Overlook Vital Things': A Few Words of Introduction," in Emma Goldman, *Anarchy and the Sex Question: Essays on Women and Emancipation, 1896-1926*, ed. Shawn P. Wilbur (Oakland, CA: PM Press, 2016), 1-14. Archival evidence does not indicate whether Warner was familiar with Goldman or other anarchist writers and activists in the 1920s; her direct work with anarchism became far more explicit in the 1930s through her Spanish Civil War work.

[15] Emma Goldman, *Anarchism and Other Essays* (New York: Mother Earth Publishing Association, 1911), 58, 59.

[16] Emma Goldman, *Anarchy and The Sex Question: Essays on Women and Emancipation, 1896-1926*, ed. Shawn P. Wilbur (Oakland, CA: PM Press, 2016), 62.

that is almost entirely absent from Goldman's heteronormative conception of anarchist sexual ethics.

In Warner's political imagination, rejection of the enchanted state is closely aligned with resistance to heteronormativity, putting her fiction into dialogue with later theorizing of queer anarchism.[17] Jamie Heckert and Richard Cleminson, for instance, have argued that the collaboration of queer and anti-statist movements forge a valuable site of resistance to the co-opting and corrupting forces of racism, nationalism, and capitalism: "the transnational (or anti-national) and anti-racist aspects of anarchism may help us address the pressing challenges of 'homonationalism.'"[18] Heckert and Cleminson borrow here from Jasbir Puah's analysis of the pernicious influence of capitalist and nationalist ideologies on radical queer movements where instead of using silence, repression, and condemnation to stymie political alternatives, the twenty-first-century state in its late capitalist mode thwarts radicalism through absorption and co-option. "Homonationalism" refers to the myriad ways that formerly radical queer energies become assimilated into mainstream success narratives and thus lose their oppositional core.[19] By contrast with the homonationalist models of success, Gavin Brown advocates for a radical queer anarchism that maintains its dissidence:

> Queer is an ethical process by which (some) gender outlaws and sexual dissidents strive collectively to reclaim and develop our ability to determine the conditions of *our own* lives. It is about attempting to prefigure in the here and now, through form and process, aspects of life beyond capitalism, and beyond the limiting range of consumable identities that are currently sold to us.[20]

Brown's notion of "prefiguring" a life beyond capitalism by living in ways that anticipate a better future gives structure and weight to Warner's more fanciful and suggestive formulation of "the political theory of heaven." Brown's word choice echoes the political eschatology we have previously considered in D. H. Lawrence's late writings, but the emphasis on queer alternatives to

---

[17] For further development of queer anarchism that transgresses academic and popular modes, see C. B. Daring, J. Rogue, Deric Shannon, and Abbey Volcano, eds., *Queering Anarchism: Addressing and Undressing Power and Desire* (Edinburgh: AK Press, 2012).

[18] Jamie Heckert and Richard Cleminson, "Ethics, Relationships and Power: An Introduction," in *Anarchism and Sexuality: Ethics, Relationships and Power*, ed. Jamie Heckert and Richard Cleminson (London: Routledge, 2011), 8.

[19] See Jasbir K. Puar, *Terrorist Assemblages: Homonationalism in Queer Times* (Durham, NC: Duke University Press, 2007).

[20] Gavin Brown, "Amateurism and Anarchism in the Creation of Autonomous Queer Spaces," in *Anarchism and Sexuality: Ethics, Relationships and Power*, ed. Jamie Heckert and Richard Cleminson (London: Routledge, 2011), 203.

capitalism from within the current capitalist system provides another avenue for theopolitical imagination. Warner's fiction, as we will see, explores the liberating potential in ambivalent alternatives to Christianity, the enchanted state, and the co-opting force of capitalism by eluding both heteronormative and homonationalist entrapments. Unlike Brown's more robust concept of collective action, however, Warner's fiction remains speculative, tentative, equivocal, and ambiguous—a fact that has perplexed and fascinated many of her critics (especially those who long for more clear-cut declarations of her politics). Holding onto this ambivalence is crucial to the aesthetic and theopolitical vision of her work which imagines possibilities valuable for radical dissidence today.

My analysis of *Lolly Willowes* focuses on Warner's halfway commitment to anarchist politics and investigates how her fictional exploration of an in-between space that rejects both the oppressive status quo and the allures of full-blown utopianism produces a never-fully-resolved political position in dialogue with queer anarchism. As I have argued in my discussions of Woolf, Lawrence, and Waugh, this liminality and in-between-ness is something to celebrate. And, as with these other modernist novelists, Warner's writing forms a vital alternative to British civil religion. Warner is distinctive, however, in how her fiction enacts queer anarchism as political theology. Instead of Woolf's immersion in the radical ordinary as a challenge to nationalistic liturgies, Lawrence's political eschatology that combines local community with cosmic aspirations, or Waugh's cynical theology which critiques all social institutions that constrain human flourishing, Warner exploits the fissures within state power to imagine alternatives to repression that come from the failures of state control, rather than imagining an overthrow of those regimes. In Warner's fiction of the 1920s, she frequently returns to the theme of productive life emerging from within the dominance of the state while never quite imagining complete revolution, and *Lolly Willowes* offers the first of her attempts to produce fiction that challenges the Christian ideologies, institutions, and traditions that construct English national identity.

Many critics have discussed the ambivalence of Warner's texts, most notably Jane Garrity, who reads her fiction as a process of "encoding bi-location."[21] Among the several ways that Warner's position is "bi-located," according to Garrity,

---

[21] Garrity adopts the concept of "bi-location" from Warner's published lecture "Women as Writers," available in *The Gender of Modernism: A Critical Anthology*, ed. Bonnie Kime Scott (Bloomington, IN: Indiana University Press, 1990), 538–46. See Garrity, *Step-Daughters of England: British Women Modernists and the National Imaginary* (Manchester: Manchester University Press, 2003), 140. See also, Jane Garrity, "Encoding Bi-Location: Sylvia Townsend Warner and the Erotics of Dissimulation," in *Lesbian Erotics*, ed. Karla Jay (New York: New York University Press, 1995), 241–68.

is her complicated relationship with imperialism, nationalism, and sexuality, despite the ways Warner gestures toward broad-minded cosmopolitanism: "it is an English conception of space that arguably authorizes Warner's universalizing gesture, in which she implicitly positions herself as a citizen of the world."[22] Garrity's argument "demonstrates the links between this concept of expansiveness, sapphic modernism, and what national affiliation means for the interwar lesbian whose metaphorical mapping of space is suffused with both progressive ideas regarding culture and politics and the conventional notion that cultural purity resides in English geography."[23] What Garrity identifies are the ways that Warner's efforts to supersede provincial nationalism are still marked by primitivism and chauvinistic patriotism. Warner is radical in her politics and nonconformist in her sexuality, but Garrity detects in her fiction a lingering patriotic streak where Englishness colors even her most cosmopolitan and internationalist energies.

Instead of seeing this strain of nationalism in Warner's work as a problem to criticize or to excuse, I read it in direct relationship with the Christianity that she never quite sheds. Nationalism persists in her work, as does Christianity, and together these forces produce the kind of civil religion we have been considering throughout this book. What makes Warner distinctive, however, is the particularly anarchistic use she makes of her national and religious ambivalence. Her ambivalence is not only a matter of personal, privatized "faith" but extends to a distinctly political theology. Many of Warner's critics have examined her politics, especially with regard to her socialism/communism, her queerness, her Englishness, her feminism, and her anticolonialism.[24] There is no doubt that her literary writings—even when she wrote about antiquity, musicology, or elfin kingdoms—were attuned to the sociopolitical forces of her day. Yet even when critics have discussed her uneasy relationship with England, the role of the church has been sidelined as merely one of the many repressive institutions Warner shirked. I wish to bring nuance to this assessment of Warner's resistance to the church by highlighting the several ways that particular church practices were compounded with English nationalist and imperialist visions. Civil religion was every bit as much a target of Warner's animosity as it was for the

---

[22] Garrity, *Step-Daughters*, 144.
[23] Ibid.
[24] See Maud Ellmann, "*After the Death of Don Juan*: Sylvia Townsend Warner's Spanish Novel," *The Journal of the Sylvia Townsend Warner Society* 17, no. 2, (2017): 1–26; Melanie Micir, *The Passion Projects: Modernist Women, Intimate Archives, Unfinished Lives* (Princeton, NJ: Princeton University Press, 2019).

writers we have considered thus far. Though a case could be made for Warner's use of theopolitical tools just like the ones we have already seen—ordinariness against sacrificial militarism, community versus soul-deadening technocracy, and satirical agnosticism over institutional disciplinarity—I will be focusing on how Warner develops a queer theological anarchism while fruitfully embracing the condition of failure.

Shaping my reading of *Lolly Willowes* is J. Halberstam's account of alternative politics in *The Queer Art of Failure*: "Under certain circumstances failing, losing, forgetting, unmaking, undoing, unbecoming, not knowing may in fact offer more creative, more cooperative, more surprising ways of being in the world. Failing is something queers do and have always done exceptionally well."[25] Halberstam refers to the new possibilities afforded by failure as "wondrous anarchy," and that anarchic impulse is richly imagined by Warner's fiction—work that counteracts the domineering forces of civil religion.[26] In *Lolly Willowes*, Warner writes of Laura Willowes's struggles to assimilate into the English middle class with its compulsory heterosexuality and Christian moralizing—until she joins a secret coven of witches and forges a pact with Satan, her "loving huntsman," to explore the fractures within the dominant power structures established by a church united with the state. Rather than overturning such structures to create an alternative kingdom, counter-hegemony, or rival utopia, Warner's fiction meditates on the awkward, unbecoming, and anarchic spaces, inviting us to imagine the possibilities of this ambivalent anarchy.

Wondrous, Mystical, Lenten Anarchy

Halberstam's praise for "wondrous anarchy" builds on James C. Scott's extensive writings on anti-statist political activities, and particularly the power of "illegibility." To be legible to the state means that a subject can be disciplined, in the Foucauldian sense, controlled by institutional structures and effectively governed. Anarchism need not always be a wholly other, utopian alternative to the current sociopolitical order, but instead operates within and around the state's defined boundaries. With a wide range of examples and depth of knowledge about their functions, Scott articulates a set of lived practices that elude the notice of the state and are thus uncontrolled. In Prussia and Saxony during the late eighteenth

---

[25] J. Halberstam, *The Queer Art of Failure* (Durham, NC: Duke University Press, 2011), 2–3.
[26] Ibid., 3.

century, for instance, "scientific forestry" exemplifies a process of reduction, focus, and simplification that turned an otherwise-unmanageable natural space into a "resource" that could be measured, commodified, and contained. Though scientific forestry was never perfectly instituted, its theorization is, for Scott, highly revealing about the way disciplinary power functions. As he puts it:

> Certain forms of knowledge and control require a narrowing of vision. The great advantage of such tunnel vision is that it brings into sharp focus certain limited aspects of an otherwise far more complex and unwieldy reality. This very simplification, in turn, makes the phenomenon at the center of the field of vision more legible and hence more susceptible to careful measurement and calculation [...] making possible a high degree of schematic knowledge, control, and manipulation.[27]

What was true for forestry commodification has also been true of cities, where urban planning manifests efforts to make legible an otherwise-convoluted human habitation. By cataloguing specific moments throughout the history of the state and across a wide global range, Scott suggests that this typical process by which the state produces legible people might give opportunities for subversion. "An illegible society," Scott writes, "is a hindrance to any effective intervention by the state, whether the purpose of that intervention is plunder or public welfare."[28] Though this statement, and many of the examples he gives, shows his recognition that the state's purposes are not always nefarious, what he offers is a tool for creating alternative spaces within the state. Rather than suggesting that large-scale revolution and a total overthrowing of the governing power is essential for rescuing oppressed individuals and communities, Scott indicates that there may be ways to live well in those unseen, illegible spaces "outside [the state's] field of vision."[29] Such eccentricity—being outside the center of mainstream institutions—can be an exclusion turned against itself and mobilized into flourishing.[30] Illegibility as a political opportunity can be understood theologically as a way to elude the enchantments of state power. Simon Critchley has described a "mystical anarchism" with echoes of both Halberstam and Scott, where "politics is perhaps no longer, as it was in the so-called anti-globalization

---

[27] James C. Scott, *Seeing Like a State: How Certain Schemes to Improve the Human Condition Have Failed* (New Haven, CT: Yale University Press, 1998), 11.
[28] Ibid., 78.
[29] Ibid., 12.
[30] Halberstam has explored such eccentricity further through the concept of "wildness" as an epistemology. See Halberstam, *Wild Things: The Disorder of Desire* (Durham, NC: Duke University Press, 2020).

movement, a struggle for and with visibility. Resistance is about the cultivation of invisibility, opacity, anonymity, and resonance."[31] Critchley's view of resistance endorses a position that thrives within dominant power structures, subverting them but not establishing a new hegemony. Critchley theorizes what he calls "anarchic meta-politics"[32] and champions an anarchism that forms as "interstitial distance within the state."[33]

Warner's phrase "the political theory of heaven" might sound, perhaps, like a sort of rival utopia, an anarchist domain separated from immanent reality and available only in the most imaginary versions of space and time. But in Warner's fiction, there is thoughtful meditation on this form of nonbelief which is not a simplistic religion-without-church but rather an indictment of the church's complicity with the state. Writing in the wake of the First World War, Warner folds into her early novels subtle but trenchant criticisms of the ways that English society has been warped by a patriotic militarism nurtured by Christianity. Her characters frequently inhabit small, anarchic spaces that are not completely free from religion and nation, but they manage to thrive in broken, adjacent relationship with these forces.

Even Warner's first published book, a volume of poetry called *The Espalier* (1925), reveals her interest in political theology that responds to the ideological wreckage of the First World War. Though Warner has been included in several anthologies of women's writing from the First World War, she has not been widely recognized as a significant voice from that conflict.[34] Her youth during the war plus her far more significant involvement with and writing about the Spanish Civil War and the Second World War have led scholars to associate her far more with those later conflicts. Prior to her novels, however, Warner wrote poetry that was explicitly theopolitical and antiwar. In "The Lenten Offering," a poem from *The Espalier*, the speaker directly addresses Christ as someone in grief and aggrieved, confronting him with the image of the church's excluded ones. The speaker's ire is like a thorn growing in part of a churchyard reserved for those more abject than Christ who died by suicide or in still-birth. These deaths extend to a broader scope through a vision of a spear more powerful than all others and capable of greater wounds—presumably even deeper than

---

[31] Simon Critchley, "Mystical Anarchism," June 1, 2012. https://theanarchistlibrary.org/library/simon-critchley-mystical-anarchism
[32] Simon Critchley, *Infinitely Demanding: Ethics of Commitment, Politics of Resistance* (London: Verso, 2014), 88.
[33] Critchley, *Infinitely Demanding*, 111.
[34] See Margaret R. Higonnet, ed., *Lines of Fire: Women Writers of World War I* (New York: Plume, 1999).

the one in Christ's side. That spear wounds more deeply because it is sharpened by massive grief. All the world's sorrow, Warner suggests, amounts to more than the individual pain felt by the individual Christ. This confrontation with Christ during Lent is personal, but naming the church's castaways and the vastness of human suffering gives the poem its political weight, which is particularly felt in the second stanza which explicitly references the Great War and its aftermaths. The speaker offers Christ more nails which cannot be removed because they are "Forged at Krupp's, Creusot's, Vickers', and tipped with gold / Pen-nibs that signed the treaty of Versailles."[35]

With this stanza Warner makes her poem a confrontation not just with Christian pieties and church practices but with the ideology of civil religious militarism.[36] The unholy trinity of firms Warner names in this stanza was responsible for producing shells during the First World War, and their work was a classic case of war profiteering, selling to all sides regardless of nationality.[37] The poem's ironies are reminiscent of trench poetry by combatants such as Siegfried Sassoon, but Warner's focus is less on the injured and angry combatant than on the whole social order being scourged and afflicted by the institutions of militarism—church, capital, and state.

Within Warner's oeuvre, "The Lenten Offering" is a bit unusual in the forthrightness of its cynicism about wartime ideologies. Though she did not undergo a phase of ardent support at the start of the war, as was common among many of her contemporaries, she also was not a committed pacifist (like Woolf) or repulsed by this particular war (like Lawrence). "The Lenten Offering" supplies a biting response to Warner's earliest piece of published writing, an essay called "Behind the Firing Line: Some Experiences in a Munition Factory" that she wrote for *Blackwood's Magazine* in February 1916. Published anonymously by "A Lady Worker," this essay described her experiences as a munition-worker modifying shells on the night shift at a weapons factory. The essay is more informative and autobiographical than argumentative, and its leading edge is the arduousness of the work rather than any real concern about the ideologies of military industry. Her descriptions, however, reveal her reaching for church language and religious imagery to make sense of the factory life. She refers to the

---

[35] Sylvia Townsend Warner, *New Collected Poems*, ed. Claire Harman (Manchester: Manchester University Press, 2008), 32.
[36] Matarasso succinctly describes the poem's targets, writing that it "compares the instruments of Christ's Passion with the inhumanities inflicted in turn by Church, arms manufacturers and politicians" ("A Recurrent Modulation," 49).
[37] See Jonathan A. Grant, *Rulers, Guns, and Money: The Global Arms Trade in the Age of Imperialism* (Cambridge, MA: Harvard University Press, 2007).

nightly routine of a cleaning man dousing their stations with his watering-pot as an "instrument of aspersion," connecting this factory work to the Christian ritual of being sprinkled with water during baptismal remembrance while also wittily invoking the more modern, negative connation of "aspersion" as harm.[38] She describes the start of her shift as a nightmare vision of judgment day worthy, of panels by Hieronymus Bosch: "Small stertorous trains trotted about in the darkness, like good housewives going to market on the Last Day: and once a crane descended on me, silently, with the deadly certainty of the Devil who had got me at last."[39] She imagines the shells as "Quakerish instruments of death"[40] while the factory of women laboring at their machines becomes church-like: "Priests of a new rite, they stand before a thousand clattering alters."[41] There is little in the essay to suggest that this religious language is intended as criticism of Christianity. Rather, it seems to be the water she swims in, an unexamined environment shaping her thought. That her autobiographical writing at this stage can be so indebted to Christian imagery suggests how thoroughly Warner was immersed in a religious world, and even though the underlying meaning of her imagery may be unintended, it clearly associates Christianity with the war effort. "The Lenten Offering" signals a sharp turn in her thinking where wartime service on behalf of the nation and for the profit of the armaments industry can no longer be casually bathed in religious language. The satire of the poem shows the distance she has crossed since the war, and it combatively responds to Christian, capitalist, and militarist ideologies that converged through religiously inflected nationalism. In her later fictional efforts she would introduce queer themes more fully, adding heteronormativity to the list of oppressive forces that construct English identity through civil religion.

Laura's Interstitial Distance

That insidious fusion of Christianity, capitalism, militarism, and nationalism— along with heterosexism—is crucial to Warner's first novel, *Lolly Willowes*, though unlike "The Lenten Offering," she handles these elements with a light touch and a veil of ambiguity. Critical discussion around the novel has focused

---

[38] Sylvia Townsend Warner, "Behind the Firing Line: Some Experiences in a Munition Factory," *Blackwood's Magazine* 199 (1916): 200.
[39] Ibid., 198.
[40] Ibid., 195.
[41] Ibid., 202.

less on these particular political dimensions and rarely dealt seriously with its theology.[42] Warner's engagement with religion does not conform to expected patterns of post-secular mysticism. Instead of a quest for unorthodox spirituality or enlightened transcendence achieved on humanistic terms, what Warner depicts in *Lolly Willowes* is an inextricable immersion in Christianity as a civic force that constitutes citizenship and upholds the heteronormative matrix. Warner's novel articulates the conundrum of being caught in civil religion while seeking alternative, ambivalent spaces that are illegible to the church and state and beyond the heterosexual marriage economy. *Lolly Willowes* is an anarchist novel that offers a political theology as resistance to the ideological network Warner satirized in "The Lenten Offering."

Scholarship on *Lolly Willowes* has typically focused on its formal playfulness and queer/feminist politics—which is understandable given the book's fantastical turns and forthright satire of patriarchy.[43] Our protagonist Laura Willowes finds herself aging past her years for respectable marriageability, a premise that creates much of the satirical comedy in the novel's first sections. For reasons never quite explained, the last third of the novel swings wildly away from its opening as Laura leaves behind her family's strictures to embrace spinsterhood in the village of Great Mop—only to learn that the town is thoroughly populated by witches and warlocks. Reflecting back on her writing career, Warner somewhat disparagingly said that "[fantasy] put its ugly face out in *Lolly Willowes*" but the disfigurement was inevitable, since fully realistic stories held little attraction for her.[44] Later critics have generally not shared Warner's judgment, finding instead that fantasy is essential to its politics and experimental form. Jane Marcus argues that fantasy animates the novel's "imaginary mythological wild space" as a "response to the phallocentric city,"[45] and Jane Garrity likewise applauds

---

[42] Pericles Lewis, for example, mentions her only in passing as a "mildly avant-garde feminist" whose seemingly conventional forms keep her at the margins of a strongly defined "modernism" (*Religious Experience*, 18). Warner also explores "religious experience" in ways that do not align with Woolf, James, etc.

[43] See Gerd Bjørhovde, "Transformation and Subversion as Narrative Strategies in Two Fantasy Novels of the 1920s: Sylvia Townsend Warner's *Lolly Willowes* and Virginia Woolf's *Orlando*," in *Essays in Honour of Kristian Smidt*, ed. Peter Bilton, Lars Hartveit, Stig Johansson, Arthur O. Sandved, Bjøn Tysdahl (Oslo: University of Oslo Press, 1986), 213–24; Meyrav Koren-Kuik, "From *Lolly Willowes* to *Kingdoms of Elfin*: The Poetics of Socio-Political Commentary in Sylvia Townsend Warner's Fantasy Narratives," in *Baptism of Fire: The Birth of the Modern British Fantastic in World War I*, ed. Janet Brennan Croft (Altadena, CA: Mythopoeic Press, 2015), 245–62; Peter Swaab, "The Queerness of *Lolly Willowes*," *Journal of the Sylvia Townsend Warner Society* 11, no. 1 (2010): 29–52.

[44] Schmidt and Warner, "Warner in Conversation," 36.

[45] Jane Marcus, "A Wilderness of One's Own: Feminist Fantasy Novels of the Twenties: Rebecca West and Sylvia Townsend Warner," in *Women Writers and the City: Essays in Feminist Literary Criticism*, ed. Susan Merrill Squier (Knoxville, TN: University of Tennessee Press, 1984), 136.

"Warner's slyness" which queers the narrative through "artful refusal, in essence, to play it straight with readers."[46] That the novel is coy and queer about its ultimate "message" has not prevented it from being labeled a "declaration of women's rights" or "manifesto" and other such epithets.[47] But, as Jacqueline Shin argues, such a reading "flattens Warner's sly, slippery, and perverse text by forcing it into the genre of the manifesto," often disappointing readers who hope for unambiguous messages rather than what Shin calls a "narrative witchcraft" that "embodies a far more subtle politics and a more deeply nuanced challenge to the unequal power relations engendered by patriarchy" than has been noted.[48]

While Warner's sly narrative witchcraft is certainly one of the tantalizing features of her novel's exploration of gender and sexuality, this witchcraft is also vital to how she engages with the forces of militant nationalism. Jennifer Poulos Nesbitt has shown how the novel constructs domestic spaces that Laura subverts, not only in defiance of patriarchy but of nationalist ideologies. Nesbitt, drawing on Partha Chaterjee, observes that "a naturalized female domesticity symbolizes the essential nation," and claims: "*Lolly Willowes* places Laura's decision to rebel in this context of shifting gender roles and geopolitics, although she doesn't realize the connection between the latter issue and her own oppression until later in the novel" while working on behalf of the war effort.[49] Nesbitt points to a moment late in Part 1 where Laura is binding parcels at a depot, serving her country during wartime in a thankless and unheroic place decorated with recruiting posters that fade throughout the war. Laura witnesses the discoloration of the posters and refuses to accept the "cheap symbolism they provoked."[50] For Nesbitt, the particular images on the posters—Britannia in a scarlet cloak and a "ruddy young man and his Spartan mother" (*LW*, 63)—manage to "elide the two meanings of domestic" while signifying that "as embodiments of the nation, women demand sacrifice, but they are also passive objects unified bodily with the territory to be defended."[51] In the space of the depot, but also in the purely domestic spaces of the home, the seemingly private life of this woman is embedded

---

[46] Garrity, *Step-Daughters*, 151.
[47] Robert L. Caserio, *The Novel in England: 1900–1950, History and Theory* (New York: Twayne, 1999), 225. See also Marion Gibson, who writes, "One way of reading Laura's witchcraft is simply as feminist empowerment, but there is also a specifically lesbian subtext," in *Witchcraft: The Basics* (New York: Routledge, 2018), 149.
[48] Jacqueline Shin, "*Lolly Willowes* and the Arts of Dispossession," *Modernism/modernity* 16, no. 4 (November 2009): 710.
[49] Jennifer Poulos Nesbitt, "Footsteps of Red Ink: Body and Landscape in *Lolly Willowes*," *Twentieth-Century Literature* 49, no. 4 (2003): 452, 454.
[50] Sylvia Townsend Warner, *Lolly Willowes; Or, The Loving Huntsman* (New York: NYRB, 1999), 64. Hereafter cited in text *LW*.
[51] Nesbitt, "Red Ink," 454.

in nationalist ideologies that manifest through small, local forms. Warner's twist on this moment, however, is important. Laura feels deeply equivocal about her patriotism, resisting the allures of "cheap symbolism" from the sight of fading recruitment posters but also reminding herself that violent sacrifice is being conducted in her name: "But blood was scarlet as ever, and she believed that, however despairing her disapproval, that blood was being shed for her" (*LW*, 64). That formulation—"being shed for her"—alludes to Christian language of salvific death and shows the enchantments of civil religion at work in Laura's midst. She continues working in this condition of ideological and emotional ambivalence, right until she hears the celebrations erupt on Armistice Day when she collapses with influenza. It is unclear at this point in the story how Laura might escape her conditions, but her wartime service and its toll on her body reveals one of the many ways that Warner constructs partial detachment from ideologies that we cannot entirely avoid. The internal struggle that Laura feels about patriotism and militarism is an inkling of the queer failure that Halberstam theorizes, a struggle that will grow larger throughout the novel as Laura is increasingly seen "failing, losing, forgetting, unmaking, undoing, unbecoming, not knowing" while she embraces "more surprising ways of being in the world."[52]

Among the elements that establish the straight, square, conventional world that Laura inherits is her family's participation in the British civil religion that helps animate mainstream society. Early in the novel, Warner describes the Willowes family's failure to become eminent, with the modest exception of "great-great-aunt Salome" who "had made the nearest approach to fame" because her "puff-paste had been commended by King George III" (*LW*, 10). Civil religion appears in Salome's even longer lasting product, her "prayer-book, with the services for King Charles the Martyr and the Restoration of the Royal Family and the welfare of the House of Hanover" (*LW*, 10–11). These services, the narrator quips, are "a nice example of impartial piety" (*LW*, 11). A modern family of little public importance thus clings to the trivial achievements of a distant relative whose mere embroideries at the edges of royalty are cherished as heroic and glorious. The portrayal of the Willowes is comic, but within the comedy is the serious recognition of how Christianity and the state powerfully combine. Prayer services for "King Charles the Martyr" are politically and theologically loaded.[53] Perhaps great-great-aunt Salome's liturgy was a form of

---

[52] Halberstam, *Queer Art*, 2–3.
[53] For the fullest account of the political theology of King Charles and his cult, see Andrew Lacey, *The Cult of King Charles the Martyr* (Woodbridge, Suffolk: Boydell Press, 2003).

peacemaking between rival visions of monarchical rule, but it seems just as likely to be equal opportunity power grabbing. This critical and satirical portrayal of civil religion in the Willowes family creates an undercurrent that will remain strong as Laura explores alternatives to the heteronormative matrix.

Very little space in the narrative is devoted to hot forms of civil religion. Laura's collapse on Armistice Day is significant but not underlined with any full account of the celebrations, and her departure from London to the rural retreat of Great Mop diminishes any chance of military commemorations in state churches. But subtler forms of civil religion emerge from the periphery of Laura's life as characters around her enact Christian practices that serve a social function. Christianity is not practiced with much ardor by the elder members of the Willowes family nor does it seem to intrude much into their relatively minimal thought or speech. It does, however, remain a constant presence in small ways that shape their activity, producing for them the kind of stabilizing force and provincial displays of Englishness we have seen in fiction by Woolf, Lawrence, and Waugh. Near the end of Part 1 of *Lolly Willowes*, there is a time shift of fifteen years that signals how the Willowes family has developed a pattern of living in different places depending on the season. They stay in a hotel at a health resort in springtime because the English spring can be unpredictable, and any uncertainty, "let alone the uncertainty of a Christian Easter, made lodgings unsatisfactory at that time of year" (*LW*, 60). Their discomforts are trivial and their obstacles to leisure few, but so long as Laura's brother Henry finds "a little unsophisticated golf and float-fishing" and her sister-in-law Caroline can read a bit while her children swim, they can enjoy their springtime retreat (*LW*, 60). Golfing, fishing, reading, swimming—and the certainty of a "normal" Easter—create the simple pastimes that confirm their existence and make them English people of a certain class. This regimen of family life also operates as a perverse parody of alignment with the natural order. Much of the novel, especially in Part 3, demonstrates Laura's mystical, bodily alignment with nature, and the Willowes family's seasonal migrations are middle-class capitalist perversions of that natural patterning, a turn to boorish physical comforts rather than an immersion in the mysteries of the primordial ecological order. Their family unit is rigidly heterosexual and self-contained, and their middle-class pastimes reproduce the conventionality of their relationships in a public form. Self-presenting as the kind of people who have taste in lodging, travel, and church, the Willowes family displays its Christianity as a public identity that builds a solid English nation in its local form with little regard for the underlying natural rhythms of the world or for the collective implications of their mundane political activity.

Much as the family's Christianity and patriotism are small and dispassionate, Laura's disconnection from her family's rituals is minor and ambivalent rather than hotly revolutionary. Early on, there are little hints that Laura is not fitting in, not only because she is the unmarried relation, but because she prefers the summer holidays to the springtime, which the narrator explains parenthetically: "the Easter holidays she never cared about, as she had a particular dislike for palms" (*LW*, 61). If the rest of the Willowes family establishes themselves within ritual patterns of English living sustained by the church, Laura continually finds herself disjointed from their patterns. Disliking palms at Easter is, the novel slyly suggests, part of the slippery slope that puts one at odds with the resurrected Christ. Her preference for summer is not because of its greater freedoms but for a widening vista of her desire. Returning to London after the summer holiday always brings her regret, and their ride back to the city in the wagonette has her reflecting on the cravings for walking and finding "strange herbs" that went unfulfilled (*LW*, 61). Her usefulness in her station as unmarried caretaker keeps her bound, and this small moment near the end of Part 1 hints at what will emerge for her, breaking free from this version of family life and into a world where solitary walks in search of unknown flora are normal habits for witches integrating themselves with the natural order. The contrast between the distasteful Christian palms and the vegetation of witchcraft shows yearnings that Laura cannot yet satisfy. As so often happens in the novel, Laura enters an in-between space, unable to fully name, much less claim, her true desires but wishing for some alternative to the surrounding Christian culture. She cannot completely free herself from Englishness or Christianity, but her thoughts, feelings, and actions create little spaces of interstitial distance from these dominating forces.

One of the clearest signs that Laura has found interstitial distance from the power of British civil religion comes as she realizes that she can be "rooted in peace" by reorienting her relationship with all the institutions that comprise her world (*LW*, 136). Warner's narrator explains that Laura knows she has changed, "ceased to triumph mentally over her tyrants, and rallied herself no longer with the consciousness that she had outraged them by coming to live at Great Mop" (*LW*, 136). This prior attitude, Laura realizes, was merely reactionary and oppositional—the sort of simplistic contrarianism that an anarchist mode avoids. Instead of acting merely to outrage the keepers of tradition, Laura begins to develop alternative spaces to thrive. Ceasing to be antagonistic to power does not, however, mean that Laura is quiescent, nor does she overlook the damage perpetuated by hostile institutions. Forgiveness for the injury caused by her family and its culture is out of the question, not only because of who Laura is but because of her political stance. She recognizes that these were not individual sins but evidence of systemic injustice, and she lists them off in a litany that Jane Marcus has described as "an exorcism."[54] Her list includes "Society, the Law, the Church, the History of Europe, the Old Testament, great-great-aunt Salome and her prayer-book, the Bank of England, Prostitution, the Architect of Apsley Terrace, and half a dozen other useful props of civilization" (*LW*, 136). These "props of civilization" are the essence of civil religion, combining legal, ecclesial, familial, and scriptural powers into one devastating force.

Resisting Banal Christian Nationalism

Inescapable Christian culture overtly appears in a few crucial moments during the brief section on the war years, a section noticeable for how it shows the intrusion of war but also its re-containment through social ritual. The war erupts during the Willowes family's summer holiday routine, and we learn from the parish magazine that "the vicar had scarcely left East Bingham when war was declared" which the Willowes feel is to his credit, since he "was made of stouter stuff than they" and refuses to give up his holiday because of the war (*LW*, 62). The only news source mentioned is the "parish magazine," and the essential public reaction is that of the vicar, rather than a political or military figure. His stoicism, and refusal to let a little thing like global war interrupt his holiday, sets a tone for the next several pages where Warner tours the various reactions of the Willowes to the war. Warner's depiction of the war is brusque: Henry and Caroline's eldest daughter Fancy marries, has a daughter, and becomes a widow when her husband is killed in combat—all in the span of a single paragraph. Fancy's story is the stuff of a splashier First World War novel that Warner never fully develops, and we learn in passing that she works with munitions "in a high-explosive shed" and later "drew on a pair of heavy gauntlet gloves and went to France to drive motor lorries" (*LW*, 63). But our titular character is trapped in something more mundane; "the war," we are told, "had no such excitements for Laura" (*LW*, 63). On Armistice Day, while the rest of London celebrates in the background, Laura collapses from influenza—a casualty of the 1919 pandemic—but this physical symptom of global crisis is as close as she comes to the adventures of wartime.

[54] Marcus, "A Wilderness of One's Own," 154.

Narratives that disconnect from the war and focus on the mundane are familiar forms of antiwar protest in modernism, but Warner suggests that stoicism and a related disconnection from political forces is just as ideologically freighted as more heated expressions. Well before the famous breaking point in *Lolly Willowes* where our protagonist falls in with Satan, the novel describes another important breakage: the rupture of the First World War and its effect on the Willowes family. The narrator walks us through Laura's realization that her family only appears to be heroic in their unflappability when really they are manifesting another version of Christian-inspired patriotism. Laura observes in Henry and Caroline "a demure Willowes-like satisfaction in the family tree that had endured the gale with an unflinching green heart" and feels familial pride: "she admired the stolid decorum which had mastered four years of disintegration, and was stolid and decorous still" (*LW*, 65). The repetition of "stolid" reinforces its constancy but also suggests it is a façade, a war record built not of service but of a determined and studious lack of affect. When asked by a woman in the country whether the Willowes go to the roof or the cellar during air raids, Henry replies: "We do neither [...] We stay where we are" (*LW*, 65). At first, Laura feels a "thrill [...] when she heard this statement of the Willowes mind" due to its air of deliberate insouciance (*LW*, 65). But she soon detects something amiss in Henry's response, an intuition that what appears on the surface as a kind of toughness or a Woolf-like "indifference" to patriotic, militaristic allures is in fact something quite similar to more recognizable displays of hot nationalism. Warner's free indirect narration shows Laura rethinking her reaction and associating the Willowes's determined inaction as part and parcel with civil religion at its hottest: "Was it nothing more than the response of her emotions to other old and honorable symbols such as the trooping of the colors and the fifteenth chapter of Corinthians, symbols too old and too honorable to have called out her thoughts?" (*LW*, 65–6). The stolidity of the Willowes family is another version of flag-waving nationalism, like ceremonies uniting military pageantry with adoration of royalty. The fifteenth chapter of First Corinthians meditates on the resurrected Christ whose triumph initiates the bodily resurrection of all people, and its famous verses, "O death, where is thy sting? O grave, where is thy victory?", which feature prominently in Christian burial rites, echo unspoken in Laura's mind, combining the postwar mourning rituals with her family's ritual stoicism.[55] What is particularly intriguing about this moment is how different it appears from the many familiar texts of modernism where war produces a social

---

[55] 1 Cor. 15:55-57.

rift. Rather than the traumatic corridor of Woolf's *To the Lighthouse* (1927) or the persecution of Lawrence's "Nightmare" chapter in *Kangaroo* (1923) or the fragmentation and constriction of Jones's *In Parenthesis* (1937), Warner exposes the folly of war through her characters' willful unflappability.

The Willowes family models in a paradigmatic fashion the ideological banality theorized by Michael Billig, where an "unwaved flag" is as potent and formational as more ostentatious displays of patriotism, and its presence is more insidious by being seemingly inert.[56] Laura's brother and his wife have a firmly established pattern of life set to rhythms based in church attendance and attitudes governed by literalist biblicism. Sundays begin with Henry winding their household clock "till only the snouts of the leaden weights were visible, drooping sullenly over the abyss of time" (*LW*, 47). Gay Wachman notes the importance of British Christianity in this scene and how "its deadly tedium is crystallized in a creepily banal moment."[57] Laura feels both wonder and dread as the Willowes family winds clocks and attends church in a clockwork manner, creating patterns that attempt to neutralize existential concerns through regularity, simplicity, and stoicism.

While the family moves in sync like the "leaden weights" of their clock, we catch a glimpse of Caroline's religiosity that contrasts with Laura's (*LW*, 47). Caroline, we are told, "was a religious woman. Resolute, orderly and unromantic, she would have made an admirable Mother Superior" (*LW*, 48). Like an abbess without a convent, Caroline carries herself with strict austerity and presumes that her family will maintain a similar orderliness. This belief in order, Laura learns, comes from values Caroline sees as biblical. Laura compliments the neatly folded clothing in Caroline's drawers, and Caroline responds that she is following a biblical example: "the grave-clothes were folded in the tomb" (*LW*, 48). This brief comment passes between the two women quite uncomfortably as a flare-up of theological conviction that threatens the static banality of their community. Never again do they speak of this moment or of Caroline's hidden convictions, but what becomes clear from this interaction is that the family's banal, clockwork Christianity is a force of cultural order and common ground shared by the less biblically minded members alongside Caroline's more thoroughgoing fundamentalism. This tiny scene of disruption transitions rapidly into a reminder about the family's legacy with great-great-aunt Salome's prayer-book and the

---

[56] Billig, *Banal Nationalism*, 6.
[57] Gay Wachman, *Lesbian Empire: Radical Crosswriting in the Twenties* (New Brunswick, NJ: Rutgers University Press, 2001), 76.

Christian rituals that preserve their family through the generations. Whatever the personal beliefs of any given member on a spectrum that appears to have Laura at one end and Caroline at the other, there is a generalized acceptance of "religion" as a sustaining force of family tradition and social respectability. Caroline is the figurehead of Willowes family piety, and her role as maternal purveyor of faith reinforces the sense that English Christianity is inextricable from heteronormative family patterns. Laura's unease with the entire matrix of her family's beliefs—their stoic response to war, their cultural Christianity, and their heterosexism—is an unease with the version of nationalism that the Willowes practice in the mundane and everyday.

Family practices, however, are not merely the private workings of a household shaped by religious pieties; they are inextricable from banal nationalism. In many subtle ways, the construction of "Englishness" forms through the social order of the Willowes's regular, weekly activities. At church services, Laura detects in her sister-in-law's practices the infusion of Christian ritual with national importance: "Religion was great-great-aunt Salome's prayer-book which Caroline held in her gloved hands. Religion was a strand in the Willowes life, and the prayer-book was the outward sign of it. But it was also the outward sign of the puff pastry which had been praised by King George III" (*LW*, 49). The continual reminder that steady religious practice involves outward appearance rather than inward belief shows how these activities are building social structures rather than leading to personal transcendence. Just as frequent are the small reminders that the family's identity is forged in Christian practices recognized by the state. Religion "is" the prayer-book famously made by their great-great-aunt, a book that is carried publicly to church in order to demonstrate a visible piety. Warner's curious formulation, though, is to say that religion "was also the outward sign of the puff pastry." Public rituals can be entered into by carrying your mildly famous relative's prayer-book to church, but that prayer-book not only trumpets one's piety but reminds others of your familial connection to royal favor. Civil religion functions in obvious, flamboyant ways during coronations or military funerals, but Warner teases out a more subtle, quiet, and banal way that seemingly private rituals become publicly meaningful, as an object like the prayer-book signifies Christian belief but also, more importantly, patriotic worthiness.

If those family practices signify patriotic Christianity in action at the small, local level, then Laura's separation from those practices can be understood as her inchoate gestures towards an alternative theology of queer anarchism. While Caroline holds the signifying prayer-book in church, the narrator reminds us of Laura's distance from her sister-in-law, and how "she was not even religious enough to speculate towards irreligion" (*LW*, 49). Laura goes with Caroline to church whenever Caroline requests, which means that she is frequently in services throughout the week—an echo of Harman's description of Warner being not very religious but "having a great deal of church." By consistently attending church services while not being committed to a faith, she occupies an in-between space. In Part 2 of the novel, Laura, age forty-seven, separates herself from her brother Henry's household and moves to Great Mop in the Chilterns, a rural setting she finds in a guidebook and that calls to her from some deep and inexplicable place. She feels discontentment in London with her family, knowing that "once again she was in for it. What It was exactly, she would have found hard to say" (*LW*, 72). Something indeterminate from the natural world calls to her, and she feels that the patterns of life established by the Willowes and sustained by patriotic Christianity are no longer tenable for her. Remaining in London with her family was a foothold into heterosexuality, a gesture toward some unseen future with a husband of her own—or at least a substantial role within heteronormative conventions. Claiming her own living space beyond her family's purview separates her from their economy, religion, and relational structures.

In moving to Great Mop, Laura stages her first big revolt from her family, but this move is not a plunge into some newfound utopia. As Heather Love has noted, much of Warner's fiction involves a "mixture of utopianism and disappointment" that "link[s] revolutionary longing to [a] history of queer longing" and "explores the dark affects that fuel social change."[58] What Laura finds, initially, are a series of little differences that amount to a minor revolution, and through much of Part 2, Warner sprinkles breadcrumbs that lead to the coming witchery. In passing through town in the evening, she hears laughing "from the taproom of the Lamb and Flag" where men are "sitting silent and abstracted with their mugs before them" (*LW*, 115). Laura senses something unusual about this behavior, but she is also struck by a strange sensation of wonder though "she was content to remain outside the secret, whatever it was" (*LW*, 117). This is a telling moment, well before the conclusion where Laura finds her ambivalent, interstitial space. Being close to an alternative community yet somehow still "outside [its] secret" enables her to feel contentment even without full belonging and thus gestures toward her latent anarchism. Her ambiguous position and indefinable emotions suggest the liminality José Esteban Muñoz

---

[58] Heather Love, *Feeling Backward: Loss and the Politics of Queer History* (Cambridge, MA: Harvard University Press, 2007), 131.

describes wherein "queerness is always on the horizon" blending "futurity and hope."[59] Laura has an inexpressible longing for an unclear goal and she inhabits a space in the village that is separate both from her former family life and from her newfound context in the town.

Warner's choice of the "Lamb and Flag" evokes religious nationalism at the mundane level of the local pub. The banner-waving *agnus Dei* comes from the book of Revelation, and its common English version shows a white lamb carrying the flag of St. George. Though the sign above a pub is clearly an "unwaved flag," it nonetheless suggests the religiously fueled imperialism of the Crusades and the apocalyptic imagery of the Bible. This symbol of militant civil religion is surprising in Great Mop, given what we learn of its satanic population, but the Lamb and Flag reminds us that the village is no simple utopia. Instead, Warner offers a conventional English village with churches and patriotic-sounding pubs, but she layers these conventions into an array of little differences that show alternatives within the conventional. To the casual observer—the tourist, say, or even the political official—this village of Great Mop is perfectly in keeping with the British mainstream. But for its inhabitants, Great Mop offers a thriving counterculture that is invisible, or in James Scott's terms "illegible," to the broader culture. The men in the Lamb and Flag who are not jovially building the nation by celebrating in the pub but instead keep a strangely austere distance from its expected conviviality are living in interstices, still present in the pub with their pints but seeming "abstracted" from the common rituals.

Many critics have read Laura's move to Great Mop as the victorious entrance into a better life—a "total fantasy gratification," as Gillian Beer puts it, which "is, uniquely among her works, about successful escape."[60] Such readings, however, oversimplify the ambiguous relationship that Laura has with witchcraft, Great Mop, and that supposed "escape." As she watches the men inside the Lamb and Flag pub, she is intrigued by their community but is most certainly not a full part of it. Likewise, her landlady Mrs. Leak, who we discover is among the town's prominent witches, is not a close friend or companion. There is a slight distance between Laura and the rest of the

---

[59] José Esteban Muñoz, *Cruising Utopia: The Then and There of Queer Futurity* (New York: New York University Press, 2009), 11.

[60] Gillian Beer, "Sylvia Townsend Warner: 'The Centrifugal Kick,'" in *Women Writers of the 1930s: Gender, Politics and History*, ed. Maroula Joannou (Edinburgh: Edinburgh University Press, 1999), 76. Diane Purkiss even claims the novel over-simplistically associates witches with anti-patriarchy. See Purkiss, *The Witch in History: Early Modern and Twentieth-Century Representations* (New York: Routledge, 1996), 40.

town, much as there was slight distance between Laura and the mainstream, heteronormative, patriotic Christianity of her family. It is with her family that people first suggest she may have leanings toward witchery. When Laura announces her intention to move to Great Mop and leave her brother's family behind, the Willowes have an array of reactions, and Henry, we are told, "rallied Laura" and decides that "at Great Mop she would start hunting for catnip again" and would "become the village witch" (*LW*, 91). Henry's dismissiveness and mocking humor are the first concrete statement about what eventually happens, and Laura's response to his jest is affirmative: "How lovely!" (*LW*, 91). The thought of Laura becoming a witch is played as a joke that Laura embraces by accepting its whimsy without its sting. Such is the off-balance, half-mocking, half-serious tone of the entire novel and of Warner's handling of the political theology of its conclusion.

Wishing to Be in Her Coven

Laura's transformation into a witch is formally marked by a sentence constructed in mock legalese: "She, Laura Willowes, in England, in the year 1922, had entered into a compact with the Devil" (*LW*, 155). That compact, described like a legal contract, emerges through Laura's participation in a Witches' Sabbath and her changing relationship with her nephew Titus, whose intrusion into the village of Great Mop signals a resurgence of patriarchy that Laura successfully routs. There is an experiential and action-oriented dimension to Laura's conversion, but throughout the novel there are also reminders that Laura has cultivated an intellect capable of resisting the patriotic Christian mainstream. The hints of Laura's intellectual life and Warner's own acknowledged source material for constructing her village of witches indicate crucial ways that *Lolly Willowes* displays learned theopolitical discourse.[61] Through her intellectually complex response to the satanic culture of Great Mop, Laura maintains her resistance to both the heteronormative mainstream of her family and the seemingly "liberated" subculture of witchery. Her ambivalence helps her hold fast to the interstitial distance from all the forces that make demands on her, becoming a continued resource for her anarchist position.

---

[61] Claire Harmon recounts a story that when Warner dined with Virginia Woolf sometime after the publication of *Lolly Willowes*, "Woolf asked how she knew so much about witches. 'Because I am one,' Sylvia replied" (*Warner: A Biography*, 66). This anecdote, unfortunately, is unverified (*Warner: A Biography*, 332n59).

Laura herself is theologically educated in the self-taught way of a woman of her time. Well before her move, when Laura is a young woman alone in her father's library, she is given free rein to read what she pleases and begins her education about witches. The first mention of witches comes early in Part 1 when we learn—breezily and in passing—that Laura has been reading freely in her father's library, aware that "the conversation at local tea-parties and balls never happened to give her an opportunity of mentioning anything that she learnt from Locke on the Understanding or Glanvil on Witches" (*LW*, 25). John Locke's *An Essay Concerning Human Understanding* (1689), with its philosophy of the *tabula rasa*, corresponds to Laura's condition as something like a blank slate, soaking in her family's culture and the intellectual life, but Locke also attempts logical proof for God's existence that ironically juxtaposes Laura's alternative religious awakening. Locke insists that reason can lead to "certain and evident truth" and "that there is an eternal, most powerful, and most knowing Being; which any one will please to call God, it matters not."[62] Locke's proofs for the existence of God (or at least some omnipresent, omnipotent, and omniscient Being) exude a religious certainty that the novel undermines, and what Laura absorbs is his pursuit of self-knowledge. Her break with her family, move to Great Mop, and eventual satanic conversion all emerge from considering her own inner constitution, and the sly irony is that, contrary to Locke, Laura's self-discovery leads not to God but to Satan.

Coupling Locke with Glanvil undercuts Locke's theology and further demonstrates Laura's erudition and association with a theology of witchcraft to counter the Christianity of her cultural context. The passing reference to Glanvil early in the novel returns with greater force in Part 3 when Laura feels herself disconnected from the mildly unsociable townspeople of Great Mop. Mrs. Leak introduces neighbors to Laura dispassionately, "rather like the Witch of Endor calling up old Samuel" (*LW*, 115). The image of Samuel with the Witch of Endor appears on the frontispiece to Joseph Glanvil's *Saducismus Triumphatus, or, Full and Plain Evidence Concerning Witches and Apparitions: In Two Parts: The First Treating of Their Possibility, The Second of Their Real Existence*, written in 1681, which Laura was presumably reading.[63] Much like her ironic treatment of Locke, Warner nods to Glanvil with a wink. Glanvil's intention for writing about witches—strenuously arguing for their existence to refute disbelieving

---

[62] John Locke, *An Essay Concerning Human Understanding* (New York: Dover, 1959), 309.
[63] Shin discusses Glanvil's frontispiece without commentary on the book itself. See "Arts of Dispossession," 711.

skeptics—was that evidence of satanic cults would imply the existence of God. Glanvil's dedication page to Charles, Duke of Richmond and Lennox, describes those intentions: "the design being to secure some of the out-works of religion, and to regain a parcel of ground which bold infidelity has invaded."[64] With contorted logic, Glanvil believed that establishing the veracity of witchcraft and Satanism would strengthen the resolve of Christian believers whose faith was slipping in the modern age: "our age, in which atheism is begun in sadducism: and those that dare not bluntly say, *there is no God*, content themselves (for a fair step and introduction) to deny there are spirits and witches."[65] What for Glanvil was a form of Christian apologetics becomes for Laura a gateway to a life adjacent to the faith of her family and nation.

While Glanvil's missional Christian approach to witches provides Laura her intellectual entry point into the theory of witchcraft, Warner's ideas about witches derived from additional sources referenced less explicitly in the novel, particularly the scholarship of the British archaeologist Margaret Murray. Upon its publication, Warner read Murray's *The Witch-Cult in Western Europe* (1921), a groundbreaking and provocative book wherein Murray distinguished between "Operative Witchcraft and Ritual Witchcraft"—the former being any sort of dabbling in "charms and spells" and the latter, which Murray calls "the Dianic Cult," being a constellation of "religious beliefs and rituals of the people known in late medieval times as 'Witches.'"[66] Through extensive research with primary source documents, Murray shows how this Dianic Cult existed before Christianity came to Europe and that many of its ways and modes persisted within Christianity despite the new religion's efforts to expunge its Dianic ancestry.[67] She would follow this book with an even more expansive argument in *The God of the Witches* (1931), claiming that there is "a continuity of belief and ritual which can be traced from the Palaeolithic period down to modern times," a consistent worship of "the Horned God" who "remained a great deity" until "the rise of Christianity, with its fundamental doctrine that a non-Christian deity was a devil" and thus "the cult of the Horned God fell into

---

[64] Joseph Glanvil, *Saducimus Triumphatus* (London: Roger Tukyr, 1700), 74. Spelling modernized.
[65] Glanvil, 82.
[66] Margaret Murray, *The Witch-Cult in Western Europe*, 1921 (Oxford: Clarendon Press, 1962), 11–12.
[67] Murray's arguments have been criticized by subsequent scholars, as Carl A. Raschke describes in a passing dismissal of Murray's work: "serious anthropological findings do not support the preexistence and persistence of the 'old religion' in the sense that the romantics have propounded." Raschke, "On Witches and Witch Hunts: Violence, Counterviolence, and the Writing of Religion," in *Religion and Violence in a Secular World: Toward a New Political Theology*, ed. Clayton Crockett (Charlottesville: University of Virginia Press, 2006), 49.

disrepute."⁶⁸ Warner drew from Murray's writings a sense of that alternative space within Christianity where rituals of the type she depicts at the end of *Lolly Willowes* can flourish unseen in a culture that militates against them.

Intriguingly, however, Warner does not embrace the totalizing, revolutionary vision of Murray's works. For Murray, the Dianic Cult of the Horned God is centuries old and merely underground, biding its time while some of its basic tenets—such as ritual sacrifice—are practiced by the state rather than the cult. Warner's relationship with this kind of religion is as partial and ironic as her relationship with Christianity. After the publication of *Lolly Willowes*, Warner sent a copy to Murray, who wrote a letter complimenting the book but, as Warner reported, "she was doubtful about my devil."⁶⁹ Mimi Winick notes that Murray's skepticism about *Lolly Willowes* derived in part from her sense that Warner had too easily adopted Christian mythology with her depiction of Satan. Instead of a rival, underground religion, Warner had reasserted the primacy of Christianity in her embrace of devilry: "the tradition of witchcraft that she embraces defines itself against Christianity and cannot escape its logic."⁷⁰ Warner and Murray met for lunch, a meeting Warner recounted to David Garnett with obvious pleasure, telling of Murray's tales of the occult—"She said things that would make the hairs of your head stand bolt upright"—and indicating how appealing she found Murray.⁷¹ "I wish I were in her coven," Warner wrote, "perhaps I shall be."⁷² This slight comment, a joking aside for Garnett, is packed with meaning. Murray was quite serious about witches and their neglected place in global history, particularly for the ways that ritual witchcraft functioned as a pre-Christian religion that continued to influence modern Christianity and society—but Murray was not a witch. Warner's comment expresses desire—slightly ironic, slightly erotic, and slightly sincere—that a community might form of women bucking against the masculinist, heteronormative mainstream. Murray's biographer notes that her books on witches were not well received by fellow social scientists who complained that she showed insufficient discernment with her primary sources,

---

[68] Murray, *The God of the Witches*, 1931 (Oxford: Oxford University Press, 1970), 13–14. Late in life Warner recalled, incorrectly, that as she wrote *Lolly Willowes* she was "very much influenced by old Margaret Murray's book, *The God of the Witches*" ("Warner in Conversation," 36). This error is revealing, however, for showing that Warner continued to follow Murray's writings even after she had moved past her own writing about witchcraft.
[69] Warner, *Letters*, 9.
[70] Mimi Winick, "Modernist Feminist Witchcraft: Margaret Murray's Fantastic Scholarship and Sylvia Townsend Warner's Realist Fantasy," *Modernism/modernity* 22, no. 3 (September 2015): 566, 582.
[71] Warner, *Letters*, 9.
[72] Ibid.

taking the recorded statements of accused witches too much at face value rather than evaluating their plausibility.[73] Whatever the merits of Murray's works as historical or anthropological scholarship, there is unquestionably something theological about them in their challenge to conceptions of the church and its function. Murray's outsider's status is clearly a point of attraction for Warner. Wishing to be "in her coven" signals Warner's interest in connecting with a woman flaunting conventions and forging her own idiosyncratic path. This desire is creatively expressed through Laura Willowes and it gestures towards queer anarchist community.[74] Being not-quite-inside a not-quite-existing coven—but desiring this community nonetheless—seems a perfect image for Warner's liminal, anarchic condition.

Though Murray's writing was clearly an influence on Warner, there was another source text for *Lolly Willowes* that Warner later claimed was even more important: Robert Pitcairn's compilation of court cases *Criminal Trials in Scotland* (1833). In later ruminations, Warner claimed that she preferred Pitcairn to Murray: "the actual speech of the accused impressed on me that these witches were witches for love; that witchcraft was more than Miss Murray's Dianic cult; it was the romance of their hard lives, their release from dull futures."[75] It is noteworthy that these accounts are far more aggressive and violent than Warner's depiction of the languid, pastoral, slightly eerie but not overtly shocking coven in Great Mop. The Pitcairn version describes the systematic torture of women suspected of witchcraft, with sleep deprivation and the padlocked iron collar known as the "witches' bridle" used to coerce confessions.[76] The harshness, insensibility, and capriciousness of the interrogations contribute strongly to their injustice and terror. In these accounts, it is not the witch who emerges as the figure of horror, but rather the interrogator, whose badgering questions and physical torment make the court records frightful. Though Murray's approach to witches is the more feminist take on the material, Pitcairn's is the more emotional. At times the witches seem sinister, but the absurdity of the charges and extremity of the punishments give them grave pathos. Murray's books grant witches a sort of superpower, making them capable of infiltrating all levels of society and, in a sense, substantiating some of their opponents' worst fears about their powers

---

[73] See Kathleen L. Sheppard, *The Life of Margaret Alice Murray: A Woman's Work in Archaeology* (Lanham: Lexington Books, 2013), 177.

[74] Sheppard relates that the mainstream scholarly guild never embraced Murray's work on witches, but many so-called Murrayites continue to be inspired by her work and the modern Wiccan movement rates her books highly (*Margaret Alice Murray*, 182).

[75] Qtd. in Harman, *Warner*, 59.

[76] Robert Pitcairn, *Ancient Criminal Trials in Scotland* (Edinburgh: Bannatyne, 1833), 50.

and influence. Laura Willowes is clearly not a powerful witch of that sort, and her smallness is what reinforces the anarchist strain of her witchery.

Many readers of Lolly Willowes have commented on the use of witchcraft in the novel as an anti-patriarchal, queer and feminist device, but witches are also figures of rebellion against church and state. A recurring motif in Pitcairn's narratives about witch trials is that these prosecutions were devised to quell dissent against the monarchy and deviance from the church's social control. Warner's reading of Pitcairn's *Ancient Criminal Trials of Scotland* appears most noticeably in her references to specific Scottish witches who were part of the North Berwick witchhunts of 1590–1.[77] As she prepares to go to the Witches' Sabbath, Laura realizes that Mrs. Leak is a witch who will accompany her, and she feels comforted because her chaperone is "a matronly witch like Agnes Sampson" (*LW*, 170). Later, when Laura debates with Satan, she remembers her youthful reading about "the happy relationship between the Devil and his servants" and decides that "If Euphan Macalzean had rated him—why, so, at a pinch, might she" (*LW*, 217). Both the cases of Agnes Sampson and Euphan Macalzean are chronicled in Pitcairn's book, and their stories evoke the "romance of hard lives" that Warner found so compelling. In Macalzean's case, Pitcairn intriguingly writes about his surprise that someone who otherwise had such high standing "should have leagued with the obscure and profligate wretches who figure in the Trials for Witchcraft at this period, for the destruction of her sovereign."[78] His gloss on her trial is as much political as personal, and Warner's reference alludes to this political dimension. Pitcairn admits that Macalzean "*believed* herself, as well as her associates, to be possessed of supernatural powers; and that she had the firmest reliance in infernal agency."[79] But, he counters this lunacy with his more rational sounding account, an account that is distinctly theopolitical: "The only reason which can be assigned for such frantic and detestable conduct seems to be, that she was devoted to the ancient Roman Catholic faith, and thus bearing personal hatred against the King and the Reformed Religion."[80] Laura suggests that she can accept Satan since the high-class Macalzean also did so, and being in league with Macalzean is also to align with subversive political theology. What makes Laura Willowes different is that she is illegible, not fully captured by Satan and blatantly invisible to her family, the novel's primary representatives of mainstream English Christianity and its heteronormative social organization.

---

[77] See Gibson, *Witchcraft: The Basics*, 148–50.
[78] Pitcairn, *Criminal Trials*, 249.
[79] Ibid.
[80] Ibid.

The scene of the Witches' Sabbath in *Lolly Willowes* was not much approved by Margaret Murray because the image of the devil was not part of an alternative, premodern religion but instead drawn from the English Christianity documented by Pitcairn and others. That Christianity continues to provide the mythical structures for Warner's anti-patriarchal fantasy is one of the reasons for the discomforting conclusion to the novel, where Christian patriarchy is not completely overthrown or supplanted. The discomforting ambivalence also emerges from the complicated presentation of the queerness of Great Mop's coven, a space that clearly defies the heteronormative marriage economy promoted by the Willowes family but does not replace that economy with any simple queer alternative.

The sabbath gathering depicts the most explicit challenge to heteronormativity—yet Laura navigates this space with reluctance, equivocation, and wariness that are far from the expected celebratory renunciation of her family. Initially, her awkwardness emerges because of the advances of a young man who touches her to initiate a dance, an overture that Laura receives with uncertainty and self-deprecation. "Even as a witch" she feels "doomed to social failure" as "her first Sabbath was not going to open livelier vistas than were opened by her first ball" (*LW*, 174). The Sabbath, despite its supposed flouting of convention, mirrors the social forms that produced and reproduced the heterosexual matrix Laura found so oppressive in her former life with the Willowes family. The balls that signified participation in a reproductive economy that builds the nation in its local forms are inverted by the Witches' Sabbath, but mere inversion is an insufficient mode of renunciation. Laura's feelings of failure are momentarily lessened by her flirtations with Emily, who seizes Laura and brings her into the dancing. This moment is the novel's most explicit homoerotic display, where the women dance "like two suns that whirl and blaze in a single destruction" (*LW*, 175). With less grand and poetical abstraction, their bodies connect in an erotic frisson absent from most of the novel: "a strand of red hair came undone and brushed across Laura's face" which makes "her tingle from head to foot" (*LW*, 175). Dancing with Emily, she thinks, could be a partnership to keep "until the gunpowder ran out of the heels of her boots" (*LW*, 175). But "Alas! this happy ending was not to be," and Laura's thrilling sexual exploration is short-lived, interrupted by other dance partners and Emily's spontaneity. Sustainability is deliberately opposed by the ritual: "the etiquette of a Sabbath appeared to consist of one rule only: to do nothing for long" (*LW*, 176). If Laura were seeking a long-term, sustainable, communal alternative to the pressures of heteronormativity, Christianity, and nation that she had endured with her family, it is not provided by the coven in Great Mop.

When Satan himself finally appears at the Sabbath, his presence increases the ambivalence of the queer alternative. His introduction comes as Emily and Mrs. Leak sit on either side of Laura, holding her arms as "Mrs. Leak patted her encouragingly, and Emily whispered rapidly, incoherently, in her ear" (*LW*, 181). This magical and erotic combination introduces the "stranger" who manifests as Satan and greets Laura "with secretive and undulating movements" and a creepily sexual "cold darting touch" on her cheek (*LW*, 182). This lick from "a fine tongue like a serpent's" repulses her, but Laura "found his hands detaining her" (*LW*, 182). The reptilian sexuality is a rupture of the decorum found in Laura's former life with the Willowes, but it is also nonconsensual, coercive, and sickening. She responds forcefully, dismisses Satan, and tells him that his Sabbath is thoroughly unenjoyable. This assertiveness fills her "with a delighted and scornful surprise at the ease with which she had avenged her dignity" (*LW*, 183). Satan's advances and all "the Powers of Darkness, then, were no more fearful than a herd of bullocks in a field?," she wonders (*LW*, 183). So Laura resists and mocks the entrapments and assaults of Satan's erotic pursuit, finding herself separated from the rites and relationships of the witches while still allying herself with them against the bondages of the heteronormative family, church, and state. She lacks the kind of full-blown community that might overtake and replace those powerful institutions that govern mainstream English society, and her position may seem isolated.

And yet, the imaginative space Warner creates by the end of the novel resonates with later theorizations of queer anarchism, such as that of Jamie Heckert who writes of "anarchy without opposition."[81] Heckert notes that "anarchist politics are usually defined by their opposition to state, capitalism, patriarchy, and other hierarchies" and urges us "to queer that notion of anarchism" in order to see "what new possibilities arise when we learn to cross, to blur, to undermine, or overflow the hierarchical and binary oppositions we have been taught to believe in."[82] Rather than defining herself solely by her opposition to the Willowes creed with its compulsory heterosexuality, Christianity, and nationalism, Laura finds another space—but she also does not assent to its strictures and guidelines, discovering a point of individual flourishing that is connected to existing powers but not motivated by them. She crosses, blurs, undermines, and overflows the homoerotic, anti-patriarchal coven as much as she eludes the heteronormative Christian nation.

---

[81] Jamie Heckert, "Anarchy without Opposition," in *Queering Anarchism: Addressing and Undressing Power and Desire*, ed. C. B. Daring, J. Rogue, Deric Shannon, and Abbey Volcano (Edinburgh: AK Press, 2012), 63.

[82] Heckert, "Anarchy without Opposition," 64.

The Anarchism of the Lovingly Hunted

The critical distance between Laura and Satan is also, in part, an echo back to the antiwar messaging of "The Lenten Offering," as the "huntsman" metaphor connects with the violence of the Great War. Satan as "huntsman" thinks how bored he has become in modernity because the hunt is no longer thrilling after "the success of his latest organized Flanders battue" (*LW*, 162). The appeal in chasing Laura comes from her being "a Solitary Snipe" rather than the mass slaughter of war (*LW*, 162). This image of Satan being jaded from his efforts at the Western Front, batting soldiers like grouse into gunfire, is a reminder that the devil of Warner's book is no straightforward symbol of peaceable, utopian politics.

By referring to Satan in the sometimes-forgotten subtitle "The Loving Huntsman," Warner even makes her title page a sly act of subversion. Would the novel have become the inaugural Book of the Month Club selection had it been titled *Lolly Willowes; Or, The Sexy Satan* ? But apart from the subversive joke of the title, the actual figure of Satan in the novel remains a puzzlement, not just for conservative readers bothered by Warner's breaches of Christian morality and narrative cohesion, but also for readers seeking to champion her progressive feminism. As Winick describes it, the "novel's witchy passivity" emerges "as a potent if fundamentally compromised form of resistance" since "in allying herself with Satan, Lolly emphatically frees herself from the demands of living according to the expectations of English Christian society. But at the same time, she corroborates some of the oldest assumptions of patriarchal Christianity."[83] In its basic outline, the novel upholds its reputation as a feminist triumph, where a nonconforming woman embraces witchcraft against patriarchy, dispatching the incursions of her nephew Titus. But it concludes with an ambiguous exchange between Laura and the distinctly masculine Satan, and there is little in the narrator's final words to reassure us of female autonomy. Laura rests amid Satan's voice above her in the trees, which is "all she would know of his undesiring and unjudging gaze, his satisfied but profoundly indifferent ownership" (*LW*, 222). This conclusion—and especially "ownership" as the novel's final word—dampens any enthusiasm for *Lolly Willowes* as a story of feminist escape. Satan is better than the other options presented to Laura by English society, and she feels that no one else would "come to her aid" in rejecting her nephew's patriarchal and

---

[83] Winick, "Modernist Feminist Witchcraft," 576, 581.

imperial advances: "Custom, public opinion, law, church, and state—all would have shaken their massive heads against her plea, and sent her back to bondage" (*LW*, 199). Being unbound by those civil religious institutions is a version of freedom, but it is not the kind of alternative anarchist community envisioned by Emma Goldman and later political radicals.

The position of Laura at the end of the novel is one of "interstitial distance" from the mainstream, heteronormative, Christian patriarchy as well as from the Satanic coven. Laura is not unequivocally autonomous, but being under Satan's "indifferent ownership" means that she has found a small site of anarchy in which to thrive. What is lacking is not so much her freedom but any real sense of community. The value of anarchism for Halberstam and Critchley is that it produces alternative communities united in "failure" or in "responsibility." Laura triumphantly fails, in Halberstam's sense, and bears some relationship with the townspeople of Great Mop, as Critchley endorses, but her anarchy remains largely individualized. To some extent this is a function of the genre of the novel itself, at least in the form Warner used in the 1920s. (She would later experiment with socialist, collective novels such as *Summer Will Show*, *After the Death of Don Juan*, and *The Corner That Held Them*.) The anarchism that Warner initiates in *Lolly Willowes* is tentative and incomplete. Laura has found a new space to thrive, illegible to the patriarchal mainstream and unfettered by her satanic life, but there is not much realization of an active, anarchist coven. Her adjacency to Great Mop's witch culture is a kind of freedom, but it is also a limitation for her political efficacy. Anarchism—at least in any collective form—remains in this novel a "political theory of heaven," desirable but fanciful. Fantasies of better political life might be doomed to failure, but by failing in the right direction, there may emerge the bases for modes of flourishing illegible to the confining powers of church and state.

For many political resistance movements, "overcoming" is a crucial rallying point, an encapsulation through a single word of the yearned-for future and a sustenance for hope. The promise that somehow, someday, "we shall overcome" the current systems of racism, sexism, homophobia, imperialism, capitalism, militarism, and nationalism has been a sustaining force in many collective actions, giving life and inspiration to political witnessing despite end-goals and outcomes that may remain largely amorphous. As a powerful inspiration for necessary political action, "overcoming" is not a concept I would want to completely reject.

And yet, we might look to a writer such as Warner for alternatives to overcoming, not because we must abandon the possibility of dismantling systemic oppression but because we may glimpse other opportunities for thriving and other modes of political witness. Latent in the notion of overcoming is a specter of failure—only a total defeat of unjust systems counts as "victory," and a utopian future stands as the only measure of success. This is not to say that all political movements must wallow in defeat if they do not perfectly achieve their goals or that an eternity of political struggle is always understood as failing, but yearning for a brand-new world where the current power structures have been revolutionized may project a single triumphant outcome that occludes other richly valuable alternatives that can flourish within and around our current world orders.

The ambiguous and challenging ending of *Lolly Willowes* offers a vital resource for theopolitical imagination, not because it casts a utopian vision of overcoming or even much support for an ongoing program of political struggle, but because it calls us into reflection about interstitial spaces for flourishing. Unseen, and thus uncontained and unbound by the state and its heteronormative, Christian strictures, Laura escapes the clutches of a particular version of national identity. But this escape is not into any unambiguous "freedom" or autonomy, and it is certainly not ascension into a rival power capable of overcoming patriotic Christianity with a new force of satanic anarchy. Warner's fictional, even fantastical depiction of a life enjoyed within the interstices imagines anarchism as a possibility not because regnant powers are demolished but because their stranglehold has slipped. That slippage could be deemed an imperfect victory for political resistance—perhaps even a failure for rival political action to achieve its longed-for goals—but it may also be lauded for its practical alternative. If the only measure of successful radical politics is the absolute, total reorganization of unjust social structures, then political victory might remain always out of reach, glinting in the mists of "heaven." What Warner's ambivalent, anarchist vision offers is a possibility for flourishing even under the imperfect conditions of the present time, striving still for perfection but not being defeated by the modesty of lesser gains. Queering the spaces un-coopted by the state becomes Warner's imaginative challenge to the nation, a richly minor political life enacted this side of heaven.

Coda: Living the Theopolitical Imagination

The acts of war memorialization with which this book began—at the Cenotaph in Whitehall and the Tomb of the Unknown Warrior in Westminster Abbey—are emblematic of the state's enchantment. Rituals of national worship that flow from these symbolic objects and help constitute the sacredness of citizenship are a means by which the past in all of its messiness is domesticated and sanctified. Such rites offer solace through their finality and sense of closure: how to face grief and loss from wartime? Assert the holiness of sacrifice for the nation and achieve the aura of afterlife even in a secular age. This will-to-closure permeates the postwar commemorations from a century ago, and its allure is found in all kinds of totalitarian political and economic ideologies. The pernicious influence of such narratives also affects our capacity to face the slow catastrophe of our climate crisis and related calamities like global viruses and increasing material disparities. Faced with life-threatening, species-threatening challenges, the enchantments of authoritarianism, science denial, and enemy-blaming often prove difficult to resist. The blending of patriotism and Christianity in the years of the Great War and its aftermath had consequences that continue to be felt today in commemorative rituals and constructions of national identity, and the modes of resistance to these ideological and ritual formations remain relevant in our current time of Christian nationalisms.[1]

Theopolitical imagination as I have discussed it throughout this book is not the only plane on which our current crises must be faced—social action that changes material conditions cannot be separated from the "merely" intellectual and affective parts of our politics. And yet, it is through the power of imagination that new thought patterns have the possibility to develop and new forms of social and economic organization can begin to take shape. Modernist

---

[1] On confronting white Christian nationalism through intersectional political theology, see Jeffrey W. Robbins and Clayton Crockett, eds., *Doing Theology in the Age of Trump: A Critical Report on Christian Nationalism* (Eugene, OR: Cascade Books, 2019).

literary styles characteristically deny closure, opening new pathways that suggest myriad connections among people, our communities, and the earth—but not in simple, idealistic, or sentimental fashion. Our bonds develop tenuously and often with great struggle, but recognizing the difficulty in producing individual and collective flourishing is a vital alternative to closed-off, unquestioning, and teleologically sealed narratives such as sacrifices to the nation-state through war, economic triumph for the entrepreneurially successful, purity for the racial/ethnic elite who secure a firm national border, stability for monogamous reproductive sexualities and blood-based family systems, and spiritual redemption for the religiously sanctified. Against such orthodoxies and the comfort they provide for the in-groups who arise victorious in their narratives of success, modernist forms explore rupture, failure, incompleteness, and emergent political and religious sensibilities. Each of the novels discussed in previous chapters adopts a formal structure that denies closure, and attentiveness to this form offers to political theology the possibility of nuance, insight, and rethinking that deepens and refines our imaginative abilities. *Jacob's Room* ends on an unanswerable question, *Lady Chatterley's Lover* on tentative hope and an em dash, *Decline and Fall* on ironic circularity, *Vile Bodies* on ever-expanding war, and *Lolly Willowes* on interstitial flourishing within the dominant culture. The political theologies these books imagine are committed to change and critical of destructive powers, but they are also open-ended and invitational rather than prescriptive or foreclosed. While this openness might seem a liability from the perspective of political action, it is an asset for refining, expanding, and giving new texture to our imagination. As Michaela Bronstein has argued, the power of certain modernist forms is their ability to "contain and strain after always-revised universalisms" without coming "to satisfyingly excerptable conclusions," instead being "processes rather than endpoints" that leave "open the possibility of new connections between transhistorical art and societal change."[2]

Literature and literary analysis offer unique contributions to theopolitical imagining. "Political theology," Luke Bretherton explains, "is an interpretive art for discovering faithful, hopeful, and loving judgments about how to act together in response to shared problems. And it is an art best practiced in the company of others, and through active listening to outsiders, whether inside or outside of our primary community."[3] Bretherton cautions that developing a political theology

---

[2] Bronstein, *Out of Context*, 220.
[3] Luke Bretherton, *Christ and the Common Life: Political Theology and the Case for Democracy* (Grand Rapids: Eerdmans, 2019), 6.

does not ensure "wise political judgment" since "the possibility of that depends on a host of other factors, including character, imagination," and many other matters of context.[4] Openness to dialogue across differences does not, however, mean disregard for injustice. Listening beyond our own primary community to build a common good still maintains shared convictions and struggle against the social, political, and economic forces that damage us. What I intend with this book is a step toward thinking more deeply about political theology as an "interpretative art" shared across different communities and genres. I concur that theopolitical interpretation should never ossify into rigid, predictable, or scrupulous doctrine, nor can it simply point to a program of action or way of living that does not also require the messiness of human community plus historical and material realities. But if character and imagination are vital parts of a responsive, productive, inclusive, and regenerative politics, then literary works along with thoughtful literary analysis help us develop the sensitivity and acuity needed for better and wiser political judgment.

Among the goals of this book is an effort to bring into conversation voices not always held together: literary criticism, theory, and literary works along with political theology that crosses boundaries of confessional difference as well as the division between sectarian and secular theologians. This book shares in spirit with Catherine Keller's claim that in order to confront political and theological narratives of "a final, one-off destruction and salvation" that abound in our apocalyptic time, we need "the theological alternatives on offer from fresh visions of the world" that "include theologies of deep pluralism, engaged in interreligious interchange and multiple secular practices."[5] A notion of interchange such as this should not be mistaken for *faux-naïf* universalism or idealized neutrality where ideological differences carry no weight. Rather, it is serious working in "deep pluralism" that can enable significant collaboration against the forces that threaten our shared existence. J. Ashley Foster writes eloquently of the legacy of scholarship and care left by Jane Marcus, her "guiding influence and a radical presence" that "allows us to think about Jane's writings and teachings in terms of linkages, networks and connections," situating "us in an elaborate web of relations that can be entered at any point and that fosters a multiplicity of perspectives and harbors a diversity of voices."[6] Rather than hierarchies that emphasize power differences, Marcus advocates a model

---

[4] Ibid.
[5] Keller, *Facing Apocalypse*, ix–x.
[6] J. Ashley Foster, "Jane Marcus Feminist University: Rhizomes, Connections, and Networks of Radical Thinking," *Virginia Woolf Miscellany* 93 (2018): 32.

based in rhizomes, "a structure that is generative and regenerative, that grows horizontally and not vertically, that subsists without a trunk or center, and that is ever expansive through roots and branches coming in contact and extending outwards."[7] This "rhizomatic structure of collectivity, collaboration, multiplicity, connections, relations, extension and expansion" calls "us to question the canon even as we insist on more works' entry into it," to "continually diversif[y] the modernist discourse, expanding its voices" and "we must also work for peace."[8] This book has been one foray into this exchange of fresh visions and an invitation for more theopolitical imagination and working for peace from beyond the regions and traditions where I have sought resources. This chapter is a "coda" rather than a "conclusion," intending a summative and suggestive set of comments rather than the foreclosing of a conversation. It is my hope that others can carry on this interchange with creative and rhizomatic attentiveness to our archives and interlocutors.

The novel is an intimate artistic form, suited to the deep exploration of character and the attachments formed between readers and texts.[9] Though there are examples of experiments with collectivist fiction—the panoramic novels of John Dos Passos or the documentary fiction of Storm Jameson's *Mirror in Darkness* trilogy—the personal and intimate forms predominate. Jessica Berman has argued that "modernist fiction can provide meaningful alternative models of community" through its formal experimentation, giving voice to the way "we move in a realm of being-in-common that rests upon the border between 'I' and 'we', a border that may not necessarily coincide with the political boundaries that surround us" and thus challenging concepts of "simple statehood."[10] This formulation of community is not mere idealism but rather is fraught and contentious since strains of exclusionary, repressive, and violent nationalism also stake their claims on us and promise captivating senses of community. Dwelling on the intimacy of such forms and the competing ideological and political strains within modernism, Sejal Sutaria describes how T. E. Hulme (and related figures) offered a "scientific exploration of ethics as a means to bringing about the radical transformation of society into one ordered by religion, discipline, and a democracy based upon Justice rather than emotion"—a totalizing and

---

[7] Ibid.
[8] Ibid.
[9] See Jessica Berman, *Modernist Commitments: Ethics, Politics, and Transnational Modernism* (New York: Columbia University Press, 2011) and Rita Felski, *Hooked: Art and Attachment* (Chicago: University of Chicago Press, 2020).
[10] Jessica Berman, *Modernist Fiction, Cosmopolitanism and the Politics of Community* (Cambridge: Cambridge University Press, 2001), 3–4.

supposedly rationalist system with a political theology that anticipates and corresponds with Carl Schmitt's theories of sovereignty.[11] Countering this austere political theology are other modes of modernist experimentation where "for Bloomsbury writers like E.M. Forster or Virginia Woolf," for instance, "fiction was a place in which the writer might try out the politics of empathy, press upon traditional relationship structures or sexual mores, and examine what Forster labeled the emotionally under-developed English heart and how it might be remedied through human exchange with more emotional cultures."[12] Staying attuned to the affective, relational, and intimate dimensions of human experience while activating strategies for political resistance and renewal is the special purview of the novel.

Numerous cross-pressures in the early twentieth century made the modernist period a time of crisis—global war, economic instability, radical social change, heated political ideology, etc. Modernist writers contended with these crises through innovative literary forms, and the intimacy of the novel allowed a fusion of the political and personal that manifested in what I have argued is a mode of political theology. Among the common stories of the twentieth century is that modernist formal innovations became canonized and exhausted, and late-twentieth-century fiction turned to recycling and pastiche that matched a cultural sensibility where formerly cherished political and religious beliefs were worn out and abandoned. Looking at a pair of late-twentieth-century English postmodernist novels, however, shows the persistence of many themes from the works I have discussed in this book—enchanted religious nationalism that sanctifies violence, a sense of desperation and crisis, and an effort toward fiction with experimental form that can express a theopolitical imagination. Jeanette Winterson's *The Passion* (1987) and Julian Barnes's *England, England* (1998) develop these themes and offer their own unique conversation points with recent political theology, and my discussion of these novels suggests avenues for further exploration of theopolitical fiction in a supposedly secular age. Their narratives enact the political value of public mourning and the radical politics discernable from within exhausted linguistic forms, giving resources for our imaginative lives today.

The Passion is a magical realist fantasia set in the Napoleonic wars that combines themes of imperial conquest, Christian sacrifice, and impossible erotic love into

---

[11] Sejal Sutaria, "Ripples in Modernist Waters: The Poetics, Ethics, & Politics of T.E. Hulme's Vision of Anti-Humanist Democracy," *Global Review* 1, no. 1 (2013): 172.
[12] Ibid.

an antiwar narrative that reflects on the enchantments of nationalism. The story oscillates between two narrators—Henri, a poor young soldier conscripted into Napoleon's personal service, and Villanelle, an androgynous Venetian boatperson who works in casinos as a gambler and courtesan. In a postmodernist approach to history and narrative, one of the novel's refrains is "I'm telling you stories. Trust me."[13] All of the character details, settings, and historical events are heightened into magical realism. Commentators on the novel have discussed its playfully transgressive exploration of gender and sexuality, but those elements of the novel are inextricable from its depiction of religious nationalism and the devastations of war.[14] Napoleon in the novel is a figure of insatiable appetite—for food, sex, and military conquest. Henri serves him meals of roasted chicken which Napoleon swallows whole without chewing, neglecting even to spit out the bones. That voracity is synecdochic of his military campaigns, where a taste for empire leads him into un-winnable battles such as the "zero winter" assault in Russia and to absorb into his army people of all nationalities. Among the many meanings of the term "passion" in the text is the intense (and ultimately soul-destroying) devotion Henri develops for Napoleon's charismatic figure and imperialist ideology, a devotion so strong that it ultimately thwarts his similarly intense love for Villanelle. Napoleonic imperialism and the enchanted nationalism that sustains it is a religious force so enthralling that it devours everything so that even when the war is over, Henri and Villanelle are unable to escape its maw. Winterson associates the Christian story with this same kind of all-consuming and destructive force where Christ's passion—trial, torture, and crucifixion—enthralls and causes self-abnegating devotion. Alongside these nationalist and religious passions is the enthrallment of romantic love, figured in the novel most evocatively with Villanelle's heart literally belonging to her former husband who keeps it in a box. Winterson offers no clear solution to the conflicts in the novel or any static philosophy for how to deal with our passions, which usually come to us unbidden and rule us without our intent. Many of Winterson's novels explore these themes of sexuality, religion, and nation, but *The Passion* is overtly charged with these themes and invites readers into sensitive and perspicacious awareness of their consequences.[15]

---

[13] Winterson, *The Passion* (New York: Grove, 1987), 69.
[14] See, for instance, Jane Haslet, "Winterson's Fabulous Bodies," in *Jeanette Winterson: A Contemporary Critical Guide*, ed. Sonya Andermahr (London: Continuum, 2007), 41–54.
[15] Another key example is her landmark debut, the fictionalized autobiography *Oranges Are Not the Only Fruit* (1985), where she explores the effects of conservative, Pentecostal Christianity and its missionary zeal during her northern English childhood as she came to terms with her queer sexuality. See also Emily McAvan, *Jeanette Winterson and Religion* (London: Bloomsbury Academic, 2020).

Through its meditations on religion, nationalism, imperialism, and sexuality within the complexities of our deepest emotional attachments and desires, *The Passion* offers a theopolitical imagination in dialogue with recent turns toward affect theory in theology. Karen Bray and Stephen D. Moore have shown the rich and diverse pathways for the integration of affect theory and theology, including avenues for affect and political theology. They suggest "reading for affect in contemporary cultural and political movements and recognizing within them religious sensibilities in certain affectual modes, such as a religious sense of supplication or lament within the moods of certain secular protests."[16] Winterson's novel is not precisely what Bray and Moore have in mind (their examples of secular protest include Black Lives Matter rallies as rituals of lament), but its literary, intellectual, and emotional exploration of affect as a religious and political phenomenon aligns with theological and theoretical investigations of affect, power, liturgy, and protest. Bray and Moore ask theologians to consider "what, for that matter, if *theological* writing is akin to a convulsed cry, but also a collective cry? What exactly might it mean to register collectively our affectivities and resistances toward religion, toward God, toward gods?"[17] *The Passion* can be read as an unresolved and exploratory response to such questions, where the personal and intimate operates within collective ideologies that generate both emotion and resistance and where religious politics give both meaning and repression. Though Winterson crafts postmodernist historical fiction that playfully imagines the Napoleonic era, her portrayal of war and its pervasive and interminable effects speaks to geopolitical violence in the 1980s and continues to be meaningful in our current century with its cycles of never-ending, once and future wars. In her account of one such unending cycle, Wonhee Anne Joh writes of the Korean War and the perpetual presence of US militarism and argues for an "affective politics that may cross time and space to possibly birth collaborative solidarity with other sites and collectives who are at the receiving end of U.S. militarized terror."[18] There are possibilities here "to engage an affective politics for critical theological studies," Joh writes, by seeking in religious narratives a "site of trauma terror and unending mourning."[19] Winterson's

---

[16] Karen Bray and Stephen D. Moore, "Introduction: Mappings and Crossings," in *Religion, Emotion, Sensation: Affect Theories and Theologies*, ed. Karen Bray and Stephen D. Moore (New York: Fordham University Press, 2019), 1–18. 7.
[17] Bray and Moore, "Introduction," 12.
[18] Wonhee Anne Joh, "Affective Politics of the Unending Korean War: Remembering and Resistance," in *Religion, Emotion, Sensation: Affect Theories and Theologies*, ed. Karen Bray and Stephen D. Moore (New York: Fordham University Press, 2019), 87.
[19] Ibid.

elliptical, sorrowful ending to *The Passion* gives imaginative expression to trauma and mourning, the consequences of perpetual, total war on the intimate spheres of the body, sexuality, and relationships.

England, England extends this postmodernist engagement with theologies of the state further through a mock epic about constructing English national identity and religious mythology. In *The Passion*, Winterson gave us a fantasy history of Europe, and Barnes plays a different chronological game by setting *England, England* in a not-so-distant future where capitalism has reached a new world-altering level that transforms all historical and cultural experiences into simulacra. An entrepreneur named Sir Jack Pitman, who bombastically asserts his authentic Englishness, though his birthplace and heritage are unknown, has conspired to draw international tourism to England by concentrating all of the most desired national tourist sites into the more manageable geographic area of the Isle of Wight. This new destination offers vacation packages where global consumers can see Dover, Stonehenge, and Buckingham Palace in one easy go while actors portraying Samuel Johnson and Robin Hood give historical and mythical color. (Sir Jack discovers that the Royal family, however, has an aura that cannot be achieved through fakery or replication, and blackmailing and bribes are required to coerce the actual monarchy to relocate to his theme park England—a turn that Barnes uses to satirize the simulacral quality of the "real" royals.) Jerry Bateson, Sir Jack's chief business consultant, announces that even though "some people out there [...] think it's [England's] job, our particular geopolitical function, to act as an emblem of decline," he can turn this narrative around through proper marketing by showing that "*we are already what others may hope to become*" and that "we must sell our past to other nations as their future!"[20] Sir Jack becomes the architect of this consumerist fantasy-nightmare, but in a spirit of openness—or, at least openness to marketing potential—likely purchasers of the vacation package "from twenty-five countries had been asked to list six characteristics, virtues or quintessences which the word England suggested."[21] The list of fifty items for appropriation and consumption comprises many predictable cultural markers including sport, literature, and historic sites, along with slanderous ethnic stereotypes (many of which Sir Jack dismisses out of hand as "the result of faulty polling technique").[22] But it also retains elements of civil religion, even in this stage of advanced capitalism and secularity, where quintessential Englishness must still include "trouping the

---

[20] Julian Barnes, *England, England* (New York: Vintage, 1998), 40–1.
[21] Barnes, *England, England*, 86.
[22] Ibid., 87.

colour" and "God Save the King/Queen," even if such mentions are outnumbered by references to "shopping," "Harrods," and "Marks and Spencer."[23]

But this postmodernist satire of global capitalism does not stop with its comic encyclopedia of English history, culture, and traits. Sir Jack's scheme is such a raging success that it acquires a life of its own and the Isle of Wight becomes "England, England" while the original island is renamed "Anglia" and becomes depopulated, keeping only its most eccentric inhabitants and anyone desiring the quaintness of a rustic, antique, and "authentic" English life. This renewed land is also filled with simulacra, but the deliberate constructedness of the lifestyles in Anglia does not take away from their power to build community, which is more about personal connections than consumer exchange value. Religion—that failed enterprise of the twentieth century that scarcely registers on Sir Jack's survey of English quintessences—also returns to a full place within the fabric of life in Anglia, but without pretensions of naive belief. The local vicar, who cuts the grass around the churchyard graves with a stone-sharpened scythe rather than the mechanical mower he also owns, has changed his name from "Jack Oshinksy" to "Jez Harris" and moved to Anglia from his corporate job in the United States, marrying an Anglian woman who has "softened and localized his Milwaukee accent."[24] Martha Cochrane, Sir Jack's former employee who becomes the novel's protagonist and moral center, moves to Anglia where she lives out the remainder of her life, a life that she acknowledges has "a strange trajectory": "so knowing a child, so disenchanted an adult," but now "an old maid" who remembers "a fashion among Christians, often quite young ones, to declare themselves—on what possible authority?—born again."[25] Martha fancies that this quaint, outdated, dubious, and even problematic theological gesture might have meaning for her: "perhaps she could be a born-again old maid."[26] This rebirth pertains not only to her age, gender, and sexuality but also to her national identity which the narrative makes inseparable from Christianity. Not, to be clear, an "original" orthodox Christianity, which the novel suggests is an impossible fiction, but a Christianity that still somehow manages to convey valuable practices, concepts, and feelings despite the world's disenchantment. Barnes's novel communicates a wistful but hopeful ending in an exhausted postmodern age, where community is fabricated from the scraps of outworn traditions and a new politics struggles into being from the wreckage of metastatic capitalism.

[23] Ibid., 86–7.
[24] Ibid., 251.
[25] Ibid., 268.
[26] Ibid.

Barnes's kaleidoscopic depiction of English nationalism as a simulacrum foregrounds the poststructural linguistic theories that animate his approach to culture, belief, and identity, in a manner that puts his novel in dialogue with radical political theologies that make similar use of Derrida to articulate theopolitical praxis for our current time. Noëlle Vahanian, for instance, gives an account of an "insurrectionist" theology geared for radical politics in the twenty-first century, not by seeking theological language that transcends its historical and material conditions and the problems inherent in this immanence but rather by "conceiv[ing] of insurrection from within—within the fourfold, within phallogocentric language, within the history of colonial oppression and white supremacy, within capitalism, within the sin of Christianity—without exoticisms."[27] A theology that foregrounds ways it is at war with itself and openly confronts the harmful ideologies from within which it speaks—this is the task of "insurrection" (rather than the more triumphalist and exculpatory "resurrection"). *England, England* stages this sort of postmodern theological encounter with great verve, imagination, and humor, never failing to show the exhaustion of our language, beliefs, and cultural forms while also entertaining ways that goodness, feeling, and community can spring from within even the most tired and unredeemable modes of speech and practice. The radical politics of this insurrection arises from an honesty about how theological and cultural identities are rooted in social and linguistic systems that cannot fully escape sexism, imperialism, racism, economic injustice, and the crimes perpetrated in the name of faith.

What these late-twentieth-century works of English fiction show is that, despite the supposed exhaustion of postmodernist form and a cultural context that Charles Taylor described as the "supernova of unbelief," literary explorations reveal the persistence of enchantment and the continued power of a sacralized state.[28] Winterson and Barnes are two examples of the novel as political theology from the end of the century, still concerned with empire, war, and market as sites of religious aura in a time of cultural secularity and transferred belief. There is ample opportunity for continuing the dialogue I have opened in this book,

---

[27] Noëlle Vahanian, "The Gospel of the Word Made Flesh: Insurrection from Within the Heart of Divinity," in *An Insurrectionist Manifesto: Four New Gospels for a Radical Politics*, ed. Ward Blanton, Clayton Crockett, Jeffrey W. Robbins, and Noëlle Vahanian (New York: Columbia University Press, 2016), 144. Like all of the authors of *An Insurrectionist Manifesto*, Vahanian seeks language for doing theology which can acknowledge, face, and contend with the many problematic aspects of Christianity and its influence in the world while still showing how radical politics can emerge from its narrative and claims: "a theology of insurrection is neither a repudiation of Christianity and an indictment of its universalism, nor is it a Christian apologetic clamoring the triumph of post-Christian, yet Christian, secular universalism" (149).

[28] Taylor, *A Secular Age*, 300.

pursuing these lines of inquiry with other theopolitical resources and other eras, regions, and genres of literature.[29]

To read fiction as political theology is not an attempt to reduce literature to propositional statements or logic-driven arguments, nor do I intend to avoid the troubling elements of modernism when turning to this mode and period for intellectual resources. Holding onto these contradictions while still seeking the value of this work as a scholar-teacher is vital, I would argue, for how we must operate in our age of crisis. Ria Banerjee urges us to speak explicitly and overtly about our most pressing political concerns, but she notes that in the spirit of modernism, we might also speak "indirectly, obscurely, making leaps of association that might not neatly connect. That famous Forsterian epigraph is, after all, wrapped in quotation marks and followed by an ellipsis; 'Only connect ...' makes no demand for success or failure of our critical enterprises beyond the imperative to try."[30] Banerjee's attentiveness to the open-ended and tentative hope in *Howard's End* supplies a model for our political imagination that seeks community without the boundaries and closure of other collective formations: "the insights we perceive by troubling established readings of our fictional repertoires can help to shape future social and emotional structures upon a reordered planet."[31] In Forster's novel, the narrator also gives that famous injunction a religious resonance: "Only connect! That was the whole of her sermon. Only connect the prose and the passion, and both will be exalted, and human love will be seen at its height. Live in fragments no longer."[32] Though ironic and offered with authorial distance from the character described, the urge to connect is a "sermon" preached in the face of failure and disconnection. Insights from troubled and troubling readings held with openness and togetherness among readers who, despite differences, seek a common good—these are the promises of a literary studies that can intervene in war, envision newly inclusive communities, reorient broken economies, contend with climate crises, and challenge the nation's sacralization with a theopolitical imagination that is dynamic, creative, and artful. It is with such resources that we may fully live.

---

[29] See, for example, Simon During, "Political Theology, Literature and the Global South," in *The Global South and Literature*, ed. Russell West-Pavlov (Cambridge: Cambridge University Press, 2018), 209–22.

[30] Ria Banerjee, "Troubling Modernism at Community College during the Sixth Extinction," *Modernism/modernity Print Plus* 7, cycle 2 (October 7, 2022). https://modernismmodernity.org/forums/posts/banerjee-troubling-modernism-community-college-during-sixth-extinction

[31] Ibid.

[32] E. M. Forster, *Howard's End*, 1910 (New York: Vintage, 1989), 195.

Bibliography

Anderson, Benedict. *Imagined Communities: Reflections on the Origin and Spread of Nationalism, Revised Edition*. London: Verso, 2016.
"Armistice Day, 1920. The Burial of the Unknown Warrior." *The Times*, Supplement. November 12, 1920.
Arkwright, John S. *The Supreme Sacrifice and Other Poems in Time of War*. London: Skeffington, 1919.
Banerjee, Ria. "Troubling Modernism at Community College during the Sixth Extinction." *Modernism/modernity Print Plus* 7, cycle 2 (2022).
Barnes, Julian. *England, England*. New York: Vintage, 1998.
Becket, Fiona. *The Complete Critical Guide to D. H. Lawrence*. London: Routledge, 2002.
Beer, Gillian. "Sylvia Townsend Warner: 'The Centrifugal Kick.'" In *Women Writers of the 1930s: Gender, Politics and History*, edited by Maroula Joannou, 76–86. Edinburgh: Edinburgh University Press, 1999.
Bellah, Robert N. "Civil Religion in America." In *The Robert Bellah Reader*, edited by Robert N. Bellah and Steven M. Tipton, 225–45. Durham, NC: Duke University Press, 2006.
Berlant, Lauren. *The Queen of America Goes to Washington City: Essays on Sex and Citizenship*. Durham, NC: Duke University Press, 1997.
Berman, Jessica. *Modernist Fiction, Cosmopolitanism and the Politics of Community*. Cambridge: Cambridge University Press, 2001.
Best, Nicholas. *The Greatest Day in History: How on the Eleventh Hour of the Eleventh Day of the Eleventh Month, the First World War Finally Came to an End*. New York: Public Affairs, 2008.
Billig, Michael. *Banal Nationalism*. London: Sage, 1995.
Blayac, Alain. "Evelyn Waugh and Humour." In *Evelyn Waugh: New Directions*, edited by Alain Blayac, 112–32. New York: St. Martin's, 1991.
Bonney, Norman. *Monarchy, Religion and the State: Civil Religion in the United Kingdom, Canada, Australia and the Commonwealth*. Manchester: Manchester University Press, 2013.
Bradbury, Malcolm. *Evelyn Waugh*. London: Oliver & Boyd, 1964.
Bradshaw, David. Introduction to *Decline and Fall*, by Evelyn Waugh, ix–xxxiv. New York: Penguin, 2001.
Bray, Karen. *Grave Attending: A Political Theology for the Unredeemed*. New York: Fordham University Press, 2019.
Bray, Karen and Stephen D. Moore. "Introduction: Mappings and Crossings." In *Religion, Emotion, Sensation: Affect Theories and Theologies*, edited by Karen Bray and Stephen D. Moore, 1–18. New York: Fordham University Press, 2019.

Bronstein, Michaela. *Out of Context: The Uses of Modernist Fiction.* Oxford: Oxford University Press, 2018.

Brown, Gavin. "Amateurism and Anarchism in the Creation of Autonomous Queer Spaces." In *Anarchism and Sexuality: Ethics, Relationships and Power*, edited by Jamie Heckert and Richard Cleminson, 200–23. London: Routledge, 2011.

Burack, Charles. *D. H. Lawrence's Language of Sacred Experience: The Transfiguration of the Reader.* New York: Palgrave Macmillan, 2005.

Burgess, Anthony. *Flame into Being: The Life and Work of D. H. Lawrence.* New York: Arbor House, 1985.

Bushaway, Bob. "Name Upon Name: The Great War and Remembrance." In *Myths of the English*, edited by Roy Porter, 136–67. Cambridge: Polity, 1993.

Butler, Judith. *Frames of War: When Is Life Grievable?* London: Verso, 2010.

Caserio, Robert L. *The Novel in England: 1900–1950, History and Theory.* New York: Twayne, 1999.

Cavanaugh, William T. *Theopolitical Imagination: Discovering the Liturgy as a Political Act in an Age of Global Consumerism.* London: T&T Clark, 2002.

Cavanaugh, William T. and Peter Manley Scott, "Introduction to the Second Edition." In *The Wiley Blackwell Companion to Political Theology: Second Edition*, edited by William T. Cavanaugh and Peter Manley Scott, 1–12. Chichester: Wiley, 2019.

Chapman, Mark D. *The Coming Crisis: The Impact of Eschatology on Theology in Edwardian England.* Sheffield: Sheffield Academic Press, 2001.

Charles, R. H. *A Critical and Exegetical Commentary on The Revelation of St. John.* Edinburgh: T&T Clark, 1920.

Clarke, Stuart N. and Jane Goldman. Explanatory notes to *Jacob's Room*, by Virginia Woolf, 291–723. Cambridge: Cambridge University Press, 2020.

Clarke, Stuart N. and Susan Sellers. Introduction to *Jacob's Room*, by Virginia Woolf, xxxvii–xcvi. Cambridge: Cambridge University Press, 2020.

Cole, Jonathan. *Christian Political Theology in an Age of Discontent: Mediating Scripture, Doctrine, and Political Reality.* Eugene, OR: Wipf & Stock, 2019.

Colley, Linda. *Britons: Forging the Nation 1707–1837.* New Haven: Yale University Press, 1992.

Cooke, Barbara. *Evelyn Waugh's Oxford, 1922–1966.* Oxford: Bodleian Library, 2018.

Cuthbertson, Guy. *Peace at Last: A Portrait of Armistice Day, November 11, 1918.* New Haven: Yale University Press, 2018.

Critchley, Simon. *The Faith of the Faithless: Experiments in Political Theology.* London: Verso, 2012.

Critchley, Simon. "Mystical Anarchism," *The Anarchist Library*. June 1, 2012. https://theanarchistlibrary.org/library/simon-critchley-mystical-anarchism

Critchley, Simon. *Infinitely Demanding: Ethics of Commitment, Politics of Resistance.* London: Verso, 2014.

Davidson, Randall Thomas. "Redeeming the Time." In *Christ: And the World at War: Sermons Preached in War-Time*, edited by Basil Matthews, 15–26. Boston: Pilgrim Press, 1917.

Davis, Robert Murray. *Evelyn Waugh, Writer*. Norman, OK: Pilgrim Press, 1981.

de Gay, Jane. *Virginia Woolf and Christian Culture*. Edinburgh: Edinburgh University Press, 2018.

Detloff, Madelyn. *The Value of Virginia Woolf*. Cambridge: Cambridge University Press, 2016.

Ehrenfried, Lara. "'There's a Song There, Really': Evelyn Waugh's Vile Bodies, the Musical Revue, and Early Sound Film." *Modern Fiction Studies* 66, no. 3 (2020): 423–49.

Ellis, David. *D. H. Lawrence: Dying Game 1922–1930*. Cambridge: Cambridge University Press, 1998.

Ferretter, Luke. *The Glyph and the Gramophone: D. H. Lawrence's Religion*. London: Bloomsbury Academic, 2013.

Ferretter, Luke. "Religion." In *D. H. Lawrence in Context*, edited by Andrew Harrison, 183–91. Cambridge: Cambridge University Press, 2001.

Fjågesund, Peter. *The Apocalyptic World of D. H. Lawrence*. Oslo: Norwegian University Press, 1991.

Forster, E. M. *Howard's End*, 1910. New York: Vintage, 1989.

Foster, J. Ashley. "Jane Marcus Feminist University: Rhizomes, Connections, and Networks of Radical Thinking." *Virginia Woolf Miscellany* 93 (2018): 31–3.

Foucault, Michel. *The Courage of Truth: The Government of Self and Others II; Lectures at the Collège de France, 1983–1984*. Edited by Frédéric Gros, translated by Graham Burchell. New York: Palgrave Macmillan, 2011.

Froula, Christine. *Virginia Woolf and the Bloomsbury Avant-Garde: War, Civilization, Modernity*. New York: Columbia University Press, 2005.

Garrity, Jane. *Step-Daughters of England: British Women Modernists and the National Imaginary*. Manchester: Manchester University Press, 2003.

Gibson, Marion. *Witchcraft: The Basics*. New York: Routledge, 2018.

Glanvil, Joseph. *Saducismus Triumphatus*. London: Roger Tukyr, 1700.

Goldman, Emma. *Anarchism and Other Essays*. New York: Mother Earth Publishing Association, 1911.

Goldman, Emma. *Anarchy and the Sex Question: Essays on Women and Emancipation, 1896–1926*. Edited by Shawn P. Wilbur. Oakland, CA: PM Press, 2016.

Greenberg, Jonathan. *Modernism, Satire, and the Novel*. Cambridge: Cambridge University Press, 2011.

Greenidge, Terence. *Degenerate Oxford?: A Critical Study of Modern University Life*. London: Chapman & Hall, 1930.

Halberstam, J. *The Queer Art of Failure*. Durham, NC: Duke University Press, 2011.

Hardy, Thomas. *Collected Poems*. New York: Macmillan, 1958.

Harman, Claire. *Sylvia Townsend Warner: A Biography*, 1989. London: Penguin, 2015.

Harrison, Jane Ellen. *Ancient Art and Ritual*. London: Williams and Norgate, 1913.

Hastings, Selina. *Evelyn Waugh: A Biography*. New York: Boston: Houghton Mifflin, 1994.

Hauerwas, Stanley and Romand Coles. *Christianity, Democracy, and the Radical Ordinary: Conversations between a Radical Democrat and a Christian.* Eugene, OR: Cascade Books, 2008.

Hayes, Carlton J. H. *Essays on Nationalism.* New York: Macmillan, 1933.

Heckert, Jamie. "Anarchy without Opposition." In *Queering Anarchism: Addressing and Undressing Power and Desire*, edited by C. B. Daring, J. Rogue, Deric Shannon, and Abbey Volcano, 63–76. Edinburgh: AK Press, 2012.

Heckert, Jamie and Richard Cleminson, "Ethics, Relationships and Power: An Introduction." In *Anarchism and Sexuality: Ethics, Relationships and Power*, edited by Jamie Heckert and Richard Cleminson, 1–22. London: Routledge, 2011.

Hiebert, Kyle Gingerich. *The Architectonics of Hope: Violence, Apocalyptic, and the Transformation of Political Theology.* Eugene, OR: Cascade Books, 2017.

Hoover, A. J. *God, Germany, and Britain in the Great War: A Study in Clerical Nationalism.* New York: Praeger, 1989.

Hudgens, Ric. "Three Cheers for Cynicism." In *Cynicism and Hope: Reclaiming Discipleship in a Postdemocratic Society*, edited by Meg E. Cox, 11–20. Eugene, OR: Cascade Books, 2009.

Hussey, Christopher. *The Life of Sir Edwin Lutyens.* 1950. Woodbridge, Suffolk: Antique Collectors' Club, 1989.

James, William. *The Varieties of Religious Experience: A Study in Human Nature.* 1902. New York: Penguin, 1982.

Jenkins, Philip. *The Great and Holy War: How World War I became a Religious Crusade.* New York: HarperCollins, 2014.

Joannou, Maroula. "Preface." In *Critical Essays on Sylvia Townsend Warner, English Novelist 1893–1978*, edited by Gill Davies, David Malcolm, and John Simons, i–vi. Lewiston: Edwin Mellen, 2006.

Joh, Wonhee Anne. "Affective Politics of the Unending Korean War: Remembering and Resistance." In *Religion, Emotion, Sensation: Affect Theories and Theologies*, edited by Karen Bray and Stephen D. Moore, 85–109. New York: Fordham University Press, 2019.

Joyce, James. *A Portrait of the Artist as a Young Man*, 1914. New York: Norton, 2007.

Kalnins, Mara. Introduction to *Apocalypse and the Writings on Revelation*, by D. H. Lawrence, 3–38. Edited by Mara Kalnins. Cambridge: Cambridge University Press, 1980.

Kearney, Richard, *Anatheism: Returning to God after God.* New York: Columbia University Press, 2010.

Keller, Catherine. *Facing Apocalypse: Climate, Democracy, and Other Last Chances.* Maryknoll, NY: Orbis, 2021.

Keller, Catherine and Clayton Crockett, "Introduction: Political Theology on Edge." In *Political Theology on Edge: Ruptures of Justice and Belief in the Anthropocene*, edited by Clayton Crockett and Catherine Keller, 1–15. New York: Fordham University Press, 2022.

Kern, Stephen. *Modernism after the Death of God: Christianity, Fragmentation, and Unification*. New York: Routledge, 2017.

Kipling, Rudyard. *Kipling: A Selection of His Stories and Poems, Volume II*. Edited by John Beecroft. New York: Doubleday, 1956.

Kumar, Krishan. *The Making of English National Identity*. Cambridge: Cambridge University Press, 2003.

Lawrence, D. H. *Apocalypse and the Writings on Revelation*. Edited by Mara Kalnins. Cambridge: Cambridge University Press, 1980.

Lawrence, D. H. "A Propos of 'Lady Chatterley's Lover.'" In *Lady Chatterley's Lover*, edited by Michael Squires, 305–35. London: Penguin, 1994.

Lawrence, D. H. *Lady Chatterley's Lover*, 1930. London: Penguin, 1994.

Lawrence, D. H. *Late Essays and Articles*, edited by James T. Boulton. Cambridge: Cambridge University Press, 2014.

Lee, Hermione. *Virginia Woolf*. New York: Vintage, 1996.

Lewis, Cara L. *Dynamic Form: How Intermediality Made Modernism*. Ithaca, NY: Cornell University Press, 2020.

Lewis, Pericles. *Religious Experience and the Modernist Novel*. Cambridge: Cambridge University Press, 2010.

Lloyd, David W. *Battlefield Tourism: Pilgrimage and the Commemoration of the Great War in Britain, Australia and Canada, 1919–1939*. London: Bloomsbury, 1998.

Locke, John. *An Essay Concerning Human Understanding*. New York: Dover, 1959.

Loubser, J. A. "D. H. Lawrence's Extra-Ordinary 'Ordinary Reading' of the Apocalypse." *Neotestamentica* 38, no. 2 (2004): 326–46.

Love, Heather. *Feeling Backward: Loss and the Politics of Queer History*. Cambridge, MA: Harvard University Press, 2007.

Lupton, Julia Reinhard. *Citizen-Saints: Shakespeare and Political Theology*. Chicago: University of Chicago Press, 2005.

MacIntyre, Alasdair. "A Partial Response to My Critics." In *After MacIntyre: Critical Responses on the Work of Alasdair MacIntyre*, edited by John Horton and Susan Mendus, 283–304. Notre Dame: University of Notre Dame Press, 1994.

Maher, Ashley. *Reconstructing Modernism: British Literature, Modern Architecture, and the State*. Oxford: Oxford University Press, 2020.

Mahon, John W. "'A Later Development': Evelyn Waugh and Conversion." In *"A Handful of Mischief": New Essays on Evelyn Waugh*, edited by Donat Gallagher, Ann Pasternak Slater, and John Howard Wilson, 62–76. Teaneck, NJ: Fairleigh Dickinson University Press, 2011.

Marcus, Jane. "A Wilderness of One's Own: Feminist Fantasy Novels of the Twenties: Rebecca West and Sylvia Townsend Warner." In *Women Writers and the City: Essays in Feminist Literary Criticism*, edited by Susan Merrill Squier, 134–60. Knoxville: University of Tennessee Press, 1984.

Matarasso, Pauline. "A Recurrent Modulation: Religious Themes in the Poetry of Sylvia Townsend Warner." *The Journal of the Sylvia Townsend Warner Society* 2016, no. 1 (2017): 35–64.

McCarthy, Helen. *British People and League of Nations: Democracy, Citizenship and Internationalism, C. 1918–48*. Manchester: Manchester University Press, 2011.

McCarthy, Justin Huntly "Armageddon." In *Songs & Sonnets for England in War Time: Being a Collection of Lyrics by Various Authors Inspired by the Great War*, edited by John Lane, 3. London: John Lane, 1914.

McCartney, George. *Evelyn Waugh and the Modernist Tradition*. 1987. Reprint, New Brunswick, NJ: Transaction, 2004.

McCarraher, Eugene. *The Enchantments of Mammon: How Capitalism Became the Religion of Modernity*. Cambridge, MA: Harvard University Press, 2019.

McDonnell, Jacqueline. *Evelyn Waugh*. New York: St. Martin's, 1988.

Meckier, Jerome. "Cycle, Symbol, and Parody: in Evelyn Waugh's Decline and Fall." *Contemporary Literature* 20, no. 1 (1979): 51–75.

Messinger, Gary S. *British Propaganda and the State in the First World War*. Manchester: Manchester University Press, 1992.

Mills, Jean. *Virginia Woolf, Jane Ellen Harrison, and the Spirit of Modernist Classicism*. Columbus: Ohio State University Press, 2014.

Milthorpe, Naomi. *Evelyn Waugh's Satire: Texts and Contexts*. Teaneck, NJ: Fairleigh Dickinson University Press, 2016.

Moltmann, Jürgen. *The Coming of God: Christian Eschatology*. Minneapolis, MN: Fortress Press, 1996.

Moltmann, Jürgen. *Theology of Hope: On the Ground and the Implications of a Christian Eschatology*. New York: Harper & Row, 1967.

Mosse, George L. *Fallen Soldiers: Reshaping the Memory of the World Wars*. New York: Oxford University Press, 1990.

Mulford, Wendy. Introduction to *After the Death of Don Juan*, by Sylvia Townsend Warner, v–xvii. London: Virago, 1989.

Muñoz, José Esteban. *Cruising Utopia: The Then and There of Queer Futurity*. New York: New York University Press, 2009.

Murray, Margaret. *The God of the Witches*, 1931. Reprint, Oxford: Oxford University Press, 1970.

Murray, Margaret. *The Witch-Cult in Western Europe*, 1921. Reprint, Oxford: Clarendon Press, 1962.

Myers, Jeffrey D. *The Nonviolent Apocalypse: Revelation's Nonviolent Resistance against Rome*. Minneapolis: Fortress Press, 2021.

Nesbitt, Jennifer Poulos. "Footsteps of Red Ink: Body and Landscape in Lolly Willowes." *Twentieth-Century Literature* 49, no. 4 (2003): 449–71.

Neverow, Vara. Introduction to *Jacob's Room*, by Virginia Woolf, xxxvii–xciv. Orlando: Harcourt, 2008.

Neverow, Vara. Notes to *Jacob's Room*, by Virginia Woolf, 189–314. Orlando: Harcourt, 2008.

Newheiser, David. *Hope in a Secular Age: Deconstruction, Negative Theology, and the Future of Faith*. Cambridge: Cambridge University Press, 2019.

Nietzsche, Friedrich. *The Birth of Tragedy and Other Writings*. Edited by Raymond Geuss and Ronald Speirs. Translated by Ronald Speirs. Cambridge: Cambridge University Press, 1999.

Nietzsche, Friedrich. *On the Genealogy of Morals and Ecce Homo*. Translated and edited by Walter Kaufmann and R. J. Hollingdale. New York: Vintage, 1989.

Parker, Peter. *The Old Lie: The Great War and the Public-School Ethos*. London: Constable, 1987.

Patey, Douglas Lane. *The Life of Evelyn Waugh: A Critical Biography*. London: Wiley-Blackwell, 2001.

Paulsell, Stephanie. *Religion around Virginia Woolf*. University Park: Pennsylvania State University Press, 2019.

Pecora, Vincent P. *Secularization and Cultural Criticism: Religion, Nation, & Modernity*. Chicago: University of Chicago Press, 2006.

Pitcairn, Robert. *Ancient Criminal Trials in Scotland*. Edinburgh: Bannatyne, 1833.

Poplawski, Paul. *Promptings of Desire: Creativity and the Religious Impulse in the Work of D. H. Lawrence*. Westport: Greenwood, 1993.

Purkiss, Diane. *The Witch in History: Early Modern and Twentieth-Century Representations*. New York: Routledge, 1996.

Query, Patrick R. Introduction to *A Tourist in Africa*, by Evelyn Waugh, xxvii–lxvi. Edited by Patrick R. Query. Oxford: Oxford University Press, 2021.

Raschke, Carl A. *Force of God: Political Theology and the Crisis of Liberal Democracy*. New York: Columbia University Press, 2015.

Raschke, Carl. "On Witches and Witch Hunts: Violence, Counterviolence, and the Writing of Religion." In *Religion and Violence in a Secular World: Toward a New Political Theology*, edited by Clayton Crockett, 46–60. Charlottesville, VA: University of Virginia Press, 2006.

Ratzinger, Joseph. *Eschatology: Death and Eternal Life*. Washington, DC: Catholic University of America Press, 1988.

Reeve-Tucker, Alice and Nathan Waddell. "Wyndham Lewis, Evelyn Waugh and Interwar British Youth: Conflict and Infantilism." In *Wyndham Lewis and the Cultures of Modernity*, edited by Andrzej Gąsiorek, Alice Reeve-Tucker, and Nathan Waddell, 163–82. Burlington, VT: Ashgate, 2011.

Roe, Sue. Notes to *Jacob's Room*, by Virginia Woolf, 157–87. London: Penguin, 1992.

Rosso, G. A. *The Religion of Empire: Political Theology in Blake's Prophetic Symbolism*. Columbus: Ohio State University Press, 2016.

Rousseau, Jean-Jacques. *The Social Contract and Other Later Political Writings*. Translated and edited by Victor Gourevitch. Cambridge: Cambridge University Press, 1997.

Saint-Amour, Paul K. *Tense Future: Modernism, Total War, Encyclopedic Form*. Oxford: Oxford University Press, 2015.

Sanders, Scott R. "Lady Chatterley's Loving and the Annihilation Impulse." In *D. H. Lawrence's "Lady": A New Look at Lady Chatterley's Lover*, edited by Michael Squires and Dennis Jackson, 1–16. Athens, GA: University of Georgia Press, 1985.

Schmidt, Michael and Val Warner. "Sylvia Townsend Warner in Conversation." *PN Review 23* 8, no. 3 (1982): 35–7.

Schmitt, Carl. *Political Theology: Four Chapters on the Concept of Sovereignty*. Translated by George Schwab, 1922. Cambridge, MA: MIT Press, 1985.

Schwab, George. Introduction to *Political Theology: Four Chapters on the Concept of Sovereignty*, by Carl Schmitt, xi–xxvi. Cambridge, MA: MIT Press, 1985.

Scott, Bonnie Kime. *In the Hollow of the Wave: Virginia Woolf and the Modernist Uses of Nature*. Charlottesville: University of Virginia Press, 2012.

Scott, James C. *Seeing Like a State: How Certain Schemes to Improve the Human Condition Have Failed*. New Haven: Yale University Press, 1998.

Shakespeare, Nicholas. Introduction to *Waugh Abroad: The Collected Travel Writing*, by Evelyn Waugh, ix–xxv. New York: Knopf, 2003.

Shea, Louisa. *The Cynic Enlightenment: Diogenes in the Salon*. Baltimore: Johns Hopkins University Press, 2010.

Sheppard, Kathleen L. *The Life of Margaret Alice Murray: A Woman's Work in Archaeology*. Lanham: Lexington Books, 2013.

Sherry, Vincent. *The Great War and the Language of Modernism*. Oxford: Oxford University Press, 2003.

Shin, Jacqueline. "Lolly Willowes and the Arts of Dispossession." *Modernism/modernity* 16, no. 4 (2009): 709–26.

Smith, James K. A. *Awaiting the King: Reforming Public Theology; Volume 3 of Cultural Liturgies*. Grand Rapids: Baker Academic, 2017.

Smith, James K. A. *Desiring the Kingdom: Worship, Worldview, and Cultural Formation; Volume 1 of Cultural Liturgies*. Grand Rapids: Baker Academic, 2009.

Spenser, Edmund. *Books I and II of The Faerie Queene, The Mutability Cantos and Selections from the Minor Poetry*, edited by Robert Kellogg and Oliver Steele. New York: Macmillan, 1965.

Springs, Jason A. "Civil Religion." In *Religion and Culture: Contemporary Practices and Perspectives*, edited by Richard D. Hecht and Vincent F. Biondo III, 29–46. Minneapolis: Fortress Press, 2012.

Stannard, Martin. *Evelyn Waugh: The Early Years, 1903-1939*. New York: Norton, 1986.

Stannard, Martin. Introduction to *Vile Bodies*, by Evelyn Waugh, xxvii–xcv. Oxford: Oxford University Press, 2017.

Stephen, Leslie. *Some Early Impressions*. London: Hogarth Press, 1924.

Sutaria, Sejal. "Ripples in Modernist Waters: The Poetics, Ethics, & Politics of T.E. Hulme's Vision of Anti-Humanist Democracy." *Global Review* 1, no. 1 (2013): 165–75.

Talbot, Edward S. "The World at the Cross-Roads." In *Christ and the World at War: Sermons Preached in War-Time*, edited by Basil Matthews, 27–38. London: Clark, 1917.

Taylor, Charles. *A Secular Age*. Cambridge, MA: Harvard University Press, 2007.

Taylor, Charles. *Varieties of Religion Today: William James Revisited*. Cambridge, MA: Harvard University Press, 2002.

Taylor, D. J. *Bright Young People: The Lost Generation of London's Jazz Age*. New York: FSG, 2007.

Taylor, Richard. *How to Read a Church: A Guide to Symbols and Images in Churches and Cathedrals*. London: Rider, 2003.

Utell, Janine. *Literary Couples and 20th-Century Life Writing: Narrative and Intimacy*. London: Bloomsbury Academic, 2020.

Vahanian, Noëlle. "The Gospel of the Word Made Flesh: Insurrection from within the Heart of Divinity." In *An Insurrectionist Manifesto: Four New Gospels for a Radical Politics*, edited by Ward Blanton, Clayton Crockett, Jeffrey W. Robbins, and Noëlle Vahanian, 143–71. New York: Columbia University Press, 2016.

Wachman, Gay. *Lesbian Empire: Radical Crosswriting in the Twenties*. New Brunswick, NJ: Rutgers University Press, 2001.

Warner, Sylvia Townsend. "Behind the Firing Line: Some Experiences in a Munition Factory." *Blackwood's Magazine* 199 (1916): 191–207.

Warner, Sylvia Townsend. *I'll Stand by You: Selected Letters of Sylvia Townsend Warner and Valentine Ackland with Narrative by Sylvia Townsend Warner*. Edited by Susanna Pinney. London: Pimlico, 1998.

Warner, Sylvia Townsend. *Letters*. Edited by William Maxwell. London: Chatto & Windus, 1982.

Warner, Sylvia Townsend. *Lolly Willowes; Or, The Loving Huntsman*, 1926. New York: NYRB, 1999.

Warner, Sylvia Townsend. *New Collected Poems*. Edited by Claire Harman. Manchester: Manchester University Press, 2008.

Warner, Sylvia Townsend. *With the Hunted: Selected Writings*. Edited by Peter Tolhurst. Norwich: Black Dog Books, 2012.

Waugh, Evelyn. *Decline and Fall*, 1928. New York: Little, Brown, 2012.

Waugh, Evelyn. *The Essays, Articles, and Reviews of Evelyn Waugh*. Edited by Donat Gallagher. London: Methuen, 1984.

Waugh, Evelyn. *Essays, Articles, and Reviews 1922–1934: The Complete Works of Evelyn Waugh 26*. Edited by Donat Gallagher. Oxford: Oxford University Press, 2018.

Waugh, Evelyn. *Labels: A Mediterranean Journal*, 1930. London: Penguin Classics, 2011.

Waugh, Evelyn. *The Letters of Evelyn Waugh*. Edited by Mark Amory. New York: Ticknor & Fields, 1980.

Waugh, Evelyn. *Personal Writings 1903–1921: Precocious Waughs*. Edited by Alexander Waugh and Alan Bell. Oxford: Oxford University Press, 2017.

Waugh, Evelyn. *Vile Bodies: The Complete Works of Evelyn Waugh, Volume 2*, 1930. Edited by Martin Stannard. Oxford: Oxford University Press, 2017.

Weintraub, Stanley. *A Stillness Heard Round the World: The End of the Great War, November 1918*. London: Dutton, 1985.

Wexler, Joyce. *Violence without God: The Rhetorical Despair of Twentieth-Century Writers*. London: Bloomsbury Academic, 2017.

Whitehead, Alfred North. *Religion in the Making: Lowell Lectures, 1926*. New York: Macmillan, 1957.

Winick, Mimi. "Modernist Feminist Witchcraft: Margaret Murray's Fantastic Scholarship and Sylvia Townsend Warner's Realist Fantasy." *Modernism/modernity* 22, no. 3 (2015): 565–92.

Winter, Jay. *Sites of Memory, Sites of Mourning: The Great War in European Cultural History*. Cambridge: Cambridge University Press, 1995.

Winterson, Jeanette. *The Passion*. New York: Grove, 1987.

Wolffe, John. *Great Deaths: Grieving, Religion, and Nationhood in Victorian and Edwardian Britain*. New York: Oxford University Press, 2000.

Woolf, Virginia. *The Diary of Virginia Woolf: Volume Two, 1920–1924*. Edited by Anne Olivier Bell and assisted by Andrew McNeillie. New York: HBJ, 1978.

Woolf, Virginia. *The Diary of Virginia Woolf: Volume Three, 1925–1930*. Edited by Anne Olivier Bell. New York: HBJ, 1980.

Woolf, Virginia. *The Diary of Virginia Woolf: Volume Five, 1936–1941*. Edited by Anne Olivier Bell and Andrew McNeillie. San Diego, CA: HBJ, 1984.

Woolf, Virginia. *The Essays of Virginia Woolf: Volume III, 1919–1924*. Edited by Andrew McNeillie. San Diego, CA: HBJ, 1988.

Woolf, Virginia. *The Essays of Virginia Woolf: Volume IV, 1925–1928*. Edited by Andrew McNeillie. Orlando, FL: Harvest, 1994.

Woolf, Virginia. *Jacob's Room: The Cambridge Edition of the Works of Virginia Woolf*, 1922. Edited by Stuart N. Clarke with the participation of David Bradshaw. Cambridge: Cambridge University Press, 2020.

Woolf, Virginia. *The Letters of Virginia Woolf, Volume II: 1912–1922*. Edited by Nigel Nicolson and Joanne Trautmann. New York: HBJ, 1976.

Woolf, Virginia. *The Letters of Virginia Woolf, Volume III: 1923–1928*. Edited by Nigel Nicholson and Joanne Trautmann. New York: HBJ, 1978.

Woolf, Virginia. *Moments of Being: Unpublished Autobiographical Writings*. Edited and Introduced by Jeanne Schulkind. New York: HBJ, 1976.

Woolf, Virginia. *Three Guineas*, 1938. Annotated and introduced by Jane Marcus. Orlando, FL: Harcourt, 2006.

Woolf, Virginia. *The Waves*, 1932. San Diego. CA: Harvest, 1959.

Worthen, John. *D. H. Lawrence: The Early Years, 1885–1912*. Cambridge: Cambridge University Press, 1991.

Wright, T. R. *D. H. Lawrence and the Bible*. Cambridge: Cambridge University Press, 2000.

Wussow, Helen. *The Nightmare of History: The Fictions of Virginia Woolf and D.H. Lawrence*. London: Associated University Press, 1998.

Žižek, Slavoj. *Trouble in Paradise: From the End of History to the End of Capitalism*. Brooklyn, NY: Melville House, 2014.

Zwerdling, Alex. *Virginia Woolf and the Real World*. Berkeley: University of California Press, 1986.

Index

Ackland, Valentine 141–4
Agamben, Giorgio 2, 13–14
anarchism 18, 102–3, 158, 165
   mystical 150–1
   queer 26, 146–9, 162–3, 169–70, 172–5
   Spanish 26, 143–4
   See also Goldman, Emma; Halberstam, Jack; Critchley, Simon; Warner, Sylvia Townsend
Anderson, Benedict 2, 11–12, 30, 91
Anglicanism 24, 30, 36, 43, 57, 68, 74, 100. *See also* Church of England; Christianity
annihilation 73, 79, 86, 136
Anthropocene 67, 96
apocalypticism 24–5, 69–76, 79–81, 92–7, 126, 134, 164, 179. *See also* eschatology
Archbishop of Canterbury 29–30, 61, 131
Arkwright, John Stanhope 6–7
Armageddon 69, 74–5, 81, 85, 92, 94
Armistice Day 1–6, 29–34, 47, 85, 156–9
atheism 21n68, 23–4, 34, 36, 100–1, 167

Barnes, Julian 181, 184–6
Bible 10, 17, 68, 76, 116, 118, 161, 164
   II Chronicles 5
   I Corinthians 160
   Psalms 29
   Revelation 25, 70, 72–4, 79
Billig, Michael 22, 161
Bellah, Robert N. 10–12
Bell, Vanessa (Stephen) 19, 31–3, 35, 56n44
Bray, Karen 24, 60–1, 183
Bronstein, Michaela 17, 178
Butler, Judith 62

Cambridge University 33–4, 48, 56–9
capitalism 22, 40, 55–6, 59n70, 62, 94, 146–7, 153, 157, 172, 174, 184–6

Cavanaugh, William T. 2, 7n22, 13, 15. *See also* theopolitical imagination
Cenotaph 1–6, 2n2, 3n7, 40–1, 177
chapel 56–9, 68, 76, 79n41, 92, 116–18
Charles, R. H. 73–4, 77–8
Christianity 17–19, 88
   in childhood of writers 65–70, 99–101, 141–3
   and civil religion 1, 3–13, 29–31, 34–6, 43, 47–53, 132, 157–8, 165–75, 177–8
   and theopolitical fiction 22–6, 39–40, 56–7, 90–1, 94, 103–21, 124–8, 135–9, 144–54, 185–6
   and war 61–2, 74–84, 159–62, 181–2
   See also Anglicanism; Congregationalism; evangelicalism; Quakerism; Roman Catholicism
church
   orthodoxy 20–1, 36, 84
   as social institution 24–6, 39–43, 46–54, 57–8, 92, 106, 113–26, 134, 136, 141–2, 148–54
   and state 13, 29–30, 33–4, 39–43, 100–2, 108–10, 129–31, 145, 157–64, 169–74, 185
   versus state 7n22, 10
   See also St. Paul's Cathedral; Westminster Abbey
Church of England 3, 30, 68, 100. *See also* Anglicanism
civil religion
   history of 8–12
   in practice 1–8, 29–34, 41–59, 90–3, 114–19, 127–30, 148–50, 155–7, 159–63
Coles, Romand 13, 24, 39–40, 55. *See also* Hauerwas, Stanley; politics of death; radical ordinary
communism 7, 109, 143–4, 148
Congregationalism 25, 76–7. *See also* Christianity
cosmopolitanism 3n6, 115, 148

Index

cosmos 24–5, 66–73, 76, 82–9, 92–4, 99, 147
crisis 2, 61, 71–2, 75, 93, 159, 181, 187
   ecological 61, 73, 95–6, 177
   end-times 74. *See also* eschatology
Critchley, Simon 7, 13, 26, 150–1, 174
Crockett, Clayton 13, 70
cynicism 26, 102n10, 102–15, 119, 121, 123–8, 130, 132–3, 136–9, 147, 152

democracy 7, 39–40, 56, 65, 82, 180–1
Diogenes of Sinope 103

ecology 23n73, 63, 67, 69, 157
elegy 24, 34, 37–9, 49, 59, 66
Eliot, T. S. 19, 24, 35
enchantment
   civil religious 156, 181–2, 186
   of nation-state 2, 5, 8–15, 26, 29, 33–5, 39–40, 51, 54–6, 63, 146–50
   of violence 80, 126, 177
Englishness 54, 110, 113, 119–20, 124, 138, 139n81, 148, 157–8, 162, 184–5
empire 17, 33, 46–7, 62, 78, 91, 119n60, 124, 139, 182, 186. *See also* imperialism
eschatology 10n32, 24–5, 70–6, 80–3, 86, 88–90, 94, 96, 99, 133, 146–7
evangelicalism 24, 36, 127–8. *See also* Christianity
experimental literary form 15, 18–20, 24, 37, 40–1, 62, 154–5, 180–1

failure
   institutional 124–30, 139
   of society 56, 111–13, 134–6, 171
   reclaimed 25–6, 147–9, 156, 174–5, 178, 187
   See also Halberstam, Jack
fascism 7, 66, 70, 79–80, 82, 143, 144
feminism 23n73, 25, 71, 148, 154, 169–70, 173–4
First World War 24, 31, 61, 73–5, 136, 151–2, 159–60. *See also* Great War
Foucault, Michel 26, 103–7, 116, 139, 149

General Strike (1926) 61, 65
gnosticism 76, 89
Goldman, Emma 144–6, 174

Great War 1–3, 29, 42, 121
   in art 85–6
   as cataclysm 34, 75, 129, 134, 173
   as religious 8, 10–11, 22–3, 69, 116–17, 152, 177
   See also First World War; Armageddon
Greenidge, Terence 107–10, 115n49
Guy Fawkes Day 42–5, 47, 58

Halberstam, Jack 26, 149–50, 156, 174
Hardy, Thomas 57, 73
Hauerwas, Stanley 12–13, 24, 39–40, 55, 58
   See also Coles, Romand; politics of death; radical ordinary
Hayes, Carlton J. H. 11
heaven 26, 76, 120, 144, 146, 151, 174–5
heteronormativity
   and anarchism 144–7
   of Christianity 162–3, 165, 170–5
   in civil religion 153–4, 157
   Lawrence and 87–8
   and nation-state 23, 55, 168
hope
   eschatological 10n32, 72–5, 81–2, 95–7
   for redemption 37, 59, 84–6, 88, 185
   political 25, 65, 78, 93, 136, 174, 178
   queerness and 136
hymnody 4, 6–7, 30, 32–4, 68

imperialism 2, 22–5, 34, 40, 52–3
   as attitude 45, 55–6, 60, 76–9, 119, 123, 127, 148
   legacy of 50, 131, 164, 174, 181–3
   and theology, 12, 17, 66, 88, 97, 133, 186
   and violence 7
   See also empire
internationalism 46–7, 78, 114–15, 133, 135, 148, 184

James, William 21, 69
Jenkins, Philip 8, 69, 74
Jesus 77–9
Jones, David 19, 161
Joyce, James 21n68, 68

Kearney, Richard 21n68, 36
Keller, Catherine 70, 86n63, 96, 179
Kipling, Rudyard 6–7

Lanchester, Elsa 107, 108n32, 109
Lawrence, D. H. *See also* Armageddon; eschatology; Moltmann, Jürgen; Nietzsche, Friedrich
   Apocalypse 25, 68–82, 85, 89, 92–7
   "A Propos of *Lady Chatterley's Lover*" 83–6
   Kangaroo 70, 161
   Lady Chatterley's Lover 24–5, 71–2, 86, 88–94
   The Plumed Serpent 65, 70–1
   religious upbringing 65–9, 72–3
   versus martyr-rulers 79–80, 97
League of Nations 114–15
Lewis, Pericles 20, 35, 154n42
liturgy
   definition 31–4
   national 2, 22, 30n5, 37–8, 40–51, 57–60, 147
   religious 117–18, 156
   theopolitical 22, 62–3, 183
   See also Smith, James K. A.
Lloyd George, David 29, 91, 119–20
Lupton, Julia Reinhard 16–17
Lutyens, Edwin 3–5

MacIntyre, Alasdair 12
Mammon 94
Marcus, Jane 154, 159, 179–80
martyrdom 10, 16, 38, 79–80, 97, 156
McCarraher, Eugene 94
memorialization 4n8, 5, 31, 49, 51, 56, 59, 157, 177
militarism
   and civil religion 33–4, 58–62, 66, 121–4, 126, 149, 151–3, 182–4
   and ecology 93, 97
   in fiction 37, 45–6, 131–6
   and nation-building 2–3, 6–7, 22–24, 40, 49–50, 55, 76, 156, 160, 174
   theological 70, 89–91, 116–18
   versus pacifism 32n17, 128
millennialism 79–81
modernism (aesthetic movement)
   as activist 8, 187
   in decline 112–13
   and form 108n32, 154n42, 160
   as political theology 15–20, 23–4, 27, 41, 106–7, 147–8, 177–81
   and religion 34–6, 69

Moltmann, Jürgen 25, 70, 80–2, 88
monarchy 5–6, 16, 29–30, 33, 41, 109, 120, 156–7, 162, 170, 184–5
mourning 2, 22, 37, 38, 62, 160, 181, 183–4
Muñoz, José Esteban 163
Murray, Margaret 167–71
mysticism 20, 34–7, 49, 57, 70, 76, 78, 85, 94, 149–50, 154, 157

nationalism
   Christian 1–2, 6–7, 11–12, 30–2, 43–5, 49–53, 66, 69, 74, 95, 99, 108–9, 111, 124–33, 138–9, 153, 172, 177, 181–3, 186
   and homonationalism 146–8
   hot and banal 22, 29, 32, 41–2, 45, 47, 49, 51, 54, 66, 161–2, 164. *See also* Billig, Michael
   as imagined community 2, 91, 101. *See also* Anderson, Benedict
   local 47, 49, 51, 101, 156–7, 162, 171
   and memorials 3–6, 46, 53–4
   and renewal 71, 78–9, 86–9
   sacrificial 38–9, 55, 59, 62, 117, 134, 155, 180
   wartime 29–34, 76
   See also civil religion
nature 35, 40, 48–53, 55, 58, 72, 85, 89, 92–3, 97, 150, 157–8, 163
neoliberalism 60–2
Nietzsche, Friedrich 73, 77, 84–5
nonviolence 78

Oxford Student Christian Union 114–15, 115n49
Oxford University 57–8, 100n3, 101n7, 107, 110–11, 113–15, 114n46

pacifism 32n17, 61–2, 152
parrhēsia 26, 105–6, 111, 114, 122, 129, 133, 139
patriotism 30–3, 47, 58, 61, 99, 101, 116, 124, 148, 151, 156–65, 175, 177
peace 30, 49–50, 61–2, 91, 115, 133, 157–8, 173, 180
Pecora, Vincent P. 19, 35n22
Pitcairn, Robert 169–71
political theology
   and affect theory 60–1, 183–4

biblical 77–9
conservative forms 99–100
definition 7–8, 12–15, 178–81. *See also* Schmitt, Carl
fiction as 7, 16–18, 22–7, 34, 37, 55, 72, 102–3, 112, 117, 124, 126–7, 130, 143, 165, 178, 181, 187. *See also* Lupton, Julia Reinhard
secular forms 40, 51–2, 67, 69–71, 73, 84, 105–6, 144, 148, 170. *See also* Critchley, Simon
See also theopolitical imagination; Cavanaugh, William T.; Hauerwas, Stanley
politics of death 24, 39–40, 47, 50, 56, 59, 63, 66
postmodernism 181–6
post-secularism 15, 35–40, 154
protest
against the Enlightenment 83
against the nation-state 2, 24, 73, 106, 136–9, 160, 183
antiwar 62
literature as 34n20, 38–9, 49–50, 59–60, 102–3
Protestantism 43, 57, 84, 88, 100, 102–3, 109–11, 138
See also Anglicanism; Christianity; Church of England

Quakerism 24, 36, 142, 153. *See also* Christianity
queer theory 26, 145–9, 153–6, 162–4, 169–72
Query, Patrick R. 137

radical ordinary 24, 39–42, 47, 51–4, 59, 63, 147
Raschke, Carl A. 7, 13, 167n67
resistance
to civil religion 23, 26, 34, 41
ideological 3, 7, 14, 16–7, 32–3, 44–5, 51, 53, 56, 59–60, 81, 97, 105, 159–65, 172–5, 183
literature as 21–3, 86, 142, 146, 154, 181
to state power 39, 41, 78, 84, 103, 148, 151
resource, literature as 3, 16, 18, 34, 41–2, 62, 67, 69, 72, 102, 112, 127, 139, 175, 180–1, 187

ritual
Christian 48–51, 56, 116–18, 161–3
commemorative 29–30, 33
communal 84–5, 183
everyday/mundane 24, 97, 158–9
national 1–10, 31–3, 37–45, 159–61, 177
pagan 88–9, 94, 167–8, 171
Roman Catholicism 11, 14–15, 25, 43–4, 74, 99–102, 108–11, 126–9, 137–8, 170
See also Christianity
Rousseau, Jean-Jacques 9–10, 12, 103

sacralized state 3, 7, 15, 23, 26, 37, 56, 97, 186–7
Satan 149, 160, 164–8, 170, 172–5
satire 26, 101–6, 112–16, 120, 124–30, 137–9, 142, 149, 153–4, 157, 184–5
Schmitt, Carl 14, 79–80, 181
Scott, James C. 149–50, 164
Second World War 34–5, 133–5, 151
secularism
anarchist 26
incomplete 5, 8–9, 29–31, 74, 177, 183–6
and nation-state 11–23, 55
See also post-secularism
Shaw, George Bernard 115
Smith, James K. A. 13, 24, 31, 44–5, 58
socialism 7, 118, 148, 174
Spanish Civil War 26, 143–5, 151
Spenser, Edmund 5
spirituality
biblical 57, 116
cosmic 83, 89–90
pluralistic 8n24, 20, 74, 154
private 15, 21, 23, 35–7, 68, 106, 110, 128, 131, 141, 178. *See also* mysticism
Stephen, Leslie 57–8
St. Paul 60, 77
St. Paul's Cathedral 42–3, 52–4, 60

Taylor, Charles 8, 19, 21n68, 186
technocracy 83, 88, 149
theopolitical imagination 177, 180–3, 187
anti-capitalist 147
Foucauldian 106–8, 137
in literature 15–18, 22–3, 26, 42, 55, 96, 100–2, 139, 142, 175

versus Carl Schmitt 80–1
  See also Cavanaugh, William T.
Treaty of Versailles 152

unisonance 30, 44–6. *See also* Anderson, Benedict
Unknown Warrior 1–6, 177
unredemption 24–5, 59–63, 65–66, 99. *See also* Bray, Karen
utopianism 25, 81–82, 88, 93–5, 144, 147, 149, 163–4, 173–5

violence
  biblical and religious 78–81, 97, 169
  imperial 7
  of modernity, 20–2, 70, 85–6, 106–11, 116–26
  national 3, 15, 17, 180–1
  wartime 39, 46–53, 74, 134–6, 156, 173, 183

Warner, Sylvia Townsend. *See also* anarchism; Critchley, Simon; Goldman, Emma; Halberstam, Jack; Murray, Margaret; queer theory; Scott, James C.
  The Espalier 151
  "The Lenten Offering" 151–4, 173
  Lolly Willowes 153–66, 170–5
  munitions work 152–3
  queer anarchism 146–7, 149
  religious upbringing 141–2
Waugh, Alec 107–8
Waugh, Evelyn. *See also* cynicism; Foucault, Michel
  conversion to Roman Catholicism 99–101, 138

  "The Cynic" 103–4
  Decline and Fall 112–24, 127
  and Englishness 99–100
  Labels: A Mediterranean Journal 137–9
  The Scarlet Woman 107–11, 119, 126, 128, 137
  Vile Bodies 124–36
Wells, H. G. 115
Westminster Abbey 1, 29, 46, 177
Wexler, Joyce 20
Whitehall 1, 4, 29, 40–1, 45–7, 134, 177
Whitehead, Alfred North 89–90
Winick, Mimi 168, 173
Winterson, Jeanette 181–3
witches 149, 154–5, 158, 163–74. *See also* Murray, Margaret
witness 41, 53, 77, 92, 105, 155
  literary mode 27, 34n20
  as political act 13, 23, 56, 63, 94, 105, 174–5
Wolffe, John 6–7
Woolf, Leonard 61, 115
Woolf, Virginia. *See also* Bray, Karen; Coles, Romand; Hauerwas, Stanley; Smith, James K. A.
  Armistice Day reactions 29–33
  and Christian culture 36–7
  Jacob's Room 33–4, 37–9, 41–61
  Mrs. Dalloway 37
  "A Sketch of the Past" 55
  Three Guineas 40–2
  To the Lighthouse 35–7

Žižek, Slavoj 13, 96n74

www.ingramcontent.com/pod-product-compliance
Lightning Source LLC
Chambersburg PA
CBHW052113300426
44116CB00010B/1655